G000244593

Basic Book-keeping and Accounts

Beryl Wilkinson,
Dip.Ed. (Adult), FSBT, MBIM
Course Director, Scheidegger Training

Stanley Thornes (Publishers) Ltd

Text and Graphics © Scheidegger International School 1984

All rights reserved. No part of this publication may be reproduced or transmitted in any form or by any means, electronic or mechanical, including photocopy, recording, or any information storage and retrieval system, without permission in writing from the publisher or under licence from the Copyright Licensing Agency Ltd. Further details of such licences (for reprographic reproduction) may be obtained from the Copyright Licensing Agency Ltd, 33–34 Alfred Place, London WC1E 7DP.

First published 1984 as Scheidegger Basic Book-keeping Course by Scheidegger Training Ltd

Revised 1986
1987
1988
1989

This edition first published 1990 by Stanley Thornes (Publishers) Ltd
Old Station Drive
Leckhampton
CHELTENHAM   GL53 0DN
England

British Library Cataloguing in Publication Data

Wilkinson, Beryl
   Basic book – keeping and accounts.
   1. Accounting
   I. Title   II. Scheidegger basic book – keeping course
   657

ISBN 0–7487–0426–4

Typeset by Opus, Oxford
Printed and bound in Great Britain at the Bath Press, Avon

Contents

Preface

This course will help you to understand and be able to apply the basic principles of book-keeping. It is quite straightforward and aims to give you an appreciation of the main factors involved in keeping the accounts of a business.

The aim of the course is not to qualify you as an accountant, but to give you a thorough and fundamental understanding of book-keeping and accounts. This will enable you to handle your own accounts or those of your employer in a commonsense way, following internationally accepted methods.

You should find book-keeping interesting because it is about money and how it is used.

Note that from time to time details change, usually as a result of the Budget or some other Act of Parliament. For this reason up-to-date rates may not be shown, although the actual principles involved are correct.

If you are preparing the books for a business you should make sure that you are using current figures, which can be obtained from the Inland Revenue, Customs and Excise and the Department of Social Security.

Short answers only are given at the end of each unit. Full model answers are available in a separate volume.

Beryl Wilkinson
Scheidegger Training Ltd, 1984

Acknowledgements

With grateful thanks to Roy Lee-Faulkner, CIMA, Cert Ed. Senior Lecturer, Manchester Polytechnic, for his contribution and help with the text of this book, also to Neill Jackson of Saline, Fife, for his patience in designing the graphics.

Other Scheidegger courses:
Intermediate Book-keeping and Accounts
Advanced Book-keeping and Accounts
Keyboard and Computer

All courses are individually structured for Industry

Unit 1

Double-entry Book-keeping and the Ledger

At the end of this Unit you will be able to:

1 Understand the subject of book-keeping and accounts, and discuss the basic principles of book-keeping

2 Prepare the cash account and other relevant ledger accounts.

Introduction

Book-keeping is a practice and all practices are relatively simple to learn. You will find it easier to learn if you bear in mind three things:

- Impression
- Repetition
- Association

- **Impression** Some of the rules you will come across in this course must be learned, as they are the foundation of book-keeping.

- **Repetition** By repeating something constantly it impresses itself on your mind. By putting what you have learned into practice the rules will soon become second nature.

- **Association** Association of one aspect of the subject with another. In book-keeping you will discover that the basic rules can be associated with other rules and if you relate one aspect of the subject to another the whole will fit together more clearly.

As you work through this course you will become familiar with the language of book-keeping and be able to communicate in a way that will form the basis of a thorough understanding of the accounting transactions of a business. A detailed explanation of the terms used can be found in the glossary at the end of this book.

What is Book-keeping?

Accounting was first invented by the Babylonians who kept very simple records of transactions between traders. Their system was used by the Greeks, the Romans, the Egyptians and other civilisations until the Italian Renaissance period. In the Fifteenth century a Franciscan friar invented the system of accounting which we know today and which is based on 'double-entry'. The system which has now evolved is in use, in one form or another, throughout the world, wherever businesses need to keep records.

With the rapid advances in computerised accounts and transmission of data across continents in a matter of seconds, integration and standardisation are becoming increasingly important. These days accountants regularly discuss and agree methods to be used. Their final decisions are published in the form of Statements of Standard Accounting Practice (SSAPs). Once such a statement has been issued all major organisations are expected to comply with it. These recommendations may eventually be incorporated in company law.

You have decided to study this subject, but how would you explain it to someone else? What is the difference between book-keeping and accounting, or are they the same thing? Well, you probably have an idea, but could not easily explain the difference.

Here is a definition of book-keeping. There is no need to learn it by heart, provided you understand it.

> **Book-keeping is recording financial information on a day-to-day basis.**

Note the word **financial**: we are not only concerned with actual cash, but anything to do with the business which can be translated into money terms.

What then is accounting?

> **Accounting is making use of financial information in order to help the owner of a business understand what has happened. It is also concerned with analysing and evaluating as well as forecasting.**

As you may know, accountants often specialise in different aspects of accounting, so you may find a large organisation employs financial accountants, cost accountants, budget accountants and management accountants. They will all use the same basic set of information (often provided by the book-keepers), but in different ways.

Why is Book-keeping Necessary?

There must be a good reason for hard-headed businessmen to pay high salaries to all these different accountants. Book-keeping and accounts are about **money** and **money's worth**, so it is basic common sense to keep a close check on the business.

Successful businessmen have three **Golden Rules** for money management:

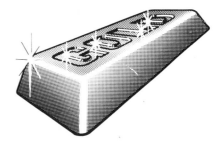

- They are very careful — critics would even say mean. Remember the motto — 'Look after the pennies and the pounds look after themselves.'
- They keep accurate records.
- They know money talks: especially to say 'goodbye'!

Never lose sight of the fact that book-keeping and accounts are meant to help manage a business: they are not the end themselves, but a means to an end. Accounts are kept to help run the business. The objectives of keeping accounts are therefore:

- To manage and control properly the finances of an organisation.
- To help the owner(s) understand the financial situation and results of trading.
- To keep a complete set of records for every aspect of the business.

Reasons for Keeping Accounts

We can summarise the need for accurate accounts as follows:

- To know the **financial position**: profit does not necessarily mean cash!
- To be able to **measure results**: particularly to calculate profits (or losses).
- To know **the worth of the business**: by looking at assets and liabilities.
- To be able to **control the business**: to check against past performance or future plans.
- To keep accurate **records of assets and liabilities**: to know how much is owed to suppliers and is owed by customers; to discourage pilfering and fraud.
- To help **make decisions**, based on fact as much as possible: to invest more capital; raise or lower prices; improve credit control, and all the other everyday decisions which must be made.
- To help **plan**: using past results and anticipated changes to set a course for the future.
- To help **check on other businesses**: to assess the credit-worthiness of prospective customers.

To sum up: the information from an accounting system should tell a business if it is going wrong and should indicate what needs to be done to get back on course.

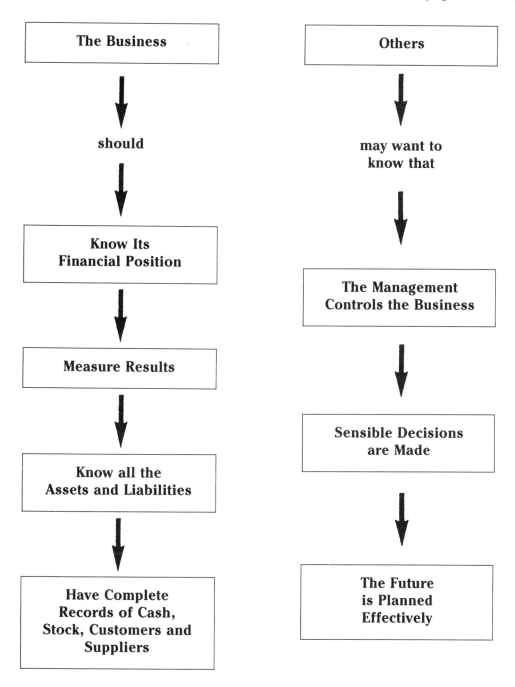

Who needs Accounts?

Accounts are essential for a successful business and are required by many different people for a variety of reasons:

- **The Inspector of Taxes**: for tax assessment.
- **Customs and Excise**: to ensure that Value Added Tax has been accounted for in accordance with Customs and Excise requirements.
- **Banks or other lenders**: to assess the viability of a loan and ensure security.

- **Creditors (Suppliers)**: to check that the business is credit-worthy and is a suitable customer.
- **Owners and shareholders**: to know how the business is doing, and that it is being managed efficiently.
- **Management**: so that it can operate the business effectively as planned, and show a reasonable level of profit.
- **Trade Unions and employees**: to know the trading results of the organisation. Their job is important in their lives, so they should know the results and the worth of the business.
- **Sellers and buyers of a business**: need to know the market value based on figures in the accounts.

WHO NEEDS ACCOUNTING INFORMATION?

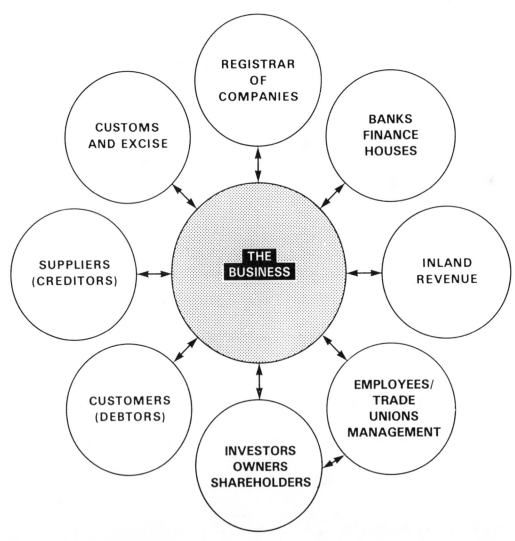

People Involved

Generally, accounts are prepared by **accountants** who are usually members of one of the professional accounting bodies. They qualify by examination and practical experience. To become a professionally qualified accountant can take five years of study. Accountants are assisted by **book-keepers, accounts clerks** or **technicians** who carry out the work of entering information into accounting records, and maintaining and balancing records accurately, under supervision. In most cases book-keeping is a routine job which is carefully supervised. Nowadays much of it is done with the help of accounting machines or computerised systems.

Big organisations employ their own accountants. Small organisations generally have their final accounts prepared by practising accountants, sometimes known as **auditors**. They are responsible for tax computations, the preparation and completion of final accounts, advice on all aspects of accounting and dealings with **tax inspectors** on behalf of their clients.

If you are employed as a book-keeper, auditors may come to check your work from time to time to see that it has been carried out correctly and follows proper accounting principles. Over the last few years the role of the auditor has changed, so you may find that they are more concerned with checking the suitability and accuracy of systems than with the absolute accuracy of the individual records. This doesn't mean, of course, that a book-keeper can afford to be careless and slapdash, but it is now recognised that it is not always cost-effective to obtain one hundred per cent accuracy.

The Books of a Business

Now that we know why accounts are prepared and who does the work, we can look at how transactions are recorded. Remember, keeping books and accounts is a *means* to an end, not an end in itself. The end is the preparation of final accounts, including the **Profit and Loss Account** and the **Balance Sheet**, to help manage the business. At this stage we only need to appreciate this aspect. We will be going into more detail later.

First of all try to get the overall picture, and once this is understood your knowledge will gradually increase.

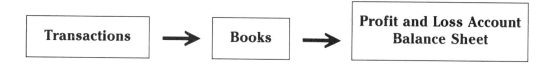

Setting up a Book-keeping System

When starting a business we require a **Ledger**. This contains all the accounts of a business and is often sub-divided into smaller books, for example the cash book. Although the cash book is classed as part of the ledger, it usually contains many cash entries and therefore is written up in a separate book.

We record all the transactions of the business in these books for a period, usually a year, although balances may be extracted regularly to check the arithmetic. At the end of the period we extract from the ledger all the information we need for the preparation of the final accounts. The ledger is the book in which every financial transaction of the business is recorded. The number and types of account will depend on the particular organisation.

In a typical company you may come across the following:

1   **Sub Sections Of The Ledger**
     a   Cash Book (A record of receipts and payments of money).
     b   Sales/Debtors (Customers) ledger.
     c   Purchases/Creditors (Suppliers) ledger.
     d   General/Nominal ledger.

2   **Books Of Original (Prime) Entry**
     a   Sales Day Book
         A record of invoices sent.
     b   Purchases Day Book
         A record of invoices received.
     c   Petty Cash Book
         Records of Credit Notes.
     d   Sales/Purchases Returns Books
         A record of small items of expense.
     e   Wages Book
         A record of wages paid.
     f   The Journal
         A memorandum book for special items.

There may also be other books derived from these, including special income books, Value Added Tax books, rent books, cost books or asset registers.

How the Books are Linked

The following diagram may help you to see how the main elements all help us to work towards our final goal.

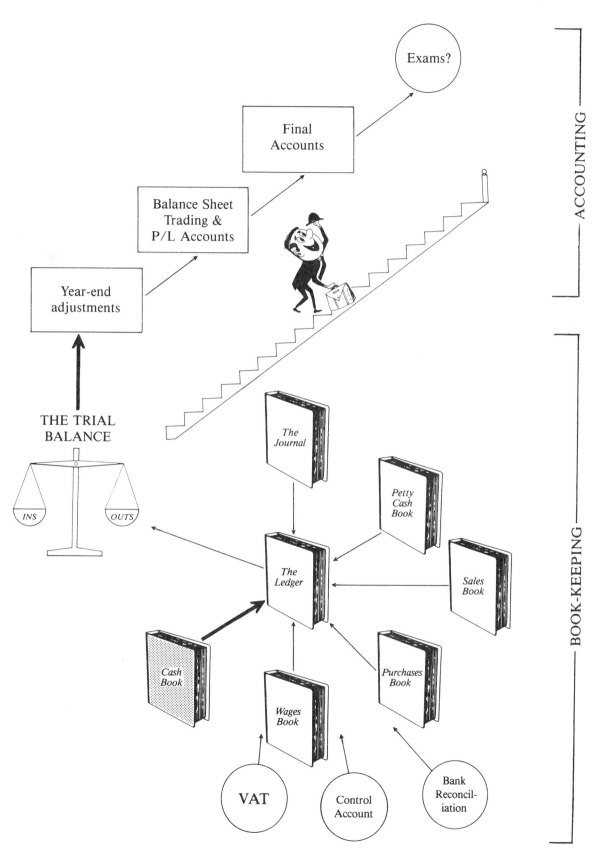

The Language of Book-keeping

You have probably noticed already such words as **credit, capital** and **purchases.** One of the difficulties for a newcomer to the world of book-keeping is to understand the language. Unfortunately, some of these words have a special meaning for the book-keeper which may be slightly different from that in everyday use.

For instance, when we talk of credit sales or purchases, the word 'credit' in this sense means that payment will be made later, so it must not be confused with the **credit side** of an account. Similarly, whenever we buy goods for resale it is a **purchase**, but if we buy an asset for use in the business (say, a motor vehicle) it is not called a purchase. Finally, the word which often causes much confusion is **capital**. From the book-keeping point of view, it is a **liability**. This is because it is a special debt owed by the business to the owner. This should become clearer when you start entering items in your accounts.

Double-entry Book-keeping

This is based on the idea that every transaction has two aspects: something of value is **received** by the business, and at the same time something of value is **given** out of the business.

A simple illustration of this is to consider what happens when you buy some goods from a shop: as far as the shopkeeper is concerned, he has **received** some cash in exchange for giving his customer goods (called **sales**).

Although this is not the only system of book-keeping, it is favoured by most medium to large size organisations. This is because it has certain advantages over single-entry systems.

Advantages of Double-entry

The main advantages can be summarised as:
- Arithmetic accuracy in recording figures.
- More detailed information of every aspect of the business and therefore better control.
- Easier to prepare final accounts to show trading results and position of the business.

Posting to the Ledger

Every time something happens in the business it must be recorded in the accounts **twice**: once to show value coming **in** and once to show value going **out**. The paper used for this is **ledger paper** and **cash paper**. For this lesson only **ledger paper** will be used, and you will see that this is different from the other types of stationery used by book-keepers. The columns are used as shown in the following example.

LEDGER PAPER

DATE		DEBITS (INS) DETAILS	*Fo	£	p	DATE		CREDITS (OUTS) DETAILS	*Fo	£	p
EXAMPLE											
19–6						**CASH BOOK**					
Mar	1	Capital		1000	00	Mar	2	Motor Vehicle		500	00
							3	Balance	c/d	500	00
				1000	00					1000	00
Mar	4	Balance	b/d	500	00						

Note *Fo: *Folio* – A means of cross-referencing. This column is also used to explain what happens to balances i.e. c/d means **carried down**; b/d means **brought down**, etc.

Notice that the **debit** side is **always on the left**, and always shows **value coming in**. This may seem confusing at first, since most people are familiar with bank statements, which show deposits as a credit. However, your bank statement is a copy of an account kept by the bank to show how much of your money they are holding. As it is your cash, the bank owes it to you: you are the creditor!

Before looking at some transactions in the ledger, there are a couple of points to bear in mind. As we are not preparing actual accounts, we can show several accounts on the same page, to avoid wasting paper. In a real system, each account would normally be on a different page. Similarly, examples in the text will not show all the columns, and will often not use pence. You should still use the correct columns on the ledger paper, and show pounds in the '£' column.

Finally, you will notice the convention that the decade is omitted from dates. So, for example, 1982 would be shown as '19–2'. This is a publishing practice. Whenever you are preparing accounts the full date should be shown as appropriate.

Examples

1 Jo Soap starts a business on 1 January 19–0 with £1000 in the business bank account.

The ledger entries for this are:

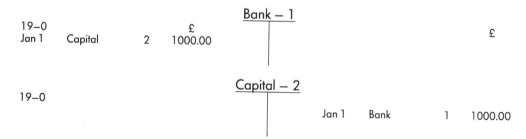

Notes 1 Each account is given a reference, in this case a number. This is used in the folio column.

2 The details column (also known as the **narrative**) shows the name of the account where the other side of the entry will be found.

3 For simplicity at this stage we are ignoring a separate cash book.

2   On January 2 Jo buys some shop fittings for £650, paying by cheque.

So the ledger entries are:

Bank – 1

19–0			£						£
Jan 1	Capital	2	1000.00		Jan 2	Shop fittings	3		650.00

Shop Fittings – 2

19–0				
Jan 2	Bank	1	650.00	

Notes   1   The same Bank account is used: it is only necessary to open a new account when there is a new aspect to record.

2   There is no change to the capital, so it is not shown again in this example.

3   £100 of the fittings are not suitable, so Jo returns them on 3 January and gets a full refund by cheque.

Bank – 1

19–0			£						£
Jan 1	Capital	2	1000.00		Jan 2	Shop fittings	3		650.00
3	Shop fittings	3	100.00						

Shop Fittings – 3

19–0								
Jan 2	Bank	1	650.00		Jan 3	Bank	1	100.00

Notes   1   It may be necessary to abbreviate in the details column, but the account titles should always be shown in full.

2   To show a reduction on an account, we make an entry on the opposite side to the original.

This process continues until the **end of a period** (usually a month), when all the accounts are balanced.

Balancing an Account

Bank – 1

19–0			£						£
Jan 1	Capital	2	1000.00		Jan 2	Shop fittings	3		650.00
3	Shop fittings	3	100.00		31	Balance	c/d		450.00
			1100.00						1100.00
Feb 1	Balance	b/d	450.00						

Notice how after debiting receipts and crediting payments we balance the account by adding up the two sides and deducting the smaller from the larger. The difference is entered and is known as a **balance**: in this case a **surplus.** Writing the balance on the credit side at the end of a period tells us the debit side is bigger, so there is a **debit balance** in this case.

After calculating this balance we bring it back across to the larger side, i.e. we have received more in than we have paid out. So we start the next period with a debit balance: a surplus. This balancing process applies to all accounts in the ledger. However, if there is only one entry on the account, as in the case of capital, many book-keepers would not balance off. If both sides of the account total the same, then it is **clear** (i.e. there is no balance) and it is necessary only to total both sides.

A single line drawn across the cash column indicates we are going to carry out some arithmetic (usually an addition, known as casting) and a double line shows a **total** figure, not the balance, although in some accounts the **total** and the **balance** are the same figure.

In the next unit we will look at more aspects of the double-entry process and learn about different types of accounts.

Questions

1 Explain book-keeping in your own words.
2 Explain accountancy in your own words.
3 Why does a businessman need to keep books and accounts?
4 What is the correct term for 'Ins' in the ledger?
5 What is the correct term for 'Outs' in the ledger?
6 What is the ledger?
7 What does balancing an account mean, and how is this done?
8 Does a credit balance on a bank account mean a surplus or an overdraft?
9 Write up the ledger for J. Craig from the following details. Balance off at the end of the month and carry the balances down to the start of the next month.

19–6
Jan 1 Started business with £500 in the bank
3 Received a loan of £2000 from NATPRO Ltd
15 Bought office fixtures by cheque £250
26 Bought a motor van £1200 by cheque
27 Returned some of the fixtures £50 receiving cheque in settlement

Notes The month should always be written in at the start of a new period, even if the account is balanced each week. The year is usually written only at the start of a new year.

10 Record the following transactions in R. Smith's ledger and balance off at the end of the month.

19–3
June 1 R. Smith commenced business with cash £400
6 Bought goods for cash £360 (remember Purchases)
12 Sold goods for cash £172 (Sales)
Bought office equipment and paid cash £50
15 Sold goods for cash £340
21 Cash sales £45
22 Paid wages in cash £27
29 Paid wages in cash £29
30 Withdrew cash for personal use £40 (Drawings)

11   Don Fisher began business with £1500 capital in cash on 1 May 19—7.

   May   1   Bought shop fittings for cash £345
          2   Bought goods for resale paying cash £1000
              Drew cash for personal use £25
          3   Sold goods for cash £21
          4   Paid rent in cash £30
          5   Bought stationery for cash £7
          6   Sold goods for cash £125
          7   Paid wages in cash £12

   Enter these transactions in the appropriate accounts and balance at the end of the week. Remember there is no need to balance accounts with only one entry.

12   For each of the following transactions, state the names of the accounts to be debited and to be credited. The first one has been completed for you below.

          1   Harry Wheeler commences business with £500 in a business bank account.
          2   Goods for re-sale are bought for cash.
          3   An owner takes goods at purchase price for his own use.
          4   A customer returns some faulty goods and is repaid the full value in cash.
          5   Insurance premiums are paid by cheque.
          6   Cash sales are made.
          7   A motor vehicle is bought, payment made by cheque.
          8   Cash is paid for an electricity bill.
          9   A bill for servicing a delivery van is paid by cheque.
         10   An outstanding loan is repaid in cash.

   Note   Any goods taken by an owner are charged at cost price.

   Answer: 1   Debit: Bank   Credit: Capital

13   Complete the ledger for Barbara Brown from the details given. Balance off all accounts at the end of the month.

   19—9
   Oct   1   Barbara set up in business with £50 in cash and £1000 in the bank
         2   A till and other shop fittings were bought for £275 paying by cheque
         4   Goods to the value of £360 were bought for re-sale payment made by cheque
         7   Cash sales for the week totalled £179
         8   Barbara took out £50 in cash and also £20 worth of goods for herself
        15   Further sales amounted to £210 in cash
        19   £300 cash paid into the bank
        23   More goods bought by cheque for £430
        27   Cash sales made totalling £515
        31   More shelving bought at a cost of £260 payment made in cash

   Each entry should show the date, details, folio and amount.

   Note   Goods taken by an owner for personal use are charged at **purchase** price, not sales price.

14 John Jones has been in business for some time. His bank account at the start of March shows a balance in hand brought forward of £2103.

From the following details of deposits and payments made by cheque complete the bank account and balance off at the end of the month.

Note that there is no need to show any of the other accounts.

19—4

Mar 1 Sales receipts deposited £562
5 Salaries paid £1427
7 Water bill paid £165
10 Goods bought for re-sale £769
11 Fixtures and fittings bought £128
14 Sales income paid in £824
17 £90 withdrawn by John for his own use
19 £50 withdrawn as cash for business use
23 Refund of £70 for faulty goods bought
27 Rent of £130 paid
29 Stationery bought totalling £63
30 Sales paid in £421

Don't forget to start with the opening balance!

15 Enter the following transactions in M. Baker's ledger. Balance off as necessary at the end of the month. Use appropriate folio references.

19—2

March 1 Commenced business with £2000
3 Bought goods for cash £750
8 Bought stationery paying cash £22
Sold goods for cash £280
15 Paid insurance cash £84
18 Paid rent, cash £55
19 Cash sales £146
21 Cash sales £234
24 Bought stamps cash £8
25 Cash sales £112
30 Bought goods for cash £420

16 Write up the bank account for Emily Sands from the following details. Balance off at the end of the month.

19—5			£
Sept	1	Balance b/d from previous month	352
	4	Paid for petrol by cheque	12
	5	Takings banked (sale)	123
	9	Bought goods paying by cheque	148
	12	Takings banked	184
	15	Paid for repairs to typewriter by cheque	25
	17	Goods returned, refund given by cheque	23
	19	Takings banked	86
	24	Cashed cheque for personal use	40
	25	Bought goods paying by cheque	260
	27	Takings banked	120

17   Brian Wyse — Newsagent

Brian Wyse decides to open a business selling tobacco, newspapers and confectionery. He has saved £3000 himself and can borrow a further £2000 from his father, at 5% interest. He will employ two assistants, one full-time and one part-time, as well as three paper boys. In the first week of trading the following transactions take place:

19–8

May   1   Opens a cash account to record his capital and the loan from his father
             Cash purchase of goods for resale to the value of £1500
             Pays rent on his premises £500
       2   Buys a van for use in the business £2000 paying cash
             Cash takings £250 (Sales)
       3   Pays insurance by cash £350
       4   Cash takings £360
       5   Pays wages £175
       6   Takes out £100 for his own use
       7   Cash takings £400

Prepare a cash account from the information given above. Balance off and bring balance down on 8 May. Then enter the information on the appropriate ledger accounts thus completing the double-entry.

Open up all the other ledger accounts and complete the double-entry but do not balance them off as we will continue to use these accounts over the next few units.

Note   For this exercise you should open each account on a separate page of ledger paper.

Answers

9   J. Craig

Balances	Debit £	Credit £
Bank	1100	
Capital		500
Loan – NATPRO Ltd		2000
Office fixtures	200	
Motor van	1200	

10 R. Smith

Balances	Debit £	Credit £
Cash	451	
Capital		400
Purchases	360	
Sales		557
Office equipment	50	
Wages	56	
Drawings	40	

11 Don Fisher

Balances	Debit £	Credit £
Cash	227	
Capital		1500
Shop fittings	345	
Purchases	1000	
Drawings	25	
Sales		146
Rent	30	
Stationery	7	
Wages	12	

---

17 Brian Wyse — Newsagent

Cash Account — 1

19–8				£						£
May	1	Capital	2	3000	May	1	Purchases	4	1500
		Loan – Father	3	2000			Rent	5	500
	2	Sales	7	250		2	Motor van	6	2000
	4	Sales	7	360		3	Insurance	8	350
	7	Sales	7	400		5	Wages	9	175
						6	Drawings	10	100
						7	Balance c/d		1385
				6010					6010
May	8	Balance b/d		1385					

Capital — 2

					May	1	Cash	1	3000

Loan — Father — 3

					May	1	Cash	1	2000

Purchases — 4

May	1	Cash	1	1500					

					Rent — 5
May	1	Cash	1	500	

					Motor Van — 6
May	2	Cash	1	2000	

Sales — 7

					May	2	Cash	1	250
						4	"	1	360
						7	"	1	400

					Insurance — 8
May	3	Cash	1	350	

					Wages — 9
May	5	Cash	1	175	

					Drawings — 10
May	6	Cash	1	100	

Unit 2

Double-entry Book-keeping (2)

At the end of this unit you will be able to:

1 Discuss further aspects of double-entry book-keeping

2 Understand different types of accounts

3 Enter a set of transactions in the ledger.

Revision of Unit 1

First of all we will recap on some of the rules of double-entry that we used in Unit 1:

Each aspect of a transaction is recorded in our books by means of **two entries.**
- The first entry has to be a **debit** to one account.

- The second entry has to be a **credit** to another account.

The first basic rule to remember is:

Every Debit has a Credit

In the text ledger accounts are shown as 'T' accounts, as we saw in Unit 1, like this:

Cash-1

Debit Side	Credit Side
Value In	Value Out

> **Credit transactions do not affect the cash book until payment is made and therefore both the debit and credit entries appear in the ledger.**

To help us post entries in the correct way, we can classify accounts. This can be done in several different ways, depending on what we are actually doing, but at this stage it will be useful to look at one way of grouping our accounts.

Classification of Accounts

Personal Accounts

These accounts are for people or other companies. People who owe us money are our **debtors**; those to whom we owe are our **creditors.**

Real (or Asset) Accounts

These are for actual things of value, such as buildings and motor vehicles, including cash.

Nominal (or Impersonal) Accounts

All other accounts are classified under this heading, including expenses such as wages, heating and income – things which cannot be seen. If this seems a contradiction, it is the cash which is real, not the wages, heating, etc.

You might like to think of the ledger as a spider's web – lots of different strands which are all part of the whole picture.

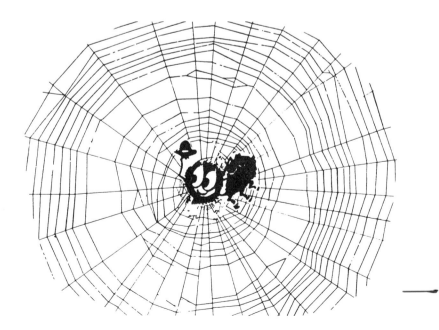

This is a quick way of showing ledger paper, and is used for the ledger accounts in this unit. Each new account has its title written across the centre of the page with a reference number. Remember that although we show several accounts on the same page, in an actual system a new page is usually used for each account.

To keep the double-entry straightforward at this stage, we will use one ledger. However, in most businesses there is a separate cash book for the cash and bank accounts, as well as a sales ledger for all the credit customers (the **debtors**) and a purchase ledger for the credit suppliers (the **creditors**). We will look at these in more detail later in the course.

The ledger is a record of all the transactions of a business, in financial terms. There is a separate account for each type and class of transaction: motor vehicles, machinery, wages, sales and office expenses, for example.

Although many organisations use computerised systems these days, the basic principles are still the same. A business of any size should keep ledgers, although smaller organisations often manage with just an analytical cash book.

Details shown in the cash or bank account are also posted to the opposite side of another ledger account. In this way separate records are kept for each aspect. Consider the way in which the double-entry system works:

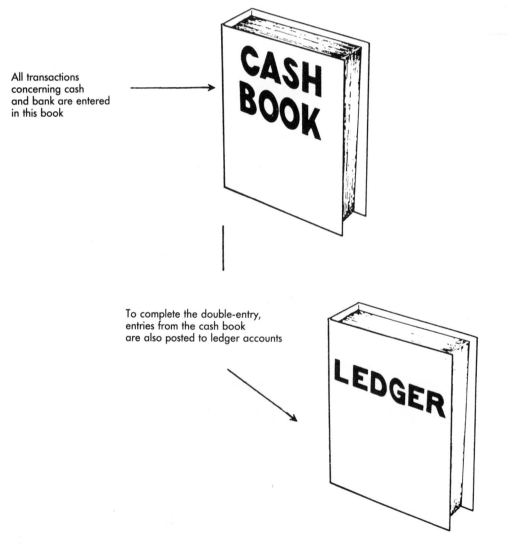

All transactions concerning cash and bank are entered in this book

To complete the double-entry, entries from the cash book are also posted to ledger accounts

There is no limit to the number of accounts which you open. Every business will open up whatever accounts it needs to suit itself. The more accounts you have, the more detail is available to prepare the final accounts (trading and profit and loss accounts and balance sheet), so it is better to have too many than not enough. A good rule to follow is this: *If in doubt, open an account!* But do check first that there isn't one already opened. For instance, you should have only one account for each customer, regardless of how much they buy from you. However, you may need several accounts for different branches of the same company.

The following rules for posting may help:

Personal Accounts:

Debited when they receive value from us;
Credited when they give us value.

Asset Accounts:

Debited when they increase in value;
Credited when they are reduced in value.

Nominal Accounts:

Debited with payments out, and losses;
Credited with income and with profits.

This book-keeper knows
the rules!

To illustrate these rules, let's look at some typical business transactions in the ledger.

Personal Accounts

We buy £500 stock on credit from J. O'Riley, and make credit sales of £440 to T. Kramer.

In the personal accounts the entries would be:

Note that we are not showing the full double-entry in these examples. We should also include dates and folios in a complete entry.

When these accounts are settled, we will pay O'Riley and Kramer will pay us, so the entries will now be:

Debit the Receiver: Credit the Giver

Asset Accounts

Office furniture bought for cash £250 is entered as:

Office Furniture	
£	
Cash 250	

If we decide to sell off some of the furniture because it is unsuitable, say £75 worth, the entry is then:

Office Furniture	
£	£
Cash 250	Cash 75

Debit Increases: Credit Reductions

Nominal Account

We pay out rent in cash of £175. This is shown as:

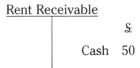

```
                        Rent
               £         │
   Cash   175           │
                        │
```

If we also let out part of our premises and receive rent of £50 in cash, this is posted to the nominal account like this:

```
   Rent Receivable
        │               £
        │       Cash   50
        │
```

Note that we need two separate accounts for the expenses (rent) and the income (rent receivable). Also, a refund of rent, for example, is shown as a credit on the rent account.

Debit Payments: Credit Receipts

These all follow the basic rule of: **Debit** showing value coming **In** and **Credit** showing value going **Out.** If this all seems a bit confusing at first, don't worry. The best way to learn is to do exercises, so the more you do it the easier it becomes, like most things in life!

Credit Transaction

In the first unit, all the transactions involved immediate payment, either in cash or by cheque. However, as you probably know, most businesses these days rely on credit transactions. By this, we simply mean that payment is made later, it does not tell us anything about the entries in the accounts, since there must still be a debit and a credit, of course.

As you can imagine, it is very important to know exactly how much we owe our suppliers, and equally important to know who owes us money, and how much. For this reason, we must have a separate account for each credit customer (debtor) and each credit supplier (creditor). Let us now look at a typical example:

Credit Purchases

On 3 March we buy goods on credit to the value of £250 from Wholesalers Ltd. On inspection, some of the goods are found to be damaged, so are returned on 5 March and a credit note for £40 received. This account is settled in full by cheque on 31 March.

The first step for these transactions would be to show the credit purchase:

Purchases — 1

			£				
March 3	Wholesalers Ltd	2	250				

Wholesalers Ltd —2

							£
				March 3	Purchases	1	250

Next, we record the returns. Notice that it is better to use a new account for this, although it is quite acceptable to show the returns as a credit on the purchases account.

Wholesalers Ltd — 2

			£				£
March 5	Returns	3	40	March 3	Purchases	1	250

Purchases Returns — 3 *

							£
				March 3	Wholesalers Ltd	2	40

Note *Alternative names for this account are 'Returns Out' or 'Outwards'. Similarly, the Sales Returns Account is also known as 'Returns In' or 'Inwards'.

Finally, settlement is posted as follows:

Bank (in the Cash Book)

							£
				March 31	Wholesalers Ltd	2	210

Wholesalers Ltd — 2

			£				£
March 5	Returns	3	40	March 3	Purchases	1	250
31	Bank	CB	210				
			250				250

Note 'CB' means **Cash Book**. Note that this account is now clear, but it is not necessarily **closed**, since we may well be dealing with this supplier again in the future. Notice also how the entry in the cash book does not tell why we have paid the cash; we only know that we have paid. To find out why, we must look at the account for Wholesalers Ltd.

Credit Sales

Since double-entry book-keeping is based on 'Ins' and 'Outs' and is very logical, sales, as you would expect, are the reverse of purchases. So, the **sales account** has **credits** to show goods going out, and the personal account is a debtor.

If we sell £370 on credit to Ivor Evans on 7 March, and he pays us £200 on account at the end of the month, his account will look like this:

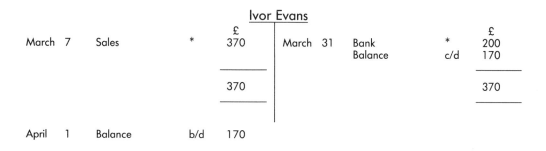

			£						£
March 7	Sales	*	370	March 31	Bank		*	200
					Balance		c/d	170
			370					370
April 1	Balance	b/d	170					

Note * No folios are shown as we are not looking at all the accounts involved in these entries.

We can now look at a full worked example to see how all these different types of transactions would be posted to the various accounts.

A Worked Example to show how to post Ledger Accounts

Simon Carter started business on 1 January with £150 capital in cash. During his first month of trading the following transactions took place. Open the necessary accounts to record these transactions and balance off wherever appropriate.

			£
January	1	Bought goods for cash	20
	2	Bought more goods on credit from Weston & Sons	85
	4	Bought fixtures for cash	15
	7	Cash sales	136
	9	Bought office equipment on credit from Remington Ltd	32
	9	Cash sales	140
	18	Paid wages in cash	33
	24	Paid Weston & Sons in cash in full	85
	25	Bought goods (on credit) from W. West	56
	25	Paid wages in cash	33
	28	Bought stationery for cash	15
	31	Cash sales	138
	31	Cash withdrawn from the business for private use by Simon Carter	30

These transactions are posted as follows:

Simon Carter

Cash — 1

Jan			*	£	Jan				£
	1	Capital	2	150		1	Purchases	3	20
	7	Sales	6	136		4	Fixtures	5	15
	9	Sales	6	140		18	Wages	9	33
	31	Sales	6	138		24	Weston & Sons	4	85
						25	Wages	9	33
						28	Stationery	11	15
						31	Drawings	12	30
							Balance	c/d	333
				564					564
Feb	1	Balance	b/d	333					

The entries are then posted to the other ledger accounts as shown:

Capital — 2

					Jan	1	Cash	1	150

* **Remember**   Use folios as a cross-reference.

These indicate an account number or a page number in the ledger and should not be entered until the double-entry is completed.

Purchases — 3

Jan	1	Cash	1	20					
	2	Weston & Sons	4	85	Jan	31	Balance	c/d	161
	25	W. West	11	56					
				161					161
Feb	1	Balance	b/d	161					

Weston & Sons — 4

Jan	24	Cash	1	85	Jan	2	Purchases	3	85

Fixtures — 5

Jan	4	Cash	1	15					

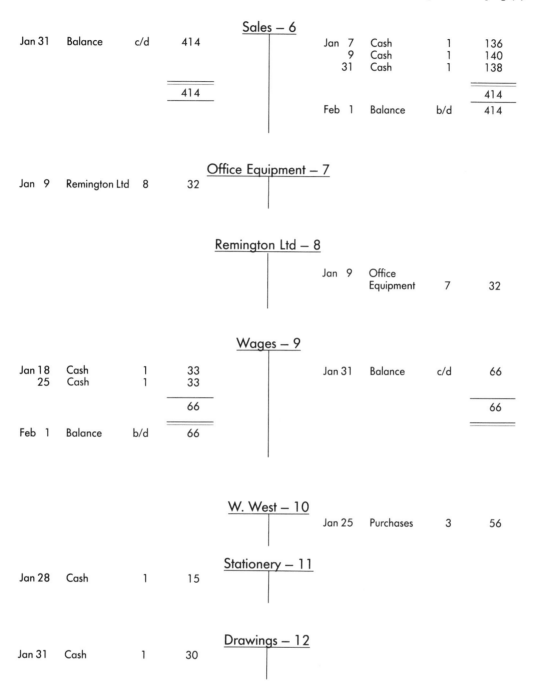

Sales — 6

Jan 31	Balance	c/d	414		Jan 7	Cash	1	136
					9	Cash	1	140
					31	Cash	1	138
			414					414
					Feb 1	Balance	b/d	414

Office Equipment — 7

Jan 9	Remington Ltd	8	32	

Remington Ltd — 8

		Jan 9	Office Equipment	7	32

Wages — 9

Jan 18	Cash	1	33		Jan 31	Balance	c/d	66
25	Cash	1	33					
			66					66
Feb 1	Balance	b/d	66					

W. West — 10

		Jan 25	Purchases	3	56

Stationery — 11

Jan 28	Cash	1	15	

Drawings — 12

Jan 31	Cash	1	30	

Note Each account is usually on a separate page in an actual ledger.

Capital

So far we have seen new businesses starting up with the introduction of capital in the form of cash or money in the bank. Alternatively, the proprietor of a business may bring in any type of asset, for instance a motor vehicle or buildings. In this case, the capital account must still be credited, but the appropriate asset account (motor vehicles or premises) is debited, since a new asset has been brought in.

Drawings

Similarly, drawings can be in some form other than cash: obviously someone running a grocery business is not going to a rival store to buy his own tea and coffee. Any goods taken from stock for the use of the owner must be treated as drawings. In this case the debit goes to the drawings account as we have already seen, but the credit entry goes to the purchases account.

In many smaller businesses this is done as an adjustment at the end of the year since it is not practical to make the necessary entries in the books every time a packet of tea is taken out of stock.

Revenue/Capital

Another way of classifying our accounts, particularly items of expenditure and income, is into **revenue** and **capital.** This becomes particularly important at the end of the year when we calculate our profit (or loss) and the worth of the business, so it is important to open the appropriate accounts and post to the right ones from the very beginning.

Capital Expenditure/Income

This is **long-term**: that is, involving **fixed assets** or **long-term liabilities**. Such items are in the business over several years. Fixed assets include premises, plant and equipment, fixtures and fittings, office equipment and motor vehicles. Long-term liabilities are such things as loans and mortgages, as well as the capital itself. Any expenditure on fixed assets, or income arising from their disposal, is not counted as part of the normal day-to-day transactions. Any cost of using such assets in running the business and therefore (hopefully) generating profits is accounted for in what is known as a **year-end adjustment** — in this case, **depreciation**.

These are **balance sheet items** — part of the **net worth** of a business.

Revenue Expenditure/Income

This is the day-to-day payments and receipts. Any such payments are written-off in the accounting period to which they relate. Once the payment is made, there is no further benefit to be gained.

Revenue expenses include all the everyday costs of running an organisation, such as salaries and wages; rent, rates and insurance; repairs and maintenance; heating, lighting and cleaning, and all the other costs associated with earning profits. **Revenue income** can be identified in our books by the word 'Received' or 'Receivable' included in the account name. The common income items (apart from sales) are rent receivable, (cash) discount receivable and commission receivable. These are **trading** or **profit and loss accounts** items.

Note It is important to make a clear distinction between these two types of income and expenditure, in order to be able to calculate accurate figures for profit and the net worth of a business.

Three-Column Ledger Account

You are probably already familiar with this style of account. This is because bank and building society statements are in this form. Most statements from credit suppliers are also set out like this.

Three-column ledger accounts follow all the rules of book-keeping. The only difference is that we are given an up-dated balance after each day's transactions. This is a big advantage for personal accounts (debtors and creditors), whenever there is a query about an outstanding balance. For this reason, it is common to find all debtors and creditors accounts kept in this style.

Example

Consider the account for Wholesalers Ltd (page 26). It would look like this:

Wholesalers Ltd – 2

Date	Details	Fo	Debit	Credit	Balance
			£	£	£
19--					
March 1	Balance	b/f			–
3	Purchases	1		250	250 Cr
5	Returns	3	40		210 Cr
31	Bank	CB	210		–

Note 'b/f' means **brought forward**. There may be extra details, such as invoice or credit note numbers, and a cheque number, but the general principles are just the same as before.
It is often necessary to indicate whether it is a debit or credit balance. A bank will show this, for example, by *o/d* for an overdraft.

Summary

We have now covered the basic principles of double-entry book-keeping. This is the foundation on which all the following units will be built. As you become more familiar with the disciplines involved, you will be able to look at accounts in isolation, without needing to see all of the double-entry. You will be able to interpret each account, and read what has happened in the business.

There are always signs and clues to read: whether an entry is on the debit or credit side, the narrative (details) used to describe the entry, and the folio which has been used. All of these points are important in posting entries to the accounts, as well as the way in which the accounts are balanced.

To help you become proficient at double-entry book-keeping, here are some golden rules. There is no need to memorise them, as long as you can understand and apply them:

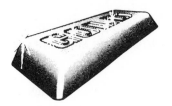

> • Every **debit** has a **credit**
> • The **debit** is always on the **left**
> • The **credit** is always on the **right**
> • **Debit** shows value coming **in**
> • **Credit** shows value going **out**
> • **Assets** and **expenses** have **debit** balances
> • **Liabilities** and **income** have **credit** balances
> • To **reduce** an account, make an entry on the **opposite** side
> • A **balance** is the **difference** between two sides
> • **Capital** is what is **owed** to the **owner**

Questions

1 What are the main books in a book-keeping system?

2 What is double-entry book-keeping?

3 What is the basic rule for double-entry book-keeping?

4 What is an account?

5 What are the advantages of double-entry book-keeping?

6 a) When money is paid out, what are the ledger entries?

b) When money is received, what are the entries?

c) J. Lester buys a second-hand motor vehicle for his business and pays by cheque. He should record this by:

   i) debiting bank account, crediting motor vehicles account
   ii) crediting bank account, debiting motor vehicles account
   iii) debiting cash account, crediting motor vehicles account
   iv) crediting cash account, debiting motor vehicles account.

d) The sale on credit of goods worth £50 to R. Brown should be recorded by:

   i) debiting sales account £50, crediting R. Brown £50
   ii) crediting sales account £50, debiting R. Brown £50
   iii) debiting purchases account £50, crediting R. Brown £50
   iv) crediting purchases account £50, debiting R. Brown £50.

7 Which accounts should be debited and credited for the following transactions? Set out your answer as indicated.

	Account to be	
	Debited	Credited
a) Cash paid into business bank account by proprietor £4000		
b) Goods bought for resale on credit from A. Smith £1000		
c) General rates paid £400 by cheque		
d) Paid A. Smith amount due by cheque		
e) Goods sold to M. Brown for £80 on credit		
f) Rent paid on premises £75 by cheque		
g) Wages paid £98 in cash		

8 Prepare the personal account for P. Combes, a credit customer, in three-column ledger style.

19–7
June   1   Balance owing brought forward from May £175
      3   Bought more goods from us £250
   15   Returned some of the goods as faulty £60
   29   More sales on credit £120
   30   Cheque received in part payment £200

9 Jane Small started up in business on 1 January 19–3 and kept a record of the following transactions for her first month's trading:

Jan   1   Introduced £1000 cash as capital
     1   Bought plant for £500 for cash
     1   Bought materials on credit from A B Supplies Ltd £1000
     7   Paid wages in cash £110
   14   Paid wages in cash £120
   21   Paid wages in cash £100
   28   Paid wages in cash £130
   28   Sold goods to G. Blaze £2600
   31   G. Blaze paid by cash £1000 on account
   31   Paid A B Supplies Ltd £800 off their account

Show all the ledger accounts to record these transactions in Jane's books and balance the accounts at the end of the month, bringing down all the balances on 1 February. Use folio references to help check your entries. There is no need to balance those accounts with only one entry.

10 Record the following transactions in double-entry form in R. Smith's ledger. Balance the accounts at the end of the month. All transactions are for cash, except where stated.

19–2			£
June	1	R. Smith started with capital	400
	6	Bought goods	360
	12	Sold goods	172
		Bought office equipment	50
	15	Sold more goods	340
	16	Bought goods on credit from J. Wilson and Co.	50
	21	Sales	45
	22	Paid rates	27
	24	Paid rent	24
	25	Bought goods on credit from R. Brown	42
	27	Paid insurance	12
	28	Paid J. Wilson and Co.	50
	30	Paid lighting and heating	18
		Took out cash for personal use	40

Note   Rent, rates and insurance can be included on one account.

11 Draw up all the necessary ledger accounts to record the following details. Balance off all accounts at the end of the month.

19–2
July 1 Ethel Shearsden has balances brought forward on these accounts:

	£
Capital	4000 CR
Cash	50 DR
Bank	1750 DR
Motor vehicles	2200 DR

   3 Paid wages by cheque £58

   7 Bought another car on credit from Wheels Ltd £3100 paying a deposit of £250 by cheque

  10 Bought goods on credit for £675 from Wholesalers Ltd

  13 Sold goods on credit to Ivor Stall £524

  14 Ethel withdrew £100 from the bank as cash for the business

  17 Paid wages in cash £62

  20 Ethel paid in £1000 cheque which she had won on the Premium Bonds to increase her capital

  21 Bought more goods on credit from Wholesalers Ltd £594

  25 Ivor Stall returned faulty goods to the value of £76

  29 Paid road fund licences by cheque £200

  31 Ivor Stall settled his account by cheque

  31 Sent Wholesalers Ltd a cheque for £500 on account

Note There are alternative ways of treating the purchase of the car (7 July), but the net result — that is, the closing balances — should be the same whichever entries are made. 'DR' means Debit and 'CR' means Credit.

12 Show the ledger account for Aye to Zed Ltd, a supplier, from the following details:

19–1
Jan 1 Balance owing, brought foward £121

   9 Purchases bought on credit £346

  11 Return of damaged goods £54

  13 Cheque sent for balance owing on 1 January, after receiving cash discount given by Aye to Zed of £5

  15 Further purchases of £273 made. Additional charge made for carriage of goods into the premises of £32

  19 Payment made on account £200 by cheque

  23 Purchase of £416 made

  31 Settled the account by cheque after taking £9 cash discount

Note This is a creditor's account. Anything which increases the amount is a **credit** entry, anything which reduces the amount due is a **debit.**

13 Draw up a full set of ledger accounts for Anil Mustafa, a clothing retailer, balancing off where necessary at the end of the month.

19–7
Aug 3 Started business with £5000 in the bank
4 Purchased a motor van £3000, paying £1000 deposit and the remaining £2000 on credit from XY motors
5 Bought goods for re-sale £2100 paying by cheque
8 Bought more goods on credit from Eezee Pay £1750
9 Paid for advertisement in local paper £75
12 Sold goods £365 for cash
14 Banked cheque for £260 for further sales
17 Received a bill from British Telecom for £45
21 Sold goods on credit to B. James £427
25 Paid salaries by cheque £983
28 Transferred £200 cash to the bank
30 Settled the British Telecom bill by cheque
31 Returned some faulty goods to Eezee Pay £124
31 B. James settled his account by cheque

Note There is only **one** possible entry for the payment on 9 August if you consider the previous entries.

14 Write up the ledger account of B. Mann as shown in the Ledger of M & N Materials Ltd (B. Mann is a customer). Balance off the account at the end of the month.

19–4
Apr 2 Opening balance on B. Mann's account (debit) £166
4 B. Mann sends a cheque for £100 on account
5 Goods sold on credit to B. Mann £14
7 Further sales on credit to B. Mann £175
10 B. Mann sends a cheque for the balance of money owed on 2 April
15 Goods returned by B. Mann as faulty value £25
27 Goods sold on credit to B. Mann £87

15 Open the necessary accounts to record the following transactions in D. Frank's ledger. Balance off the accounts where appropriate.

19–7
Jan 1 Commenced business with £1200 cash.
Bought office equipment on credit from Type Supplies Ltd £280
3 Bought goods on credit from A. Tubbs £164
8 Cash sales £52
Sold goods on credit to W. Minns £64
16 Paid Type Supplies Ltd in cash £280
20 Bought goods for cash £76
23 Cash sales £48
28 Paid A. Tubbs in cash £100

16 Brian Wyse — Newsagent

The activities for the second week of trading are as follows:

May	8	Pays Rates for 6 months £375
	9	Buys more stock for cash £1000
		Buys stock from A. Jones £1200 on credit
	10	Cash takings £370
		Pays window cleaner £5
	11	Buys petrol for van £15
	12	Cash takings £255
	13	Pays wages £180 and takes £110 drawings
	14	Cash takings £310

Complete the accounts for the second week and balance off. Take care with the date on which the balances are brought down.

You should continue to use those accounts already opened in the ledger: purchases, sales, cash for example.

There is no need to do anything with those accounts which are not involved in the above activities (i.e. capital).

Answers

8   P. Combes   Balance   285 Dr

9   Jane Small   Balances

	Debit £	Credit £
Cash	240	
Capital		1000
Plant	500	
Purchases	1000	
Sales		2600
G. Blaze	1600	
A. B. Supplies Ltd		200
Wages	460	

10	R. Smith	Balances	Debit £	Credit £
		Cash	376	
		Capital		400
		Purchases	452	
		Sales		557
		Office equipment	50	
		Rent, rates and insurance	63	
		R. Brown		42
		Lighting and heating	18	
		Drawings	40	

Have you noticed that the total of the debit balances is the same as the total of the credit balances? This is an important way of checking the arithmetic, which will be explained later in the course.

---

16 Brian Wyse — Newsagent

Cash — 1

19–8				£						£
May	8	Balance	b/f	1385	May	8	Rates	12	375
	10	Sales	7	370		9	Purchases	4	1000
	12	Sales	7	255		10	Cleaning	13	5
	14	Sales	7	310		11	Motor expenses	14	15
						13	Wages	9	180
							Drawings	10	110
						14	Balance	c/d	635
				2320					2320
May	15	Balance	b/d	635					

Purchases — 4

May	1	Cash	1	1500	May	14	Balance	c/d	3700
	9	"	1	1000					
		A. Jones	11	1200					
				3700					3700
May	15	Balance	b/d	3700					

Sales — 7

May	14	Balance	c/d	1945	May	2	Cash	1	250
						4	"	1	360
						7	"	1	400
						10	"	1	370
						12	"	1	255
						14	"	1	310
				1945					1945
					May	15	Balance	b/d	1945

Wages — 9

May	5	Cash	1	175	May	14	Balance	c/d	355
	13	"	1	180					
				355					355
May	15	Balance	b/d	355					

Drawings — 10

May	6	Cash	1	100	May	14	Balance	c/d	210
	13	Cash	1	110					
				210					210
May	15	Balance	b/d	210					

A. Jones — 11

				May	9	Purchases	4	1200

Rates — 12

May	8	Cash	1	375

Cleaning — 13

May	10	Cash	1	5

Motor Expenses — 14

May	11	Cash	1	15

Note Only those accounts which have changed in the second week are shown.

Note also the use of folios as an extra check on the double-entry.

Unit 3

The Cash Book and Petty Cash

At the end of this unit you will be able to:

1 Show the different types of cash books used in business

2 Study the use of these cash books

3 Understand where the double-entry from a cash book is entered

4 Show how to write up cash books and also explain the imprest system of petty cash.

Two Golden Rules for the Cash Book

1 When money is received, debit the cash book and credit the account in the ledger to which the income relates.

2 When money is paid out, credit the cash book and debit the account in the ledger to which the expenditure relates.

The Two-Column Cash Book

As the business grows larger we keep a more detailed cash book and take into account all cash, including physical money, cheques received and paid out, as well as other bank transfers, such as standing orders.

It is good administrative practice to bank all money as it is received, on a daily basis. Should we receive cash as part of sales it is good accounting practice to bank these takings gross rather than deduct any amounts to cover cash expense. Conversely, as far as possible we should make all payments by cheque, as this offers greater security and acts as evidence of payment.

Example

Cash Book

DR			Receipts		CR			Payments	
Date	Details	Fo	Cash	Bank	Date	Details	Fo	Cash	Bank
19–5			£	£				£	£
June 1	Balances	b/d	257.00	1640.00	June 1	S. Dixon - Rent	R1		200.00
6	Bank	¢	50.00		6	Cash	¢		50.00
8	Sales	S1	135.00		7	Water rate	R2		37.50
15	Sales	S1	48.00		18	Window cleaner	M1	10.00	
22	Sales	S1	50.00		19	B. Ginner	P1		67.00
23	A. Bright	C1		26.75	26	Wages	W1		55.00
29	Cash	¢		200.00	28	Repairs	M1	11.80	
					29	Bank	¢	200.00	
					30	Balances	c/d	318.20	1457.00
			540.00	1866.75				540.00	1866.75
July 1	Balances	b/d	318.20	1457.25					

Three-Column Cash Book

The three-column cash book that you see below is one that you will find in businesses which do not bank all cash received each day. In this particular case they keep the cash in the till and from time to time bank some of it. The remainder is used for paying expenses. In the example you will also see that, in addition to cash and bank columns, a column is provided for cash discount.

Cash Book

Date	Particulars	Fo	(Cash) Discount (allowed)	Cash	Bank	Date	Particulars	Fo	(Cash) Discount (received)	Cash	Bank
19–2			*	*	*						
June 1	Balances	b/f		92	510	June 13	Wages	4		104	
4	Sales	3		342		16	Shell Ltd	PL5	16		304
7	Sales	3		371		20	Rent	6			140
22	L. Bitman	SL5	4		76	28	Bank	¢		1000	
26	Sales	3		476		30	Drawings	7			200
28	Cash	¢			1000		Pim Ltd	PL8	8		312
							Balances	c/d		177	630
			3	4	1281	1586			24	1281	1586
July 1	Balances	b/d		177	630						

↓ To Ledger (in total)   ↓ To Ledger (in total)

Note The two discount columns are never balanced but **totalled**, so there is no balance to bring down in respect of discount — they are two quite distinct accounts.
* From this point is it no longer necessary to use £ signs in actual accounts, although they will still be used in certain circumstances.

Cash Discounts

Discounts Allowed are in respect of a cash deduction made to your customers for their prompt payment. For example, if they pay within seven days of the date of the invoice we may allow a 2½% discount. Both the cheque and discount are posted to the customer's account in the debtors' ledger. Discounts allowed are debited as an expense in the discount allowed account and credited to the debtors' ledger account. Conversely, if we pay promptly our suppliers (creditors) may allow us to make a deduction from the bill. This is known as **Discount Received.** Both the cheque and discount are posted to the supplier's account in the creditors' ledger. Discounts received are debited to the creditors' account and credited to the discount received account.

Cash discounts are shown in the cash book and are **Memorandum** columns which do not take part in the totals or balances. They are added up and posted in total to the nominal ledger. When we refer to a memorandum column, it indicates that this is an 'aide memoire' (a reminder). In a three-column cash book it shows at a glance how much discount we have allowed or received. It also keeps relatively small amounts out of the actual ledger accounts, which can then be posted in total at the end of each month.

Example Explained

Look at the three-column cash book on page 41 in detail and study the columns.

Please go through each item and make sure you understand each aspect of the entry.

1 **The Date column** records when the cash entry takes place.
2 **The Particulars column** records details of transactions and describes the nature of the entry, whether that be a cash sale or a receipt from a customer.
3 **The Folio column** is for cross-referencing to indicate where the opposite entry has been posted into the ledger. SL would indicate posting has been made from the cash book to the sales ledger. A number indicates a page number or an account.
4 **Cash Discount column** is for recording amounts of discounts received and allowed. Remember, these are memorandum columns, and *not* the actual accounts, which are kept in the ledger.
5 **Cash column** is for recording actual money (e.g. notes and coinage) received and paid.
6 **Bank column** is for recording all money (cheques and cash) paid in to or from the bank.

In the example we start off with both a cash and bank balance. The £92 refers to cash in a cash box or till and the £510 relates to cash in the bank. Any payments for cash are shown on the credit side in the cash column (i.e. wages £104) and you see how the £1000 cash is paid into the bank column on 28 June. This is known as a **Contra Entry** and appears on both sides, again crediting the cash book cash column and debiting the cash book bank column. To explain this, we are taking money out of the till and putting it into the bank. The entry is reversed if we take money out of the bank and put it in the till.

Balancing

To ascertain the balances of cash in the cash book (or till) and at the bank, we **balance** both columns of the cash book. Remember that a balance is where one side (in this case £177 cash and £630 at the Bank) exceeds the other side.

Folio Column

Remember that the function of the folio column is to show where the item has been posted in the ledger.

Value Added Tax

In many businesses you will also find a column in respect of Value Added Tax, but in order not to complicate matters at this stage we will leave VAT for the moment and look at it in the next unit.

Analytical Cash Books

For some businesses it is more convenient to maintain details of cash income and expenditure analysed over different headings, particularly VAT.

As with the discount columns in a three-column cash book, the totals of each of the columns are posted to the actual accounts in the main ledger, or in a small business are totalled at the end of the year and used to prepare the final accounts. Such cash books are similar to petty cash accounts.

Example

Analytical Cash Book

Receipts	Sales	VAT	Date		Details	Payments	Purchases	Wages	Sundries	VAT
£	£	£			£	£	£	£	£	£
300.00			June	1	Balance b/d					
151.80	132.00	19.80		2	R. Hope					
				2	M. Beveridge	115.00	100.00			15.80
				3	R. Mather	75.50		75.50		
				3	Rail fares	24.00			24.00	
193.20	168.00	25.20		4	M. Axon					
				5	W. Bagley	312.80	272.00			40.80
103.73	90.20	13.53		6	W. Thompson					
				7	Balance c/d	221.43				
748.73	390.20	58.53				748.73	372.00	75.50	24.00	55.80
221.43			June	8	Balance b/d					

This basic idea can be extended to incorporate as many different analysis columns as the particular business requires. Notice that normally there are more expenditure columns than there are income columns. Notice also that the 'Receipts' and 'Payments' columns are the only ones that are balanced. The totals of all the analysis columns (e.g. sales, purchases, VAT) are posted to the appropriate ledger accounts.

Receipts Voucher File

It is common practice to have a document or voucher retained on file so that the entry into the cash book can be checked. This may be used by an auditor or a VAT inspector. Such vouchers may be a remittance advice from a customer, a Government grant letter or a memorandum note of cash paid in by a proprietor.

Payments Voucher File

For recording every item paid out a payments voucher file is maintained. This may be in a lever-arch file and should show the cheque number as a means of cross-referencing the voucher with the entry into the cash book. An example would be an invoice or bill.

Petty Cash

The petty cash book is maintained for the small payments which it would be inconvenient to enter into the main cash book.

It is generally kept by one employee who looks after the petty cash box and is responsible for all relatively small payments such as stamps, coffee and tea supplies, cleaning materials, etc., as well as keeping the account in order and submitting claims for reimbursement to the cashier.

Petty Cash Vouchers

Here is an example of an 'internal' petty cash voucher:

Petty Cash Voucher	15 May 19–2	
For what required	**Amount**	
	£	p
Stamps	1	20
Envelopes	1	15
	2	35

Signature: S. Stevens
Authorised by: D. Luke.

A voucher should be completed as evidence of payment for all items of expenditure. Vouchers should be signed by the recipient and authorised for payment by a senior manager. Users of petty cash should be instructed to obtain receipts as proof of the expenditure. An example is given below.

Customer's Receipt for Cash Purchase 14 July 19–6	Store Name and Address Stamp
2–40 Watt Electric Light Bulbs @ 0.30	0.60
1–Candle Lampshade	3.35
1–13 amp Plug	0.45
For F.W. Worth & Co. Limited	£4.40
Received With Thanks L. Pattison	Amount

All expenditure vouchers over £10 must have a VAT number shown. You may have noticed that the till receipts from many large stores actually show the VAT registraton number to comply with this requirement. The petty cash should be kept up-to-date and balanced either weekly or monthly, or when more cash is needed.

Petty Cash Voucher File

All payments out will need a voucher or receipt and these are generally filed in the petty cash voucher file and cross-referenced with the entry in the petty cash book. File them in date and numerical order. These are evidence to the auditors and the VAT inspector of amounts actually paid out.

Now complete what you think a petty cash item would be, using the voucher on page 45 as an example for your layout.

Petty Cash box — keep locked away

Remember: Vouchers + Cash = Amount of Imprest (or Float)

The Imprest System

This is a system of maintaining a float at a set level. To exercise control so that a check can easily be made, and also for convenience, many firms use the imprest system where a fixed amount is maintained in the petty cash box – for example £50. Any senior person checking the petty cash should therefore find that the total of paid vouchers and cash in the box always equals the amount of the imprest (or float) i.e. £50. This will show if everything is in order, or alternatively that there is something wrong (e.g. money or a voucher missing) and is an effective way of controlling the petty cash system.

The advantages of an imprest system are:
- Control
- Facility
- Spotlighting Errors

See how the imprest is shown on this example of the analysed petty cash book.

Petty Cash Book

Float	Date	Details	PCV	Total	Postage and Phone	Fares	Cleaning	Sundry Expenses	Stationery and Equipment	Folio	Sundry Ledger a/cs	VAT
£	19–2			£	£	£	£	£	£		£	
50.00	May											
	25	Stamps	1	1.50	1.50							
	26	Postage	2	0.65	0.65							
	26	Cleaning	3	0.45			0.45					
	27	Sundries	4	0.32				0.32				
	27	Fares	5	1.45		1.45						
1.00	28	Personal Phone Calls	GL6									
	28	A. Kell	7	1.34						PL2	1.34	
	29	Cleaning	8	0.65			0.65					
	29	Sundries	9	0.40				0.40				
	29	Travelling	10	1.65		1.65						
	30	Envelopes	11	0.45					0.45			
	30	Office Equipment	12	1.65					1.65			
	30	Sundries	13	0.15				0.15				
	31	Totals		10.66	2.15	3.10	1.10	0.87	2.10		1.34	
	31	Balance	c/d	40.34	GL6 ↓	GL2 ↓	GL4 ↓	GL3 ↓	GL5 ↓			GL10 ↓
51.00				51.00	Postage a/c	Travel a/c	Cleaning a/c	Sundries a/c	Stationery & Equipment a/c			VAT a/c
40.34	June 1	Balance	b/d									
9.66	1	Cash	CB7									

Note The amount required to restore the float is the difference between the amount actually spent (£10.66) and any income in the period (£1).

By using analysis columns as in the main cash book a great deal of work is saved by posting the totals of expenditure from the petty cash book to the debit side of the appropriate ledger accounts. In this system of recording, the petty cash book is a ledger account — the petty cash account — and forms part of the double entry. The complete double entry is:

i)   Credit the cash book and debit the petty cash with sums paid into the float.

ii) Credit the petty cash book with expenses paid and debit the totals to the appropriate ledger expense accounts.

The column headed 'Sundry Expenses' is for unusual items which may need to be debited individually to ledger accounts.

Petty Cash

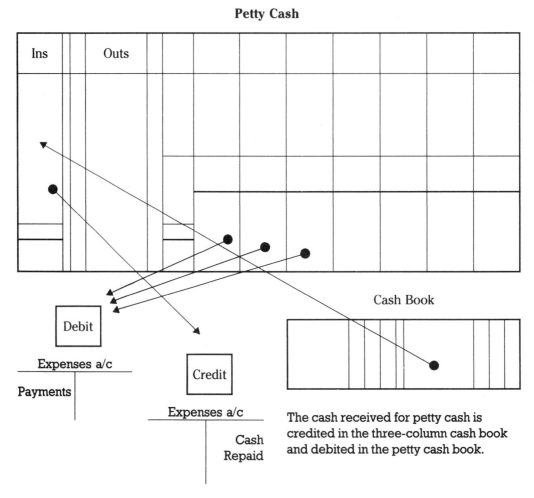

The cash received for petty cash is credited in the three-column cash book and debited in the petty cash book.

Self-Balancing

Note particularly how the totals of the columns added across equal the total of the payments added downwards. This is important as a cross-check. Note also how the balance is the **difference** between the expenditure and the receipts for a period. The balance is brought down to start the beginning of the next period's transactions. Like the cash book, the Balance is the **excess** of receipts over expenditure.

Note also the Value Added Tax column which will be dealt with in the next unit.

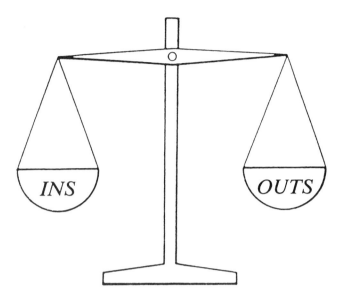

At the end of a period, all the accounts are balanced.

Questions

1 What is a petty cash book?

2 Why is it necessary to use petty cash vouchers?

3 Explain the imprest system.

4 Where are items posted from the petty cash book?

5 Write up the following transactions in a two-column cash book (with cash and bank columns) and balance off.

19–2

Jan 1 Cash in hand (balance at start of year) £42
1 Cash at bank £120
2 Paid M. Smith by cheque £21
3 Paid transport expenses in cash £2
4 Received a cheque from L. Brown £31
5 Paid M. Stewart by cheque £40
9 Cash sales £18
10 E. Rogers paid his account by cheque £60
15 Bought goods and paid by cheque £76
22 Cash sales £10
26 Paid cash for postage stamps £2
31 Withdrew cheque for personal use £15
31 Paid wages in cash £18
31 Paid cash into bank £20

6 Enter the following items in J. Smithson's three-column cash book and balance off at 26 October.

19–2

Oct 1 Balances in hand, cash £14 and bank £1790
2 Paid to R. Fairley by cheque £424, discount £20

4   Received from J. Thorpe cheque for £82. Allowed him discount of £2
5   Drew £60 from bank for office cash (contra entry)
6   Paid water rate £16; paid for repairs to office safe £10; paid office cleaner £7; all payments made in cash
7   Paid T. Williams cash £40, received discount £4
9   Received cheque from Swift & Sons £42, allowed discount of £4
10 Received from C. Conran cash £30, gave discount £3
17 Paid to P. Stevens cheque for £720, discount £16
25 Paid cheque to S. Walters £22
26 Drew cheque for wages £32, paid into bank from office cash £30, drew cheque for personal use £50 (drawings)

7 Enter the following items in petty cash book which is kept on the imprest system. At the end, balance off the book and restore the original imprest. Use analysis columns for travelling, postage, sundry expenses, stationery and ledger accounts and appropriate folio numbers and petty cash voucher numbers.

19–2

Oct   1   Drew imprest from cashiers £20
2   Paid fares £1.06; bought postage stamps £0.76
3   Paid for office teas £0.90; paid for stationery £1.32; paid for ball of string £0.30
4   Paid fares £2.30; paid for glue for office £0.46
5   Bought postage stamps £0.56; paid national insurance £1.70; paid L. Phillips £2.16
6   Paid fares £0.66; paid cleaner £0.50; paid refuse department £0.20

8 Enter the following in a petty cash book with six columns, for postage, fares, office sundries, cleaning, repairs and ledger accounts. Use appropriate folio numbers and petty cash voucher numbers.

19–2

Oct   15   Drew petty cash imprest £100, paid postage £7
16   Paid taxi £0.96; bought ball of string £0.30; paid office cleaner £0.50; and paid a creditor W. Black £11.30
17   Paid postage £3.10; bought envelopes £3; bought cleaning materials £1.30
18   Paid M. Allsop £3.20; member of staff paid £0.90 for private telephone call; paid fares £0.60
19   Paid fares £5.50; paid cleaner's wages £12.70; paid for repairs to window catch £1.70; paid T. Brown £8.30; paid for stamps £1
Balance the book and restore the imprest.

9 From the details shown below, complete the three-column cash book for Bea Dill, balance off the cash book and show the ledger account entries to record the total of cash discounts at the end of the month.

19–7

Sept   1   Balances brought forward: Bank   £1050 CR
Cash   £78   DR

2   J. Clarke settled his account for £640 by cheque after taking 2.5% discount.

3   Bea transferred £2000 into the bank account from her own building society deposit account

6   Bea sent out cheques to the following suppliers, deducting cash discount as indicated:

F. Blythe   £150   2%
R. May   £300   3%
S. Topp   £240   2½%

9   Withdrew £50 from the bank for business use

12 Paid outstanding electricity bill £123 by cheque

16 Paid casual wages in cash £43

19 Received a cheque from P. Big for £179 in full settlement of his account of £185

21 B. Read sent a cheque to settle her account of £400 after deducting cash discount at 5%

29 Cash sales for the month paid direct to bank £620

30 Bea took £40 from the till for her own use

Note   Use folios to indicate postings to the ledgers, 'GL' for the General Ledger and 'CB' for the Cash Book.

Remember that the discount columns in the cash book are memo only, so the general ledger postings are as shown.

10   Frank Cray maintains a cash book for recording all bank entries, and a separate petty cash book for all cash items. His cash book has columns as shown:

Date	Details	Fo	Disc	Amount	Total
			£	£	£

Individual items are listed in the amount column, with the daily banking figure shown in the total column. Record the following items:

19–3

Apr 1   Balances brought forward: Cash Book   £507 DR
                                      Petty Cash   £32 DR

2   Cash float re-imbursed to the imprest level of £100

3   Cash sales £362
    Cheque received from D. Gray £190 (discount allowed £7)

4   Bus fares paid in cash £3; typing paper £15 cash

5   Cheques sent out as follows:

P. Snow   £162   discount received £3
L. Blake   £395   discount received £4
S. Stuart £ 62   no discount

6   Cash sales £417
    Cheque received from W. Walls £342 in full settlement of an account for £350
    Cash payments made for envelopes £18, stamps £24, and train tickets £35

7   Cheques sent out for insurance premiums £210 and electricity £162
    Re-imbursed the petty cash float and balanced the accounts

    Vat should be ignored.

What is the advantage of balancing a cash book on a weekly basis?

11   Record the following transactions for the first month of a new business using a two-column cash book and ledger. Balance off at the end of the month.

19–6

Mar   4   P. Phogg started a business with £20 in cash and £650 in the bank. On the same day he negotiated a loan of a further £1000 from Natpro Bank.
      5   Purchased stock £320 by cheque and £506 on credit from P. Bailey. Bought office equipment on credit from Office Supplies Ltd £439
      6   Cash sales £212, credit sales £418 to B. Rae
      8   Further credit purchases of stock from P. Bailey £186 and F. Gee Ltd £395
      12 Credit sales made to R. Brown £98 and D. Little £166
      14 Wages paid in cash £52, Peter Phogg took £75 cash for himself and paid out a further £10 cash for postage stamps
      17 Cash sales £223, £32 goods returned by D. Little
      19 Bought a motor vehicle on credit £4200 from Temple Motors paying £750 deposit by cheque
      23 Received a cheque from B. Rae in full settlement
      25 Returned faulty goods to P. Bailey £72
          Bought more goods for cash £154
      27 Paid wages in cash £61
      29 Sent out cheques to Office Supplies and F. Gee to settle their accounts
      30 Cheques received from Brown and Little in full settlement
      31 All cash in hand paid into the bank

12   Write up the following transactions in the books of Alan Gordon. Enter the items in a two-column cash book with columns for bank and discount (no cash column) and post to the ledger. Balance off accounts on 7 May 19–4.

May   1   Bank balance b/f £382
      4   A. White settled his account b/f of £80 paying £76
      5   C. Brown settled his account b/f of £120 less 5% discount
          Paid D. Black £228 in full settlement of his account b/f of £240
      6   Paid F. Green his account b/f of £100 less 5% discount

13   Round and Diamond are two traders. At 1 November Diamond owed Round £340. During the month of November the following transactions took place:

Nov   6   Round purchases goods from Diamond £400
      13 Diamond sells goods to Round £160
      16 Round pays diamond £380 cash, discount allowed £20
      21 Round returns goods to Diamond £32
      25 Diamond sells goods to Round £420

a)   Prepare Round's account in the books of Diamond.
b)   State which party is indebted to the other at 30 November.

14   Brian Wyse – Newsagent

Brian Wyse decides to maintain a separate three-column cash book in order to provide more detail and give more control and security if he needs to employ book-keeping staff in the future.

Enter the following transactions in a three-column cash book, balancing at the end of each week.

Notice that the first week is just the same as a two-column book. Why is this, do you think?

May	15	Enter the balance from Unit 2 in the cash column. Transfer £600 cash into the bank (a contra entry)
	16	Sales banked £470
		Magazines bought on credit from Smethurst & Co. £750
	17	Paid window cleaner in cash £5
		Bought petrol and oil for the van £18 paying cash
	18	Bought sweets paying by cheque £260
		Banked his takings £425
	19	Van needed new tyres paid by cheque £35
		Withdrew cash ready to pay various expenses £250
	20	Paid out wages in cash £190
		Bought tea and coffee by cash (sundries) £4
		Paid takings into the bank's night safe £495
	21	Paid the milkman in cash for staff refreshments £6
		Banked the day's takings £215
	22	Sent out bills to various credit customers:
		J. Wright £100
		D. Brown £240
		P. Green £160
		In order to encourage fast payment he decides to offer a cash discount of 5% if settled within 7 days
	23	Sent cheque to Smethurst & Co. to settle his account taking 2% discount
		Settled his account with A. Jones who has allowed 5% discount, by cheque
	24	All three credit customers send in their cheques taking the discount offered
	25	Banked takings for past 4 days £825
	26	Paid wages by cheque £185; paid milkman £5 cash
	27	Banked his takings of £230
	28	Banked the day's takings £205

Complete and balance the ledger postings including the discount accounts. Do not forget to use folio references, or to open an account for Smethurst & Co. (16 May). Remember that you have already opened some accounts in Unit 2. To continue, you can either use your previous work, or open this unit's accounts with the balances brought down on 15 May.

Why do you think Brian balances his cash book each week?

Answers

5	Feb 1		Balances	b/d	Cash	28	DR	Bank	£ 79 DR
6	Oct 27		Balances	b/d	Cash	1	DR	Bank	£636 DR
7	Cash to reimburse on October 7								£12.88
8	Cash to reimburse on October 20								£59.56

14 Brian Wyse – Newsagent

Debits			*Credits*		
	£				£
Purchases	4710				
Rent	500	(no change)	Capital	3000	(no change)
Motor vehicles	2000	(no change)	Loan	2000	(no change)
Insurance	350	(no change)	Sales	5310	
Wages	730		Discount		
Drawings	210	(no change)	Received	75	
Rates	375	(no change)			
Motor expenses	68				
Cleaning	10				
Sundries	15				
Discount allowed	25				

Note If the debit balances for cash and bank are included in the above list,
the total of the debits is the same as the total of the credits.
You may like to consider this fact.

Brian Wyse's Cash Book

19–8	£	£	£		£	£	£
May 15 Balance b/f		635		May 15 Bank ¢		600	
Cash ¢			600	17 Cleaning		5	
16 Sales			470	Motor expenses		18	
18 Sales			425	18 Purchases			260
19 Bank ¢		250		19 Motor expenses			35
20 Sales			495	Cash ¢			250
21 Sales			215	20 Wages		190	
				Sundries		4	
				21 Sundries		6	
				Balances c/d		62	1660
		885	2205			885	2205
May 22 Balances b/d		62	1660	May 23 Smethurst & Co.	15		735
24 J. Wright	5		95	A. Jones	60		1140
D. Brown	12		228	26 Wages			185
P. Green	8		152	Sundries		5	
25 Sales			825	28 Balances c/d		57	1335
27 Sales			230				
28 Sales			205				
	25	62	3395		75	62	3395
May 29 Balances b/d		57	1335				

Unit 4

Bank Reconciliation

Revision of Units 1–3

At the end of this unit you will be able to:

1 Understand the importance of reconciling the bank account with the bank's records

2 Understand the procedure and steps involved in completing the reconciliation

3 Feel confident in your grasp of the important basic concepts learnt in Units 1–3.

Bank Reconciliation

This is an internal check which ensures that nothing has been omitted either from the cash book or from the bank statements, and that any errors of entry are spotted and corrected.

Regular items are paid by the bank (i.e. standing orders or direct debits) which are not always notified to the firm until a bank statement is sent. It is at the end of the month that these amounts can be entered into the cash book. Other transactions such as interest on an overdraft and bank charges are not known until a bank statement is received.

Accordingly, one of the most important tasks of the cashier is to make sure that the procedure of reconciling the bank statement with the cash book is carried out promptly whenever a bank statement is received.

A simple bank reconciliation is shown below:

Example

Bank Reconciliation Statement
at 30 June 19–2

			£
Balance of cash at Bank as shown in cash book			1000

Stage 1

Add Back
Cheques paid to creditors, but not yet cleared through bank

		£	
20 June	J. Bird	25	
29 June	I. Fry	102	
29 June	T. Bone	67	194
		—	——
			1194

Stage 2

Less
Amounts paid into bank, but not yet shown on statement

29 June	Bankings	130	
30 June	Bankings	75	(205)
		—	——
Balance as per bank statement			
			989
			——

Note If the firm has an overdraft we would **deduct** Stage 1 and **add** Stage 2 (i.e. the reverse procedure).

Let us follow each item through, but first learn **The Golden Rules:**
- Each item appearing in the cash book must be ticked when it is agreed that the cheque paid or received has gone through the bank and is shown on the statement.

- Once the item has been ticked in the cash book, tick the equivalent item on the bank statement.
- Items on the bank statement but not in the cash book will need to be entered on the date that it was balanced (i.e. bank charges, standing orders).
- If you have closed off the cash book, any items which are in the cash book but not on the bank statement will be listed. Also, items on the bank statement but not in the cash book will be listed. These are of three types:
  a) Cheques paid out but not yet cleared by the bank.
  b) Charges and banker's order payments made by or to the bank.
  c) Those items paid into the bank but not yet shown on the bank statement.

These three items are the key factors in a bank reconciliation statement.

Note Get the bank statement as early as possible and try not to close off (add up and balance) your cash book until your bank statement is received. Many book-keepers leave a space before starting the next period in order to bring the cash book up-to-date. This makes the reconciliation easier.

Stages in a Bank Reconciliation

Start with the cash book bank balance which in the example given is a surplus. If the bank balance is a deficiency (i.e. an overdraft), the items mentioned below will be reversed.

Add Back those payments made which are in the cash book but are not on the bank statement. This is to increase the bank balance in the cash book because the cheques you have paid out have not been presented. **Deduct** amounts which have been paid into the bank account but which are not shown on the bank statement.

Example

**Bank Account
as shown in the
Cash book**

19–2			£				£
June	1	Balance b/f	200	June	1	J. Green	26
	10	R. Lynn	60		5	Gas Board	50
	18	J. Robinson	90		6	Bankers Order	
	26	J. Bloggs	1000			(Leasing Co)	25
	27	C. Coombes	92		25	N. Harris	62
	30	J. Smith	67		28	F. Howard	50
					29	J. Hall	750
					29	A. Kell	87
					29	P. Cannon	75
					30	Balance c/d	384
			1509				1509
July	1	Balance b/d	384				

On examination of the bank statement it is found that:

a) the payments into the Bank on 27 June (C. Coombes) and 30 June (J. Smith) are not shown.

b) the cheques paid out on 29 June have not been presented to the Bank.

c) the bank charges of £62 are not entered into the cash book.

Remember when preparing bank reconciliation statements you must ask yourself these two questions:

- If the amounts paid out were through the bank statement, would it increase or decrease the bank balance?
- If the items paid in were through the bank statement, would it increase or decrease the balance?

Try this commonsense view and it will help you to understand bank reconciliation statements.

Remember also when dealing with bank statements that the bank is showing the financial picture from the bank's point of view. Thus cash paid in by a customer is shown as a credit on the statement, increasing the bank's indebtedness to the customer, whilst it will be debited to his own cash book. In effect, you are a creditor of the bank.

The example [on this page] can now be dealt with as follows:

1 Re-open the cash book.

Cash Book

19–6			£				£
June	30	Balance b/d	384	June	30	Bank Charges	62
					30	Balance c/d	322
			384				384
July	1	Balance b/d	322				

Note that all the entries to bring the cash book up-to-date are made on the date it was originally balanced-off.

2 Draw up a reconciliation statement as follows:

Bank Reconciliation Statement
on 30 June 19–6

		£	£
Balance as per cash book			322
Add Back			
Unpresented cheques:			
29 June	J. Hall	750	
29 June	A. Kell	87	
29 June	P. Cannon	75	912
			1234
Deduct			
Deposits not yet entered:			
27 June	C. Coombes	92	
30 June	J. Smith	67	(159)
Balance as per Bank Statement			1075

If the firm is overdrawn and working on an *overdraft*, the statement would be as follows:

Bank Reconciliation Statement
on 30 June 19–6

		£	£
Overdraft as per cash book			106
Deduct			
Unpresented cheques:			
29 June	P. Gold	35	
30 June	H. Moore	25	(60)
			46
Add			
Deposits not yet entered:			
30 June		29	29
Balance as per bank statement (overdraft)			75

Note This is the reverse procedure of the preceding statement.

Reconciliation

Reconciling statements is one of the most common tasks in accounting work and forms part of the internal control of any organisation.

Other examples of reconciliaton would be:

- Sales representatives' cash paid into the bank against their gross takings, less expenses.
- Reconciling credit suppliers' statements.

Try to cultivate your ability at reconciliation. Do not get embroiled in figures, but use a common-sense approach. Methodically tick off each item appearing on both statements.

When the statements do not balance it is usually because something has been entered twice, omitted, ticked when in fact it was not appearing in one of the statements, or wrongly entered in the cash book or bank statement. Look out for all of these difficulties and this will help your work. Remember that this is a check both on your own accuracy and that of the bank – they do sometimes make mistakes!

If you do not do so already, reconcile your own bank or building society statements. It is good practice, and should be done regularly.

The Stages in Bank Reconciliation

Cash Book

? Unpresented cheques Deposits not yet shown

Original Balance

↓

Updating

↓

Amended Balance

Stages

1 Check off those items in both the cash book and the bank statement

2 Up-date the cash book

3 Prepare the reconciliation statement

Reconciliation Statement

Balance from Cash Book

↓

Unpresented cheques and Deposits not shown

↓

Balance as Bank Statement

Bank Statement

? Charges
Interest
R/D Cheques
Standing
Orders etc.

Closing Balance

Note Debits in the cash book are shown as credits on the bank statement, and vice versa.

Revision

We have now looked at the way we record cash and credit transactions in accordance with the principles of the double-entry system. Before we go on to discuss some of the other books used in a business, let us take a second look at some of the foundations upon which we are going to build.

The main book of account is the **ledger** and this contains accounts for all the transactions of a business. All other books are known as 'subsidiary books' or books of original (or prime) entry.

The ledger may be divided into several sections:

- Nominal (or Impersonal) accounts and Real Accounts are recorded in the **General Ledger.**
- Accounts of credit customers (Debtors) are recorded in the **Sales Ledger.**
- Accounts of credit suppliers (Creditors) are recorded in the **Purchases Ledger.**

The **cash book** is both a book of original entry and part of the ledger. In Unit 1 we considered the cash and bank accounts as ledger accounts written in the same style as all the other ledger accounts. In Unit 3 you were introduced to the **two-column** and **three-column** cash books in which the cash and bank accounts are displayed side-by-side. It is sensible to keep a separate cash book, partly because the transactions recorded in these accounts are so numerous, and also because it allows a reliable cashier to look after these transactions.

All items appearing on the debit side of the cash book must be posted to the credit side of the appropriate account in the ledger in order to complete the double-entry. Similarly, all items appearing on the credit side of the cash book must be posted to the debit side of the appropriate account in the ledger.

The exception to this is when money is transferred from the office cash to the bank or when money is drawn out of the bank to replenish the office cash. In the first instance, we must credit the cash column in the cash book (as the office cash is *giving*) and debit the bank column (as the bank is *receiving*). The reverse happens when money is withdrawn from the bank and put into the office cash. In both instances '¢' is entered in the folio column against both the cash and bank entries. '¢' means 'contra' (opposite) and indicates that the other half of the double-entry is on the opposite page, with no further posting to the ledger being necessary.

Example

1 On 2 July, M. Pierce transfers £356 from his cash till to the bank.
2 On 24 July, M. Pierce withdraws £100 from the bank for office use.

Cash Book

	Fo	Cash	Bank		Fo	Cash	Bank

July 2 Cash
     24 Bank
	¢
	¢
		100	£
			356
				July 2 Bank
				     24 Cash
					¢
					¢
						£
						356
							£
							100

The narrative (details), as always, indicates the name of the account where the other half of the double-entry is to be found. Although the cash books we have looked at use one column for cash and one column for bank on both sides, it may well be the case in a business that all receipts are paid into the bank at the end of the day and all payments are made by cheque (any cash payments being recorded in the petty cash book).

If there are no cash payments being recorded in the cash book, there will be no need for a cash column on the credit side. On the debit side, the cash column can be re-named 'Details' and will be used to record all the day's receipts prior to these being totalled and the total entered in the bank column.

Credit Transactions and Cash Discount

Let us consider the following:

1 On 3 June, M. Lloyd buys goods on credit from National Suppliers for £500.
This must be recorded in the ledger in accordance with the double-entry principles:

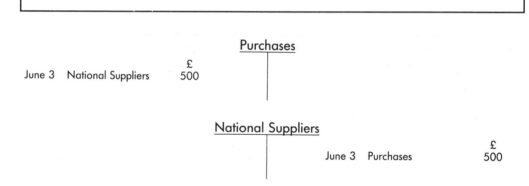

The purchases account gives an on-going record of all goods bought, whether for cash or on credit terms. If we buy goods for cash, we credit the cash book and debit purchases; if we buy goods on credit terms we credit the supplier's account and debit purchases. When we come to do our final accounts, the purchases account will tell us the total cost of goods purchased this year.
As the supplier's account (National Suppliers) stands at the moment, it reveals that M. Lloyd owes National Suppliers £500.

2 On 15 June, M. Lloyd pays National Suppliers taking 2½% discount.
The amount actually paid is credited to the cash book and debited to National Suppliers' account.

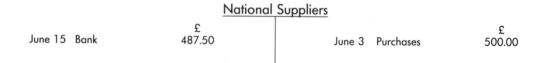

If National Suppliers' account was balanced off now, it would show that M. Lloyd still owed National Suppliers £12.50. This is not the case, however, as this amount was taken as discount and M. Lloyd does not in fact owe anything to National Suppliers. The discount received must be recorded in National Suppliers' account so that the account 'clears'.

National Suppliers

		£			£
June 15	Bank	487.50	June 3	Purchases	500.00
	Discount received	12.50			
		500.00			500.00

There remains the double-entry of the discount received to be recorded. At the time a payment is made or received, any discount is recorded in the cash book alongside the relative payment or receipt. It is entered here purely for the sake of convenience to ensure that the entries for the discount are not omitted from the books. The discount columns in the cash book are not part of the double-entry. To complete the double-entry in our example we must credit the discount received account with £12.50. In practice, the discount received account would only be credited at the end of a week or month with the total of the discount column in the cash book. This saves filling the account with a large number of small amounts.

3 On 2 June M. Lloyd sold goods on credit to B. Thompson for £100.

This must be recorded in the ledger in accordance with the double-entry principles.

Debit the Customer : Credit Sales

B. Thompson

		£		
June 2	Sales	100		

Sales

				£
		June 2	B. Thompson	100

The sales account gives an ongoing record of all income from goods sold, whether for cash or on credit terms. When we sell goods for cash, we debit the cash book and credit sales; when we sell goods on credit terms, we debit the customer's account and credit sales.

As the customer's account stands at the moment, it reveals that B. Thompson owes M. Lloyd £100.

4 On 10 June B. Thompson settles his debt, taking 5% discount.

The amount actually received is debited to the cash book and credited to B. Thompson's account.

B. Thompson

		£			£
June 2	Sales	100.00	June 10	Bank	95.00
				Discount allowed	5.00
		100.00			100.00

The discount allowed is also credited to B. Thompson's account, so the account is clear. Finally, the double-entry is completed by debiting the discount allowed account.

Questions

1 What is a bank reconciliation statement?
2 What is the purpose of such a statement?
3 What items are likely to be on a bank statement but not in the cash book?
4 What is a contra entry?
5 What are the entries for the following?
   a) Buying goods on credit
   b) Selling goods on credit
6 When allowing discount to a customer, what entries would we show and where would we enter them?
7 The following shows the bank account in A. Shaw's cash book for March:

19–2			£				£
March	1	Balance b/f	230.00	March	5	Drawings	40.00
					15	Bigg	160.00
	16	Black	50.00		15	Richards	50.00
	25	Caine	370.00		29	Lowe	190.00
	31	Magee	572.00		29	Perrin	30.00
					31	Balance c/f	752.00
			1222.00				1222.00

Early in April he received this statement from his Bank:

A. Shaw: In Account With The Milshire Bank PLC

19–2			Debit £	Credit £	Balance £
March	1	Balance forward			230.00
	5	Self (A. Shaw)	40.00		190.00
	17	Sundries		50.00	240.00
	18	Richard	50.00		190.00
	18	Bigg	160.00		30.00
	26	Sundries		370.00	400.00
	28	Cheque returned unpaid	50.00		350.00
	31	Charges	8.00		342.00
	31	Perrin	30.00		312.00

Tick off the entries corresponding in both the cash book and bank statement, then draw up a cash book, starting with the present balance of £752.00 and correct such differences as are caused by a lack of knowledge of the bank's activities. Then reconcile the revised cash balance with the balance at the bank in a bank reconciliation statement.

8 Set out below are extracts from the cash book (bank columns only) and bank statement of C. Crowe. Draw up a bank reconciliation statement.

Cash Book

19–6		£	19–6		£
Jan	1 Balance b/f	916.40	Jan	2 Wages	96.00
	28 M. Dunn & Co.	97.34		9 Drawings	100.00
	29 Simpson & Co.	196.00		10 Moffatt & Co.	202.50
	30 T. Harker	417.60		14 S. Way	568.30
	31 Smith & Co.	169.40		16 Wages	101.00
				21 Black Bros.	82.00
				31 Wages	98.00
				Balance c/d	548.94
		1796.74			1796.74
Feb	1 Balance b/d	548.94			

Bank Statement
C. Crowe: In account with Yorkshire Bank PLC

19–6		Debit £	Credit £	Balance £
Jan	1 Balance			916.40
	3 Wages	96.00		820.40
	10 Self – C. Crowe	100.00		720.40
	12 Moffatt & Co.	202.50		517.90
	17 Wages	101.00		416.90
	23 Black Bros.	82.00		334.90
	29 M. Dunn & Co.		97.34	432.24
	30 Simpson & Co.		196.00	628.24
	31 T. Harker		417.60	1045.84

9 The following are copies of the bank column of T. Smith's cash book and his bank statement as rendered by the bank. Bring the cash book up-to-date and agree the remaining items in a bank reconciliation statement.

Cash Book (Bank Columns Only)

Dr 19–6		£	Cr 19–6		£
April	20 Balance b/f	396.80	April	21 Mason	13.12
	25 Jackson	56.92		23 Norman	34.64
	30 Lemon	29.20		29 Pollard	59.08
				30 Balance c/d	376.08
		482.92			482.92
May	1 Balance b/d	376.08			

Bank Statement

19–6			Debit £	Credit £	Balance £
April	20	Balance forward			396.80
	23	Mason	13.12		383.68
	25	Jackson		56.92	440.60
	29	Pollard	59.08		381.52
	30	Bank of England		35.10	416.62
	30	Service charge	9.30		407.32

10 From the following transactions write up a suitable cash book to record the following in the business of Perry and Sons. Balance off at month-end.

19–6
July 1   Started business with cash £1500
      2   Bought goods from A. Jones £296 on credit
      3   Paid electricity by cash £28
      4   Paid £1000 cash into bank
      6   Sold goods to A. Smart £54 on credit
      8   Bought postage stamps £15 by cash
      9   Cash sales £89
   11   Goods returned to A. Jones £20
   12   Sold goods to B. Good £66 on credit
   13   Building repairs paid by cash £39
   14   A. Smart returned goods to us £12
   17   Paid A. Thomson for purchases by cheque £297
   21   Cash purchases £19
   29   Bought typewriter by cheque £302
   30   Paid motor expenses by cash £9
   31   Bought van on credit from T.M.S £567

11 From the following transactions of Albert Ltd construct an analytical cash book using debit columns headed Total, Capital and Sales, and head credit columns Total, Purchases, Heat and Light, Insurance, Motor Expenses, Postage and Sundries. Balance the cash book at month end and carry balance down.

19–9
June 1   Started business paying cash into bank £5000
      2   Purchased stock for resale by cheque £960
      3   Paid electricity bill by cheque £32
      7   Sales for the week banked £755
      9   Bought new tyres for car by cheque £52
   10   Sales banked £257
   12   Paid business insurance by cheque £207
   14   Bought stamps by cheque £36
   15   Sales banked £305
   17   Purchased further stock for resale by cheque £669
   20   Bought cups and saucers for use by business £6.50
   22   Paid for petrol by cheque £16.50
   23   Cost of despatching parcel £9.90 paid by cheque
   24   Banked money from sales £222
   26   Repairs to motor car paid by cheque £67

28   Cleaning materials and coffee paid by cheque £3.25
30   Sales banked £506

12   Enter the following items in the three-column cash book, balance off the book on 5 June and post to the ledger, including discount accounts, using folio references as appropriate.

19–2
June   1   T. Murphy commences business with £20 000 cash; he pays £19 000 into the bank account from the cash book (contra entry), buys goods (purchases) for £4600 by cheque, and buys goods on credit from T. Blake for £500.

June   2   He pays rent of £450 and legal costs of £180 both by cheque. He purchased goods to the value of £250 on credit terms from R. Tomlinson. He also sold goods on credit to P. Read for the sum of £100.

June   3   He settles the debt of £250 due to R. Tomlinson by cheque, deducting discount of 5%, and sells goods on credit to B. James for £200.

June   4   P. Read settles his debt of £100 by cheque, less 5% discount. B. James settles his account by cheque, taking 7½% discount.

June   5   Pays wages in cash £500 and draws £200 for personal use (drawings) from the cash box. He also settles T. Blake's account by cheque taking 2½% discount.

13   Tom Brown's bank account and bank statement are shown below. You are asked to up-date his account and reconcile at the end of the month.

Bank

19–9			£					£
June	1	Balance b/f	675	June	3	Wages		120
	3	Sales	125		4	Rent		80
	5	R.Doe	315		6	Motor repairs	72	
	7	Sales	249		11	C. Blue		156
	15	A-Z Ltd	621		12	Wages		120
	19	Sales	352		15	Purchases		395
	23	F. Seaman	77		16	Office		
	24	Sales	784			equipment		420
		W. Ince	95		20	J. Brown		260
		R. Mills	283			E. Grey		25
	27	Sales	164		23	Wages		120
	29	Rent			28	Water		88
		receivable	50		29	D. Black		682
	30	Balance c/d	885			F. White		317
					30	Salaries		1820
			4675					4675

Unit 4

Bank Statement

			Withdrawals	Deposits	Balance
			£	£	£
June	1	Balance b/f			2425
	2	1267		125	
		003457	1750		800
	3	003458	120		680
	6	003460	72		
		1268		315	923
	7	1269		249	1172
	13	003462	120		
		Interest		25	1077
	20	1271		352	
		1270		621	
		003464	240		
		003459	80		1730
	24	003463	395		
		1272		77	
		1273		784	
		003466	25		
		003467	120		2051
	25	SO – B. Frear		179	
		DD – B.G. Loan Co.	415		
		1274		378	2193
	27	1275		164	2357
	29	003469	682		1675

Note
- Cheque 003457 (£1750) must relate to *May* since the opening balances differ by this amount.
- Paying-in slip 1274 must include Ince and Mills.
- Incorrect posting for cheque 003464 needs further investigation; either the cash book needs to be amended or the bank should be informed.

14 Anne Burton maintains three-column ledger accounts for all her personal clients. From the following details complete the accounts for Colin Howard, a creditor, and Philip Fyfe, a debtor.

19–1			£
October	1	Balances b/f: C. Howard	1270
		P. Fyfe	650
	3	Credit sales to Fyfe	345
	6	Purchases from Howard	834
	9	Sales made to Fyfe	962
	11	Further sales to Fyfe	140
	14	Returns made to Howard	36
	17	Returns made by Fyfe	24
	19	Additional charge made by Howard for error on invoice on 6 Oct	101
	23	Cheque received from Fyfe for balance owing at start of month, less 2% cash discount	?

	27	More purchases from Howard	723
		plus charge for carriage in	32
		and cost of packages	45
	29	Credit received for returned packages	42
		Charge made by Howard for late payment	15
	31	Amount sent on account to Howard	1000

15 Steve O'Hare has received a bank statement which shows that he is overdrawn by £336. According to his records he should have a balance of £537 in hand. After investigation the following points came to light:

a) Cheques written by Steve totalling £174 have not yet shown up on the statement.
b) Deposits paid into his account have not been cleared by the bank. These come to £1066.
c) Charges made by the bank for the quarter are £25.
d) A standing order for £46 for hire of equipment has not been entered in the cash book.
e) A payment for motor repairs was entered in the cash book as £218 although the cheque was actually made out for £128.

Draw up a statement to reconcile the figure according to Steve and his bank statement.

16 Using a three-column cash book and ledger, record the following transactions for Joy Bee and Co.

19–7				£	
Feb	1	Balances brought forward: Cash		25	DR
			Bank	650	DR
			R. Lee	420	DR
			P. Smith	740	DR
			S. Hand	335	CR
			Capital	1500	CR

2	R. Lee settled his account by cheque taking 5% discount		
			£
4	Sold goods on credit: R. Lee		320
		P. Smith	280
		Q. May	540
7	Banked takings for the week £1340		
8	Bought goods on credit: S. Hand		£585
		F. Howe	£880
10	Paid three months rent by cheque £900		
14	Cash takings totalling £920 banked after paying out £140 for repairs to equipment		
19	Bought more goods on credit from Hand £220		
21	Banked week's sales £1156		
25	Smith settled his account after deducting 5% discount		
27	Sent out cheques to pay the creditors as at 15 February after allowing for 2½% cash discount from them both		
28	Banked takings for the week £842 in total after paying £175 for purchases		

Balance off all those accounts at the end of the month which have more than one entry. Use folios as appropriate.

17 Pam Edwardes receives her bank statement for June. She is surprised to see that she is overdrawn, since her records show that she is £363.10 in hand. From the details given, calculate how much is shown as the closing balance on her bank statement.

	£
Standing order paid out for hire of machinery	55.00
Bank charges and interest for the quarter	17.20
Cheques returned marked R/D: Jones	124.00
Clark	72.85
Payments made by Pam not yet shown on the statement:	
Motor repairs	263.80
Purchases	874.45
Rent	120.00
Cash and cheques paid into the bank not yet posted to Pam's	
account: 29 June	747.40
30 June	682.90

Upon checking the statement against her own figures, Pam also discovered that a cheque which she issued for £274.15 has been entered in her cash book as £247.15

---

18 Brian Wyse – Newsagent

On 29 May Brian Wyse transfers £30 from the till to keep as a petty cash float in a separate cash box. During the following week he pays these items out of petty cash:

May 29 Petrol for the van £12
     30 Tea and coffee for the staff £3
     31 Window cleaner £5

June 1 Milkman £3.10
        Received £2 from assistant for private telephone call
      2 Postage stamps £5
        Bus fares £0.90 and cleaning materials £2

Expenditure is analysed over cleaning, motor expenses, postage and telephone, and sundries.

Draw up the petty cash account, balance off on 2 June and show the reimbursement on 3 June.

On 29 May the bank sends a statement for the month. After checking, Brian notes that the bank charges come to £3 and there is a standing order paid out for the hire of equipment of £25. The bankings made on 27 and 28 May are not shown, nor is the cheque sent to Smethurst & Co. According to this statement his bank balance is £1607. Is this figure correct? Check it by bringing the cash book up-to-date and preparing a bank reconciliation statement.

Note VAT is ignored in these petty cash exercises. At this stage, in practice, any registered trader must separate the VAT element of all expenditure.

Answers

7 A. Shaw Up-dated cash book balance £694
Unpresented cheques £190
Deposits not yet credited £572

8 C. Crowe Unpresented cheques £666.30
Deposits not yet credited £169.40

9 T. Smith Up-dated cash book balance £401.88
Unpresented cheques £ 34.64
Deposits not yet credited £ 29.20

10 Perry & Sons August 1 Balance b/d
Cash £479 DR Bank £401 DR

11 Albert Ltd July 1 Balance b/d £4985.85

12 T. Murphy June 6 Balance b/d
Cash £300 DR Bank £13 325 DR

---

18 Brian Wyse – Newsagent

Petty Cash Account

Float	Date	Detail	fo	Total	Cleaning	Motor Expenses	Postage Telephone	Sundries
				£	£	£	£	£
30.00	19–8 May 29	Cash	CB					
		Petrol	1	12.00		12.00		3.00
	30	Tea & coffee	2	3.00				3.10
	31	Window cleaner	3	5.00	5.00			
2.00	June 1	Milk	4	3.10				
		Private 'phone call	GL					
	2	Stamps	5	5.00			5.00	0.90
		Bus fares	6	0.90				
		Cleaning	7	2.00	2.00			
				31.00	7.00	12.00	5.00	7.00
					GL	GL	GL	GL
		Balance	c/d	1.00				
32.00				32.00				
1.00	June 3	Balance	b/d					
29.00		Cash	CB					

Cash Book (Bank Columns Only)

		£			£
May 29	Balance b/d	1335	May 29	Bank charges	3
				Equipment hire (SO)	25
				Balance c/d	1307
		1335			1335
May 30	Balance b/d	1307			

Bank Reconciliation Statement
on 29 May 19–8

			£
Balance as per cash book			1307
Add back			
Unpresented cheque: Smethurst & Co.			735
			2042
Deduct			
Deposits not yet entered:			
	£		
27 May	230		
28 May	205	(435)	
Balance as per bank statement		1607	

Unit 5

The Purchases and Sales Day Books

At the end of this unit you will be able to:

1 Deal with the accounting transactions for buying goods and dealing with suppliers

2 Keep a purchases day book and a purchases ledger

3 Understand credit control

4 Understand the accounting transactions for selling goods and dealing with customers

5 Keep a sales day book and a sales ledger.

Suppliers and Goods Received

Any firm or company must buy goods and services to enable it to operate. A company selling goods will obviously first buy goods to sell or will obtain raw materials which it will convert into finished goods. Additionally, businesses have various other expenses, i.e. heating and lighting, rates and insurance, and these also have to be properly recorded. It is **essential** that all expenditure is properly and accurately recorded.

When purchases are made direct for cash, these appear in either the cash book or the petty cash book. The majority of purchases, however, are usually made on a **credit basis** whereby the goods are received or obtained and payment is made some time later, usual terms of trade allowing 30 days to pay.

INVOICE No. 71575

SCHEIDEGGER TRAINING LIMITED
108 VAUGHAN WAY
LEICESTER
LE1 4SH

ACL
Colour Print

25 Boston Road, Gorse Hill Industrial Estate,
Beaumont Leys, Leicester LE4 1AW,
Telephone: (0533) 351010.

195STA   PKU/467/PR   13 June 19—2

Quantity	Description	VAT Rate	£	p
500	Sets of Computer Sheets	15%	600	00
2,000	A4 Letterheading	15%	39	20
1,500	A4 Folders — Red	15%	171	00
1,500	A4 Folders — Green	15%	171	00
4,000	Stock Returns	15%	40	00
5,000	Salary Claim Forms	15%	319	00
		Goods Total	1340	20
	Terms net 28 days	VAT at 15%	201	03
		Invoice Total	1541	23

ACL

VAT Registration No. 371 8076 42.

Creditors' Invoices

Before entering invoices in the books, it is necessary to check that the goods have actually been received. Accordingly, the following procedures should be adopted:

Authorisation

Make sure that the person responsible for ordering the goods checks the invoice and signs it, thus authorising payment.

'Goods Received' Notes

For all goods received there should be **evidence of receipt**. This could be in the form of a delivery note as illustrated:

DELIVERY NOTE			
Date	Supplier's Name	Description of Goods	Signature
30 July 19—2	Snow White Launderers and Dry Cleaners	Chef's Jacket Apron Cabinet Towel	*[signature]*

Check that there is evidence of receipt of goods **before** an invoice is passed for payment.

Some firms also have a **goods received book** so that a record of all goods entering the premises is kept and can be checked:

GOODS RECEIVED BOOK			
Date	Supplier's Name	Description of Goods	Signature
30.7.	Snow White Launderers and Dry Cleaners	1 Chef's Jacket 1 Apron 1 Cabinet Towel	*L. Gordon*
2.8.	Northern Cutlery Supplies	2 doz Serving Spoons	*J. Lythe*

Note Delivery Notes and Goods Received Books do not usually show any financial details.

Checking the Invoices

See that the items charged on suppliers' invoices have been correctly priced in accordance with the agreed order, price list or quotation previously received from the supplier. When the prices have been verified, it is then necessary to check the calculations on the invoice since these may be incorrect. Care should be taken to see that all the items have been properly priced, and that the arithmetic is correct.

The Double-entry

Remember this important rule:

> **If we buy goods on Credit we debit the Purchases Account and credit the Supplier**

Purchases a/c

	£
Purchases 27	

Debit the purchases
to the purchases
account

A. Jones a/c

	£
	A. Jones 27

Credit the personal
account of each
creditor who has
supplied goods

When we buy goods we therefore have to originate the entries in our books, and we do this by first entering the transaction in a **Purchases Day Book**, a book of original entry.

The purchases day book can also be called The Purchases Book, or Purchases Journal or the Creditors Book, Creditors Day Book or Creditors Journal.

Purchases Day Book

A purchases day book is a list of all the goods or services we buy on credit. An illustration is given below. **This is not part of the double-entry**. Each entry in the purchases day book must therefore be recorded in **two** places in the ledger to complete the actual double-entry.

	Purchases Day Book					Page 1
Date	Name and Details	Folio	Details	Net Amount	Vat @15%	Gross Total
19–3 Jan 1	R. Brownley & Co. 2 doz lined pads @ £1.50 each	PL1		£ 36.00	£ 5.40	£ 41.40
17	Peter Young Ltd 4 doz diaries @ £3.50 2 doz pillowcases @ £0.10 each	PL2	168.00 2.40	170.40	25.56	195.96
21	Ambrose Smithy Ltd 6 doz notebooks @ £0.20 each 3 doz rubbers @ £0.15 each	PL3	14.40 5.40	19.80	2.97	22.77
31	Major & Co. Ltd 'Bettawear' 12 machines @ £27.10 each Less trade discount @ 33 1/3%	PL4	325.20 108.40	216.80	32.52	249.32
				443.00	66.45	509.45
				GL1	GL2	

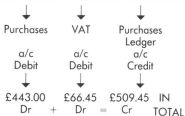

↓ ↓ ↓
Purchases   VAT   Purchases
Ledger
a/c   a/c   a/c
Debit   Debit   Credit
↓ ↓ ↓
£443.00   £66.45   £509.45 IN
Dr   +   Dr   =   Cr   TOTAL

Note The folio column is still used for cross-referencing. Enter in this column the reference number of the account in which the entry can be found in the ledger. PL stands for **Purchases Ledger** a separate part of the ledger containing all the personal accounts of our supplier.

The entries in the ledger from this purchases day book would be as follows:

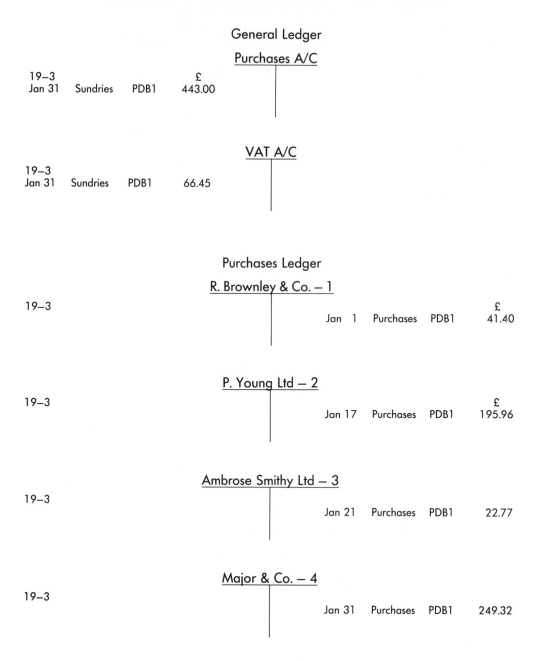

General Ledger

Purchases A/C

19–3			£
Jan 31	Sundries	PDB1	443.00

VAT A/C

19–3			
Jan 31	Sundries	PDB1	66.45

Purchases Ledger

R. Brownley & Co. – 1

19–3				£
	Jan 1	Purchases	PDB1	41.40

P. Young Ltd – 2

19–3				£
	Jan 17	Purchases	PDB1	195.96

Ambrose Smithy Ltd – 3

19–3				
	Jan 21	Purchases	PDB1	22.77

Major & Co. – 4

19–3				
	Jan 31	Purchases	PDB1	249.32

The total of these individual credit side postings agrees with the **total** in the general ledger, i.e. the total of **two** debits = the total of **four** credits, so we are still following the basic Golden Rule that:

Every Debit has a Credit

We will look at VAT in more detail in Unit 8.

Credit Notes

Sometimes goods have to be returned because they are unsatisfactory or because they are incorrectly priced. The supplier will need to issue a **Credit Note** which is the opposite to an invoice and so reduces the amount owed to the supplier.
A credit note looks like this:

Credit Note					No: 4539		

TO
Messrs Jarrow & Smith
16 Ord Road
Newery
Essex

FROM
Darren & Co
High Street
Durham

VAT Reg No: 118 7314 79

Date: 30 July 19—6   Rep: A. Brown

No.	Description	Code	Price each	Trade Discount	Net Total	VAT 15%	Gross Total
			£		£	£	£
3	Dining Chairs (damaged in transit)	X2351	22.00	6.00	60.00	9.00	69.00
1	Dining Table (wrong style)	X2357	95.00	15.00	80.00	12.00	92.00
				Total	140.00	21.00	161.00

Credit notes are often printed in red. When you receive a credit note this has the effect of reducing the amount owing. The entries in the accounts are:

> **Debit the Supplier**

> **Credit the Purchases Returns**

An illustration is as follows:

Suppliers a/c

19–6		£			
July 30	Returns	64.50			

Purchases Returns a/c

19–6				July 30	Suppliers	£ 64.50

The credit notes are entered in the **Returns Out(Ward) Book.** This is maintained separately by some companies, or alternatively at the back of the purchases day book. It looks like this:

	Purchases Returns			Goods	VAT @ 15%	Total
19–3 Jan 7	R. Miles 1 packing crate	PL5		£ 0.50	£ 0.08	£ 0.58
11	M. Joynson 2 boxes address cards (incorrectly displayed)	PL7		2.50	0.38	2.88
29	R. Brown 1 doz boxes invitation cards (on approval – not required)	PL11		4.25	0.63	4.88
				7.25	1.09	8.34

Purchases Returns a/c Credit + VAT a/c Credit = Individual Creditors a/c Debit

Purchases returns are also referred to as **Returns Out** or Outwards. In a small business with few returns, the credit entry can be posted to the purchases account instead.

Remember a useful rule to reduce an account:

> **Put an entry on the opposite side of the Account**

Discounts Received

Later in this unit we will see that it is essential to get our money from customers as soon as possible. Suppliers feel the same way about us, and accordingly may offer an incentive to us to pay promptly, perhaps within seven days. If we take advantage of this it is known as a **cash discount** and is posted in the books as **Discounts Received**.

The entry looks like this:

Debit the Creditor's Account

Credit the Discounts Received Account

A. Creditor a/c	Discount Received a/c
£	£
Discount 15	A. Creditor 15

Note If a three-column cash book is used (Unit 3) the original entry for the discount is posted to the **Memorandum** column and transferred **in total** to the actual discount accounts at the end of the month.

Expenses

Expense items like telephone, heating or lighting bills can also be obtained on credit.

In such circumstances the entries can be made through an **Expenses Day Book** with similar rulings to the purchases day book, or a separate section of the purchases day book for non-trade creditors. Alternatively, some businesses use a **Purchases Analysis Book** (similar to the analytical cash book).

Example

Analytical Purchases Day Book

Date	Details	Gross	Purchases	Heating and Lighting	Motor Expenses	Sundries	VAT
		£	£	£	£	£	£

How we pay Creditors

At the end of each month, in accordance with the terms and conditions of supply, we should pay our suppliers. They normally send us a statement of account which we would reconcile with our ledger account and then draw a cheque (less any discount due).

The entries for this would be:

Cash Book (Bank Column)		Supplier a/c	
	£	£	£
Supplier 175		Bank 175	Purchases 175
			(made earlier)

Sometimes we have direct debits or bankers orders made payable to suppliers. These would be posted from the cash book in the same way.

Dealing with Customers

Credit Control

It is important in business never to let customers have goods unless you are sure they can pay for them. Additionally, always ensure that you obtain your money when it is due. Letting customers have extended credit is a hidden cost, and you pay dearly if you let this continue for too long.

For this reason a good credit control system is needed. This involves obtaining credit references from a bank or traders who know prospective customers. You may also contact credit associations or trade associations for trade references.

References

Suppliers of goods require a reference before they allow credit terms to a customer. A 'trade reference' is given by someone reputable or well-known to the supplier, usually another trader. A 'bank reference' enables the supplier, through his own bank, to find out from the customer's bank if they are a good payer. Status enquiry agents will make private enquiries into the financial standing of customers and report back to the supplier.

Sending Invoices

Once the customers have opened an account with you, ensure that you send out invoices promptly. The sooner you invoice for goods, the sooner you will get paid. Any system which involves delays in sending out invoices is a bad one. An invoice should be sent on the same day as the goods are despatched. In certain circumstances consider the advisability of sending out invoices in advance of the goods. If a supplier does not know a customer, he may send a 'Pro Forma' invoice, which means the goods have to be paid for before they are supplied. Alternatively, the supplier can ask for payment by means of a banker's draft, which is a cheque issued by a reputable bank on its own account.

Invoices should be checked before they are sent out, to make sure that all the details and arithmetic are correct. If incorrect invoices are regularly sent out, customers may go elsewhere.

Customers and Statements

A **statement** is a summary of your transactions with the customer, showing what he owes. It is a copy of his personal account in your ledger. Make sure that statements go out at the end of each month as a reminder and a summary of what is owed by your customers. Again, delays result in late payment.

Here is an example of a statement:

Statement
Mark Stevenson Limited
Wholesale Warehousemen

Polygon Stores
1 High Street
London
SW3 4DX

30 July 19—2
The Old School House
Main Street
Bradford

Date	Details	Debit	Credit	Balance
		£	£	£
July 1	Balance From Previous Month			540.00 Dr
8	Cheque		513.00	
	Discount		27.00	Nil
20	Goods Inv. 14855	276.00	–	276.00 Dr
21	Returns CR 616		73.60	202.40 Dr

The final amount shown in this column is now due.

Compare a bank or building society account statement.

Invoice Sets

As far as possible in the design of any stationery, aim for a system where invoice copies are automatically produced as a by-product.

The copies may be:

- the original invoice
- a statement and remittance advice
- a delivery note

- an advice note
- accounts department copy
- a stores note.

A pictorial representation of this is:

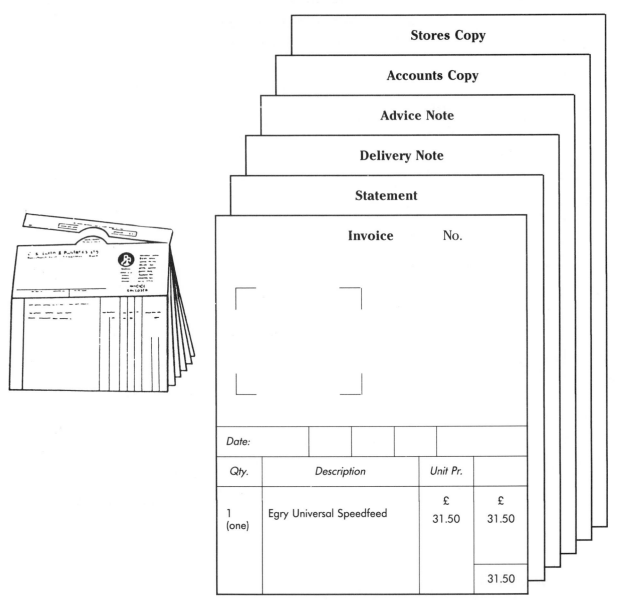

Note Each sheet could be a different colour for easy identification.
Invoice sets are often produced on NCR paper (no carbon required).

Sales Day Book

We can now study posting sales invoices into the books. When invoices are sent out, copies are maintained for our own accounts. The copy invoices are sorted in numerical sequence and chronological (e.g. date) order and posted to the sales day book. Remember, as with the purchases day book, this is not part of the double entry. Note the difference between a sales ledger and a sales day book: a sales ledger is where we keep the customers' personal accounts; a sales day book is as shown below in the example. The sales day book is almost identical to the purchases day book. However, the posting will be:

Debit	**Credit**
Individual personal accounts in the sales ledger with amount due.	The sales and VAT accounts in the general ledger with totals.

Sales Day Book   **Page 1**

Date	Name and Description	Folio		Goods	VAT	Gross Total
19–2			£	£	£	£
July 1	R. Mott & Co. Ltd					
	1 set roll-over doors	SL27		17.50	2.62	20.12
4	M. Brownlee					
	6 sets roll-over doors		105.00			
	6 sets keys		1.50			
			106.50			
	Less 20% trade discount		21.30			
		SL3				
				85.20	12.78	97.98
11	T. Dixon Ltd					
	1 set lift doors 10' wide	SL15		86.50	12.98	99.48
31	A. Kell & Co.					
	3 sets roll-over doors	SL17		52.50	7.87	60.37
				£241.70	£36.25	£277.95
				GL46	GL39	

We Then Post   To Individual Debtors a/cs   in the sales ledger

	Sales a/c	VAT a/c	Sales Ledger a/cs
	Credit	Credit	Debit
	£241.70	+£36.25	= £277.95 (In Total)

From the sales day book the appropriate ledger entries would be to

---

Debit the Debtor

Credit the Sales Account

Unit 5

Example:

General Ledger

Sales – 46

19–2				£
	July 31	Sundries	SDB1	241.70

VAT – 39

19–2				
	July 31	Sundries	SDB1	36.25

Sales Ledger

R. Mott & Co. Ltd – 27

19–2			£
July 1	Sales	SDB1	20.12

M. Brownlee – 3

19–2			£
July 4	Sales	SDB1	97.98

T. Dixon Ltd – 15

19–2			£
July 11	Sales	SDB1	99.48

A. Kell & Co. – 17

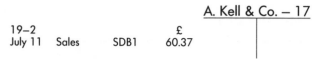

19–2			£
July 11	Sales	SDB1	60.37

Note   The total of the debits to these individual accounts equals the total posted to the credit of the sales and VAT accounts.
So, £20.12 + £99.48 + £97.98 + £60.37 = £241.70 + £36.25 = £277.95
The individual customers' accounts are debited **individually** and the sum total of the month's transactions is posted as **one amount** to the sales account.
The sum total of the Value Added Tax column is **Output VAT** and is credited to the VAT account.

Returned Goods

Sometimes the goods supplied by us are not satisfactory or are of the wrong kind, and accordingly are returned. When this situation arises we issue a returns note or a credit note (see example on page 79).

Accounting Entries

When a credit note is entered in the ledger we:

Debit the Sales Returns

Credit the Customer

An example looks like this:

```
        Sales Returns a/c              Customer's a/c
                £                                    £
A. Customer    35                      Returns      35
```

The effect of this is to reduce our sales and to reduce the amount owed by the customer to us.

Remember that a credit note entry is the **opposite** to an invoice entry.

Sales returns can also be called **returns in** or **returns inwards**.

Getting Money In

Discounts Allowed

An efficient firm ensures prompt payment from its customers.

As an incentive to get our money in quickly, we may sometimes allow a discount to our customers for early settlement of the account. This is known as Discounts Allowed, and is the opposite to Discounts Received.

Correspondence

If your customers do not pay by the due date, send them a polite reminder letter. For example:

Dear Customer

Amount Owing £

We are sorry to note that you have not paid our account which is now overdue.

We shall be most grateful if you will let us have payment as soon as possible.

Yours faithfully

Alternatively, many companies send out statements of overdue accounts with a special sticker or rubber stamp to highlight the fact.

If payment is still not made, send out a letter in stronger terms.

For example:

Dear Customer

Amount Owing £

We very much regret that your account with us has not been settled and is now extremely overdue.

We shall be grateful if you will give this matter your earliest attention and look forward to receiving your cheque by return of post.

Yours faithfully

If these two letters produce no result, an even stronger letter may be needed, threatening legal action.

The Best Approach

It has been found that a far better approach to collecting money is by establishing personal contact with customers, either by going to see them or by telephoning them. If you can telephone them in a nice friendly way and establish a bond, it is more likely that they will pay you.

Questions

1   When you buy goods on credit what are the entries?

2   When you sell goods on credit what are the entries?

3   What is a credit note?

4   What entries are made when goods are returned to a supplier?

5   You win a motor car worth £3000 and decide to incorporate it into your business. What would the entry be?

   Note: The owner is introducing a new asset.

6   Which one of the following is **not** a book of original entry?
   a)   The cash book
   b)   Purchases day book
   c)   The ledger
   d)   The sales day book
   e)   Returns In book
   f)   Returns Out book.

7   Why are folio references necessary?

8   What information must be shown on an invoice?

9 Enter the following into the purchases day book and post to the appropriate ledger accounts.

D. Hunter is a pet shop owner. He buys the following items:

19–2

2 June	1 gorilla at £200 plus VAT from Animal Suppliers Ltd
13 June	1 dozen minks at £3 each plus VAT from M. Furr Ltd
14 June	6 Labrador puppies at £40 each plus VAT from Cruft Ltd
24 June	24 yellow canaries at £2 each plus VAT from J. Bird & Co
26 June	100 rabbits at 50p each plus VAT from I. Stewart
30 June	2 horses at £100 each plus VAT from P. Haydock & Co Ltd

10 The credit sales and purchases of J. Sarson Ltd for November 19–4 were as follows:

19–4   Including VAT @ 15%

		£
Nov 2	Sold to T. Hallem & Co.	345
4	Bought from G. James Ltd	483
6	Sold to P. Fennell & Co.	690
9	Bought from A. Hensman Ltd	460
16	Sold to T. Hallem & Co.	138
17	Sold to P. Fennell & Co.	230
23	Bought from G. James Ltd	253
25	Sold to R. Gains Ltd	92
27	Sold to T. Adamson Ltd	161
30	Sold to N. Jackson & Co.	276

You are required to calculate the VAT, enter up the appropriate day books and post the items to the appropriate ledger accounts (including VAT).

11 The following credit sales and purchases were made by P. Adcock Ltd during November 19–4. All items are shown inclusive of VAT @ 15%

19–4   £

		£
Nov 1	Bought from Abbey Ltd	470.00
	Bought from Olympia Ltd	355.00
	Sold to Twinfit Ltd	680.00
	Bought from United Suppliers	125.00
10	Bought from Olympia Ltd	575.00
12	Sold to Roncount Ltd	424.00
18	Bought from United Suppliers	240.00
22	Sold to Twinfit Ltd	491.00
30	Bought from Abbey Ltd	286.00

You are required to calculate the VAT, enter up the day books and post to the ledger.

Note   To calculate VAT on each of the above items, multiply by $\frac{3}{23}$. This is discussed in Unit 8.

12 From the following details complete Stephen Bardsley's day books and show the appropriate ledger entries to record the double-entry. All transactions are subject to VAT at 15%. Folios should be used in all cases. Balance all personal accounts at the end of the month.

Sales Day Book

Date	Details	List	Trade Discount
19–3		£	
Nov 3	G. Peake	54	33⅓%
9	N. Hartwell	150	20%
16	R. Buckley	78	—
24	A. Clegg	200	25%
28	G. Peake	180	33⅓%

Purchases Day Book

Date	Details	List	Trade Discount
19–3		£	
Nov 1	J. Brown	480	25%
5	C. Chaplin	40	30%
11	H. Lloyd	210	10%
17	C. Chaplin	120	30%
26	J. Brown	280	25%

Cash Book

Nov 15   Hartwell sent £100 on account

Nov 30   Bardsley settled Chaplin and Lloyd's accounts taking 2% cash discount in both instances

Note   There is no need to show the cash book.

13   Post the following day book details to all necessary ledger accounts, using appropriate folios. At the end of the month balance off accounts with more than one entry.

Purchases Book

Date	Details	Total
19–5		£
Feb 3	A. Arkwright	175
11	P. Edwardes	63
16	P. Edwardes	240
23	D. Wright	161
27	A. Arkwright	84

Sales Book

Date	Details	Total
19–5		£
Feb 2	R. Moody	720
17	T. Hope	146
18	R. Moody	350
26	T. Hope	640

Purchases Returns Book

Date	Details	Total
19–5		£
Feb 18	P. Edwardes	13
25	D. Wright	29
28	P. Edwardes	34

Sales Returns Book

Date	Details	Total
19–5		£
Feb 9	R. Moody	36
19	T. Hope	23

14 Complete the sales book for B. Midler and show the ledger entries from the following information.

19–1

January 3   Sales to B. Forsyth list price £240 trade discount 25%

         7   VAT inclusive price to J. Tarbuck £184

      11   Trade discount of 12½% allowed to W.C. Fields on sales of £960

      18   J. Tarbuck bought another consignment at an inclusive price of £368

      22   Sold goods to S. Laurel at a list price of £270 allowing him 33⅓% trade discount

      26   M. Steel purchased goods at a total price of £483

      30   B. Forsyth bought goods at the list price of £320. Midler allowed him 25% trade discount

            All the above transactions are subject to VAT at 15%.

Note   Some of these figures have to be calculated from list prices, others have to be worked back from the total inclusive prices quoted.

15 Record the following items in the appropriate day books of M. Board and post to the ledger. All figures are inclusive of VAT.

			£
August	8	Claimed and received a reduction in price for damaged goods delivered by B. Rook	52.50
	10	Goods returned to S. King as being of poor quality	204.00
	14	Credit note received from D. Castle for goods incorrectly priced	11.50
	18	K. Knight returned damaged goods	49.68
	20	Credit note issued to W. Bishop who was dissatisfied with the price charged	34.50
	27	Returned wrong goods to B. Rook	207.00

16 Refer to the invoice shown on Page 75. Scheidegger returned all the green folders to ACL Colour Print on 18 June as they were the wrong size. Draw up an appropriate credit note.

17 Brian Wyse – Newsagent

In June Brian Wyse makes the following credit purchases:

June 3   Bought goods from W. Cookson £400 less 20% trade discount

       5   Purchased goods £360 from J. Quicks Ltd, no trade discount

       9   Bought goods £720 from P. Likely & Co., with 40% trade discount

     20   Purchased goods £120 from F. Bickerstaff, no discount offered

     28   Bought goods £840 from R. Giles, discount at 25%

> VAT is charged on all the above at 15%
> Prepare a day book from this information and post to all the appropriate
> ledger accounts, classifying them into general and purchases ledger sections.

Answers

9   Total purchases   £   774.00
     Total VAT   £   116.10

10 Total sales   £ 1680.00
     Total VAT   £   252.00

     Total purchases   £ 1040.00
     Total VAT   £   156.00

11 Total sales   £ 1386.96
     Total VAT   £   208.04

     Total purchases   £ 1783.50
     Total VAT   £   267.50

17   Brian Wyse – Newsagent

Purchases Book

Date	Details	Fo	List	Disc	Net	VAT	Gross
			£	£	£	£	£
19–8							
June 3	W. Cookson	PL1	400.00	80.00	320.00	48.00	368.00
5	J. Quicks Ltd	PL2	360.00	–	360.00	54.00	414.00
9	P. Likely & Co.	PL3	720.00	288.00	432.00	64.80	496.80
20	F. Bickerstaff	PL4	120.00	–	120.00	18.00	138.00
28	R. Giles	PL5	840.00	210.00	630.00	94.50	724.50
			2440.00	578.00	1862.00	279.30	2141.30
					GL1	GL2	

General Ledger

Purchases — 1

19–8			£	
June 30	Total	PB	1,862.00	

VAT — 2

19–8			£	
June 30	Total	PB	279.30	

Purchases Ledger

W. Cookson — 1

19–8				£
	June 3	Purchases	PB	368.00

J. Quicks Ltd — 2

19–8				£
	June 5	Purchases	PB	414.00

P. Likely — 3

19–8				£
	June 9	Purchases	PB	496.80

F. Bickerstaff — 4

19–8				£
	June 20	Purchases	PB	138.00

R. Giles — 5

19–8				£
	June 28	Purchases	PB	724.50

Unit 6

Control Accounts and the
Trial Balance

At the end of this unit you will be able to:

1   Appreciate the importance of internal 'control' systems

2   Understand how, by keeping control accounts, we can check that the work has been correctly done

3   Understand how we can build in self-checking mechanisms within a book-keeping system

4   Prepare a trial balance and explain its importance in a book-keeping system

5   Understand how the trial balance proves that the arithmetic in the ledger has been done correctly

6   Show an awareness of the sorts of errors which can be made.

Control Accounts

As a business grows and the number of creditors and debtors increases, it becomes necessary to check the work of the individual book-keeper keeping the personal accounts. Checking is important throughout the field of accounting work, and even more so since the introduction of computers.

Mistakes occur easily in office work, possibly because of boredom or fatigue, lack of concentration or because of the complexity of systems. It is therefore advisable to prepare control accounts.

The following example will help you to understand why control accounts are necessary and the book-keeping entries required for each transaction.

Sales (Debtors) Ledger Control Account

This is also known as the Sold Ledger Control Account.

Example

During January N. Wood & Co. sold goods to various companies as follows:

Goods Sold on Credit

		£
Jan 1	A. Batt & Co.	200
Jan 1	E.F. Brown	150
Jan 1	Maxi Ltd	300
Jan 10	F. White Ltd	400
Jan 10	Wright Ltd	350
Jan 17	Jay & Co.	250

Invoices were prepared by N. Wood & Co. and sent to the companies above. Their accounts in the sales ledger were then debited and the sales account credited.

During February, the following payments for goods sold on credit started to arrive in N. Wood's office.

Payments Received

		£
Feb 3	A. Batt & Co.	200
Feb 3	F. White Ltd	200
Feb 12	Maxi Ltd	300
Feb 12	Wright Ltd	150

These were debited to the cash book and credited to the respective sales ledger accounts.

F. Batt & Co.

		£				£
Jan 1	Goods	200		Feb 3	Bank	200

E.F. Brown

		£
Jan 1	Goods	150

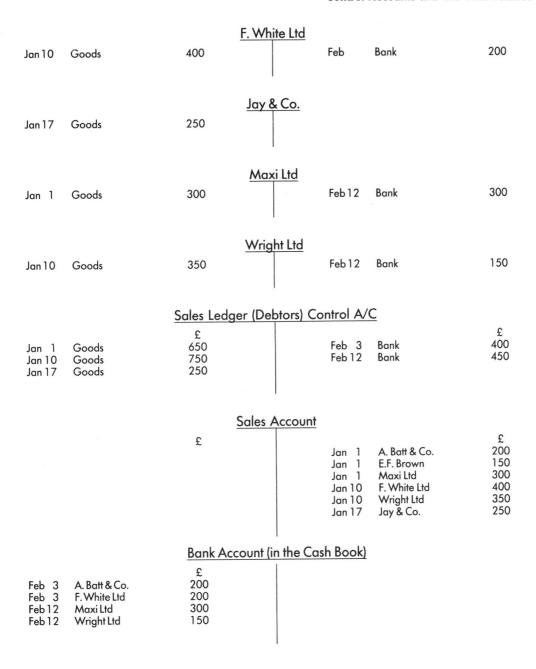

F. White Ltd

Jan 10	Goods	400		Feb	Bank	200

Jay & Co.

Jan 17	Goods	250

Maxi Ltd

Jan 1	Goods	300		Feb 12	Bank	300

Wright Ltd

Jan 10	Goods	350		Feb 12	Bank	150

Sales Ledger (Debtors) Control A/C

		£				£
Jan 1	Goods	650		Feb 3	Bank	400
Jan 10	Goods	750		Feb 12	Bank	450
Jan 17	Goods	250				

Sales Account

	£				£
			Jan 1	A. Batt & Co.	200
			Jan 1	E.F. Brown	150
			Jan 1	Maxi Ltd	300
			Jan 10	F. White Ltd	400
			Jan 10	Wright Ltd	350
			Jan 17	Jay & Co.	250

Bank Account (in the Cash Book)

		£
Feb 3	A. Batt & Co.	200
Feb 3	F. White Ltd	200
Feb 12	Maxi Ltd	300
Feb 12	Wright Ltd	150

In addition to these double entries, a total of each batch of invoices or payments posted or received each day must be entered in the control account as a single entry.

Example:

Jan 1   A total of £650 worth of invoices was debited to the debtors accounts and credited to the sales account. Therefore £650 must be entered as a debit to the control account.

Feb 3   A total of £400 worth of cheques was received and credited to the debtors accounts and debited to the cash book. These must therefore be entered as a credit to the control account.

Having entered the sales invoices and cash received, it is now possible to check the accuracy of the postings. This would be done by balancing each individual account and listing the balances to a total. Then balance the control account and if the balance agrees with the total of the individual account balances, the postings and figures will be correct. If the two do not agree then there is an error or more than one error to seek.

As an exercise, balance the accounts on the previous page and the control account and check that all is correct.

Separate Records

The control account balances are the totals of our debtors and creditors balances listed in the Trial Balance (see page 103). You can imagine the situation where we have a book-keeper keeping the individual accounts for 500 customers. Posting of invoices, credit notes, receipts, adjustments, discounts allowed etc. would involve a lot of work and it is quite likely that mistakes or errors could occur. What is done individually in each account is therefore reflected in total in the control account.

The accountant or the chief book-keeper will therefore keep independent control accounts and post to them items in total from the cash book, the sales day book, purchases day book and the returns book, as well as other special items.

At the end of the period the book-keeper will list the balances of all the individual personal accounts in the ledger and this should agree with the closing balance on the control account. This will not necessarily ensure that all the work has been done correctly. For example, mis-postings in the sales ledger or compensating errors will not be highlighted. Such errors may affect the recoverability of debts. It is therefore essential for the book-keeper to check and re-check the work carefully. This will help you to understand the importance of the control function.

There are further advantages from keeping control accounts. If the control account balances agree with the totals of the individual debtor and creditor accounts, this means that the debits must equal the credits. Therefore, if the trial balance does not agree, control accounts help to **isolate errors**. In order to manage a business successfully, figures are needed as soon as possible. Control accounts provide **quick balances** for debtors and creditors.

Items Found in Sales Ledger Control Accounts

Dishonoured Cheques

Sometimes a customer will pay but the cheque will 'bounce' (be dishonoured) and be referred back to the drawer (the customer). This is usually referred to as an R/D cheque, (Refer to Drawer).

In such an instance you would credit the cash book and debit the debtor's account. Dishonoured cheques appear on the debit side of the debtor's ledger control account. This posting reinstates the original debt.

Bad Debts

When a customer goes bankrupt, absconds or simply refuses to pay, the debt is **bad** and therefore must be written off. This should only be done by senior authority, and after it is certain that there is no chance of receiving the money. The entries would be to:

Credit the Debtor's Account

Debit the Bad Debts Account

Discount Allowed

Remember the cash book (Unit 3)

Debit Discount Allowed Account

Credit the Debtor's Account

Example:

Sales Ledger Control Account

		£				£
19–2						
Jan 1	Balance b/f	7471	Dec 31	Bad debts written off	220	
Dec 31	Interest	7		Bills receivable	5020	
	Bill receivable dishonoured	575		Receipts	14 308	
	Cash repaid to			Discounts allowed	526	
	Debtors	75		Sales returns	302	
	Bank (R/D cheques)	25		Creditors ledger		
	Sales	20 051		set-off (contras)	1017	
	Bad Debts recovered	8				
				Balance c/d	6819	
		28 212			28 212	
19–3						
Jan 1	Balance b/d	6891				

Note This account should always have a **debit balance**.
This balance should agree with the **total of the list of individual debtors' balances.**

A **Bill of Exchange** is similar to a cheque but payable some time in the future. The customer gives us a bill which we do not present for payment until, say, three months later. In the meantime the account is considered paid, the debtor is credited and we open a **Bills Receivable Account** with a debit balance. This account is still a type of debtor.

Credit the Debtor

Debit Bills Receivable Account

Returns Inwards

If customers return goods as being unsatisfactory or not ordered, a credit note has to be issued which is known as a Returns Inward or Sales Return. The entry in the ledger is to:

Credit the Debtor's Account

Debit the Sales Returns

Contras (Set-Offs)

Sometimes a customer is also a supplier to us, and at the end of the month, rather than us sending him a cheque and him sending us a cheque, we **contra** the two outstanding amounts. If we owe the supplier less than he owes us, we transfer from our purchases ledger to the sales ledger the amount of the contra (the smaller of the two amounts). Similarly, if we owe more than he owes us, we transfer the smaller amount from the sales ledger to the purchases ledger. The entries would be:

Credit the Debtor's Account

Debit the Creditor's Account

The contra has to be shown in the two control accounts, as a **debit** on the purchases control and a **credit** on the sales control.

Bad Debts Recovered

Sometimes after writing off a debt, it is eventually paid and we would debit the bank and credit the debtor's personal account. Therefore we would also have to debit the debtor's account and credit the bad debts account in order to write back the debt and thus clear the debtor's account.
In such circumstances the entry is:

Credit the Debtor's Account

Debit the Bad Debts Account

This item has to be shown on the control account as a debit entry.

Interest

If you charge interest on an overdue account:

Debit the Debtor

Credit the Interest Receivable Account

This, again, will be reflected in the control account as a **debit**.

Study the examples above and be sure that you understand each of the entries.

Summary

Anything that **increases** the debtor's debts is a **debit** entry.

Anything that **reduces** the debtor's debts is a **credit** entry.

For example:

Debtor's Account

Debits	**Credits**
Increases in the amount owing	Reductions in the amount owing
e.g. Sales	e.g. Returns
	Receipts
	Discount

Golden Rules for Control Accounts

Whatever goes into the individual personal accounts is posted to the
control account in total as follows:

Sales Ledger Control a/c

	£		£
Sales	90	Receipts	20

General Ledger Sales a/c

	£
SDB	90

Example

1 We sell goods to:
   A – £10,   B – £20,   C – £60   (Total £90)
2 Cash was received from:
   A – £5,   B – £7,   C – £8   (Total £20)

So the postings would be:

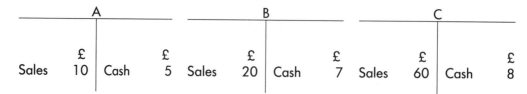

A				B				C		
	£		£		£		£		£	£
Sales	10	Cash	5	Sales	20	Cash	7	Sales	60	Cash 8

The double-entry is:

When we sell goods on credit:

> **Credit the Sales Account**

> **Debit the Debtor's Account**

When payment is received:

> **Credit the Cash Book**

> **Credit the Debtor's Account**

Purchases Ledger Control Account

With a large number of creditors it is also necessary that an overall check should be kept on the accuracy of the record keeping in the individual purchases ledger accounts. You will remember that it is essential in accounting always to ensure the accuracy of our postings. If these are incorrect we might pay more to a creditor than we owe him, or not get the benefit of such things as returns or credit notes in respect of errors on the account.

A Purchases Control Account (sometimes known as a Bought Ledger or Creditors Ledger Control Account) is a **total account** which reflects the position of the total amount due to the creditors. As with the debtors, what is entered individually into each creditor's personal account is entered in total in the control account.

An illustration of a purchases ledger account is as follows:

Purchases Ledger Control Account

19–2		£				£
Dec 31	Payments		Jan 1	Balance b/f		5751
	(to creditors)	12 538	Dec 31	Purchases		15 477
	Discount received	328				
	Balance c/d	8362				
		21 228				21 228
19–3			Jan 1	Balance b/d		8362

Note This account should always show a **credit balance**; this balance should agree with the **total of the list of individual creditor's balances on the personal accounts**.

Other Uses for Control Accounts

Incomplete Records

For a small business which does not keep complete double-entry accounts, control accounts can be used at the year-end to calculate missing figures. For instance, if a business has creditors of £5000 at the start of the year, £6000 at the end of the year and payments to creditors during the year of £20 000, we can deduce that the purchases for the year are £21000.

Purchases Control Account

	£			£
Payments	20 000	Creditors at start of year		5000
Creditors at year end	6000	Purchases for year		21 000
	26 000			26 000

Computer Packages

Modern software packages are often sold as sets, with separate disks for, say, sales ledger, purchases ledger and general (or Nominal) ledger. In order to produce a full set of final accounts from one disk (the general ledger), it is necessary to incorporate sales ledger control and purchases ledger control accounts, as well as a cash control account in the general ledger program.

The Trial Balance

At the end of each trading period the businessman needs to check his position and any profit or loss he has made. Having posted entries to the ledger throughout the trading period, he will now be in a position to prepare his final accounts. However, before he does this he needs to make sure that the entries in the books are arithmetically correct and that all the checks implicit in double-entry book-keeping have been carried out. To do this, therefore, the book-keeper will take out a trial balance.

> ## A Trial Balance is a List of Accounts taken from the Ledger showing the Debit and Credit Balances

The purpose of the trial balance is to prove the arithmetic of the double-entry. If both sides agree, it tells us that our entries are arithmetically correct.

Study the Golden Rules and method of extracting the trial balance. Remember these, as they will help you to identify the various types of accounts and decide whether they are debit or credit balances.

The Preparation of The Trial Balance

Go through the ledger and balance each account. This means adding up both sides of the ledger account (both the debits and the credits) and deducting the smaller amount from the bigger amount. The difference is the **balance**.

Here is an example:

Ledger Account

Debits	£		**Credits**	£	
Sundries	20		Sundries	10	
			Difference	10	= Balance
	—			—	
	20			20	
	—			—	
Balance b/d	10				

Note   This is a debit balance, as the debit side exceeds the credit side by £10. We therefore enter this as debit on the trial balance.
The balance is brought down and it is the side on which it is brought down which reflects the balance for entry into the trial balance, just as in the cash book.
A balance is the **excess** of one side over the other.

Check your additions and subtractions carefully. Ensure that your work is neat and that your figures are clear. If you have made an error, do not write over the figure but instead cross it out and insert the new figure, or use an accepted method of correction. Ensure when entering figures that units, tens, hundreds, thousands, etc. are placed underneath each other and properly aligned. This helps your arithmetic, avoids errors and looks neat.

Having balanced each account, the ledger balances can be transferred to the trial balance. Do not forget to include the balances from the cash book – this is part of the ledger.

Golden Rules for the Trial Balance

Debit balances on accounts indicate assets, expenses or losses. (i.e. motor vehicles, rent, loss on disposal of an asset).

Credit balances on accounts represent liabilities, income or gains. (i.e. bank overdraft, discount received, profit on disposal of an asset).

Example

Trial Balance
31 December 19–2

	Dr £	Cr £
Capital		7800
Drawings	400	
Premises	3000	
Fixtures & fittings	1500	
Motor vehicles	600	
Office equipment	1100	
Stock 1 January 19–2	1000	
Sales		7000
Purchases	3535	
Wages	730	
Advertising	105	
Rates	160	
Insurance	25	
Stationery	72	
Motor expenses	140	
Debtors	1076	
Creditors		876
Cash	23	
Bank	2210	
	15 676	15 676

Trial Balance not Balancing

If your trial balance does balance – well done! But this does not necessarily mean that the actual accounts are correct. If it does not balance, it indicates that you have made one or more errors. Such errors usually come from carelessness and inaccuracies and you should guard against these. A typical error is one of **transposition** where you write 71, for example, instead of 17. Very often this occurs when you bring a total forward to another page. It is useful to remember that differences caused by transposition errors are always divisible by 9. It may also be that your arithmetic is incorrect and you have either added or subtracted wrongly.

It is worth taking great care in ensuring:

- that your arithmetic is right

- that you post accurately

- that you total correctly.

If care is not taken to avoid these errors it will make extra work, and it is better to be thorough. The study and practice of accounts will encourage you to be orderly and systematic.

Headaches if you do not balance

Transposition

Inaccuracies

Shoddy work

Mistakes

Arithmetical errors

Carelessness

Exercise care when writing up accounts and balancing

Errors

Sometimes your trial balance balances but it can still be wrong. In book-keeping there are certain other errors made. Books are kept by human beings, who are not perfect. Perfection is not a human attribute, and accordingly through boredom and fatigue, lack of attention, poor training, or complex and complicated systems, errors are made.

It will help if you understand the types of errors which may occur, and your awareness will enable you to identify them or prevent them happening again. We will look at these in detail in the next unit.

Suspense

If great care has been exercised and all of the entries appear correct, but the trial balance does not balance, we need to open a suspense account to reflect the difference and make it balance, so that we can prepare the final accounts quickly. We then go ahead and prepare the final accounts in order to ascertain the results of the business. Afterwards, once these have been produced, we can go back and try to locate the error. Sometimes it pays to be sensibly approximate and have information now, when it is needed, rather than to be meticulously accurate but have information when it is too late.

Remember that if your books are wrong, then the final accounts must also be wrong.

It is sometimes commonsense to write the amount off rather than spend too long looking for a small difference. However, this should only be done when thorough checking has taken place, and if the difference is not large. By 'written off' we mean that an expense is charged to the profit and loss account. This is discussed further in Unit 11.

We will look at the suspense account in more detail in the next unit.

Questions

1 Explain a contra set-off entry.

2 What purposes do control accounts serve?

3 State the procedure for month-end 'balancing'.

4 What is the purpose of the trial balance?

5 If the trial balance balances, will the books be correct?

6 What is a suspense account?

7 The following is a summary of the transactions in the debtors' and creditors' ledgers of D. Smith. Write up the control accounts.

		£
Balance as at 1 January 19–3	Debtors	6850
	Creditors	3720
Credit sales for January		8072
Credit purchases for January		3690
Cash and cheques from debtors		7626
Cheques paid to creditors		3780
Credit notes from creditors		206
Credit notes to debtors		180

8 You are required to prepare a sales ledger control account from the following for the month of July.

19–3		£
July 1	Sales ledger balances	4936
	Totals for July:	
	Sales journal	49 916
	Returns inwards journal	1139
	Cheques and cash received from customers	46 490
	Discounts allowed	1455
	Bad debts written off	99
	Balances in the sales ledger set off against credit balances in the purchases ledger	259
July 31	Sales ledger balances	5410

9 You are required to prepare a purchases ledger control account from the following for the month of June. The balance of the account is to be taken as the amount of creditors as at 30 June.

19–9		£
June 1	Purchases ledger balances	3676
	Totals for June:	
	Purchases journal	42 257
	Returns outwards journal	1098
	Cheques paid to suppliers	38 765
	Discounts received from suppliers	887
	Cash paid twice in error to a supplier, now refunded	188
	Balances in the purchases ledger set off against	
	balances in the sales ledger	77
June 30	Purchases ledger balances	?

10 Open the appropriate accounts in T. Brown's ledger (including the cash book) and enter the following transactions. Balance off the accounts, and prepare a trial balance at the end of the month. Use a two-column cash book, with columns for cash and bank.

19–3
March 3 Brown commenced business paying £3000 into a bank account as his capital
    4 Bought goods on credit terms from Shaw and Gregory Ltd £180.15
    5 Paid by cheque £32.15 for stationery (office expenses a/c)
    5 Paid by cheque £18 for insurance premium (insurance a/c)
    8 Cashed cheque for £50 and put the money into an office cash box
    9 Paid £3.25 from cash for miscellaneous office expenses
    12 Sales £36.80 payment received in cash
    14 Sold goods on credit terms to C. Jones £68.42
    14 Paid wages from cash £18.20
    18 Sales £19.65 payment received in cash
    20 Paid £40 cash into bank account
    21 Bought goods on credit terms from Peters and Lord Ltd £635.25
    24 Sales £14.90 cheque received and paid into bank
    25 Bought delivery van for £852 paying by cheque
    28 Paid wages from cash £16.80
    28 Sold goods on credit terms to W. Roberts £88.42 and C. Webb £162.14
    29 Sales £42.15 payment received in cash
    29 Paid into bank all of the office cash except £20
    31 Received cheque from C. Jones for £68.42
    31 Sent cheque for £635.25 to Peters and Lord Ltd

11 Turn to Unit 4, Question 12. From your ledger postings and the cash book, extract a trial balance on 5 June 19–2, balancing the ledger accounts.

12 Freda Bryant's trial balance fails to agree. Prepare her debtors and creditors control accounts from the following information.
Indicate where the difference may be and by how much.

	£	£
Opening balances:	Debtors 9625	Creditors 15 348
Total credit sales/purchases	83 187	98 689
Returns in/out	456	237
Payments/receipts	85 261	82 377
Discounts received/allowed	160	175
Bad debts written off		480
Debtors balances off-set against creditors balances		1895
R/D cheques		640
Overpayment to creditors refunded		210

Total of balances extracted from sales ledger at end of month £8069
Total of balances extracted from purchases ledger at end of month £26 964

13 Construct the trial balance on 31 March 19—6 for P. Phogg for Unit 3, Question 11.
Explain the steps which should be taken if the trial balance does *not* balance.

14 From the following balances in Bob Lee's ledger, construct a trial balance on 30 April 19—2 and indicate how much capital is invested in the business.

	£
Cash	45
Bank overdraft	1683
Debtors	23 318
Creditors	41 169
Stock	31 091
Wages	1101
Rent	520
Insurance	218
Discount allowed	27
Discount received	340
Sales	161 790
Purchases	121 213
Sales returns	614
Purchases returns	2318
Premises	45 100
Motor vehicles	8600
Plant and Equipment	3200
Drawings	800
Sundry expenses	1450
Postage	65
Motor expenses	340
Premises repairs	598

Explain why capital has the balance that is does.

15 David Green's trial balance failed to agree. In order to isolate the error he decided to draw up control accounts. Using the information provided, indicate in which part of the ledger there is an error in the double-entry and the extent of that error.

		£
Balances agreed on 1 Jan 19—0	Sales ledger	35620
	Purchases ledger	67350

Day book totals for the year ended 31 Dec 19—0:

Sales day book	482100
Purchases day book	923580
Sales returns book	1300
Purchases returns	3240
Receipts from debtors	431890
Payments to creditors	896970
Bad debts written off	10700
Bad debts recovered	26300
R/D cheques	1340
Discount received	16820
Discount allowed	5420
Set-offs	6800
Interest charged by suppliers on overdue accounts	180

Balance extracted from the accounts at 31 December 19—0:

Sales ledger	66480
Purchases ledger	67280

Note The balances extracted from the ledger are **not** part of the control accounts. They are used to check the closing balances.

16 The office manager of a retail business has drawn up the sales ledger control account for the month of May. Unfortunately he is not an experienced accountant. In addition, the book-keeper made various errors during the month which were subsequently discovered.

From this information draw up a corrected control account and adjust the list of balances extracted from the ledger in order to reconcile the two figures.

Sales Ledger Control

19—3		£			£
May 1	Balances b/f	3675	May 31	Discounts received	210
31	Sales	5420		Returns out	365
	Contra set-off	240		Bad debts written off	580
	Discount allowed	185		Cash and cheques received	4010
	Returns in	40		Cheques returned R/D	320
				Balances c/f	4075
		9560			9560

List of balanced prepared by the book-keeper £4276

Errors discovered:

* Discounts allowed had been undercast in the cash book by £100

111

- A cheque received from a customer for £356 had been posted to his account as £635.
- The contra set-offs had not been posted to any individual accounts.
- Total receipts include a cheque for £125 for a bad debt recovered. Apart from the double-entry for this receipt no other entry has been made in the accounts.
- Interest of £55 charged on overdue accounts has not been included by the office manager in his total figures.

---

17   Brian Wyse — Newsagent

At the end of his first year of trading, Brian Wyse has the following balances in his books:

	£
Capital	3000
Cash	105
Bank	723
Purchases	28920
Sales	51640
Rates	750
Rent	5500
Postage & telephones	790
Discount allowed	156
Discount received	1820
Loan	1500
Motor vehicles	5000
Fixtures and fittings	2100
Wages	7255
Cleaning	950
Drawings	5100
Insurance	720
Motor expenses	1560
Creditors	2120
Debtors	175
Sundries	276

Set them out in the correct form for a trial balance.
List each of the above accounts under appropriate headings as follows:

Assets   Liabilities   Expenses   Income

Note   There is no opening stock shown, as this is the list of balances after the *first* period of trading.

Answers

7	Debtors control balance	£7116 DR
	Creditors control balance	£3424 CR
8	Sales ledger control totals	£54 852
9	Purchases ledger control balance	£5294 CR
10	Trial balance totals	£3612.63
11	Trial balance totals	£20 325

17   Brian Wyse – Newsagent

Brian Wyse's Trial Balance On 30 April 19–9

	£	£
Capital		3000
Cash	105	
Bank	723	
Purchases	28 920	
Sales		51640
Rates	750	
Rent	5500	
Postage & telephone	790	
Discount allowed	156	
Discount received		1820
Loan		1500
Motor vehicles	5000	
Fixtures and fittings	2100	
Wages	7255	
Cleaning	950	
Drawings	5100	
Insurance	720	
Motor expenses	1560	
Creditors		2120
Debtors	175	
Sundries	276	
	60 080	60 080

Assets	*Liabilities*	*Expenses*	*Income*
Cash	Capital	Purchases	Sales
Bank	Loan	Rates	Discount received
Motor vehicles	Creditors	Rent	
Fixtures & fittings		Postage & telephones	
Drawings		Discount allowed	
Debtors		Wages	
		Cleaning	
		Insurance	
		Motor expenses	
		Sundries	

Note   Drawings are actually a reduction of the liability 'capital'.

Unit 7

The Journal and Correction of Errors

At the end of this unit you will be able to:

1 Use the Journal

2 Recognise different types of errors

3 Correct errors

4 Use a suspense account.

The Journal

So far, we have looked at various day books: the sales, purchases and return books, and the cash book, which is the only part of the ledger which is *also* a day book. The journal is the last of the day books which needs to be considered. Any entries which do not go through one of the other day books (books of original entry) should go through the journal. This provides additional information to explain why entries are being made in the ledger and will, therefore, serve two main functions:

- To explain why certain entries have been made by providing more details, which means that the book-keeper does not have to rely on his memory if asked for an explanation (e.g. by an auditor).

- To help prevent errors, fraud or other irregularities by giving details of supporting evidence, and requiring more detailed information than would be given by a direct entry in the ledger.

Uses of the Journal

The main uses are to record:

- Acquisition and disposal of fixed assets, such as motor vehicles or plant and equipment.

- Opening and closing balances to start a new set of books, to close a business, or at the beginning and end of each trading period.

- Correction of mistakes.

- Transfers, particularly between cost centres in a cost accounts system.

That is to say, anything relatively unusual which will not be recorded in one of the other day books. Don't forget that the cash book is also a day book.

Using the Journal

The Journal is usually prepared on journal paper, which can also be used as two-column cash paper. The layout is as follows:

The Journal

Date	Details	Folio	Debit		Credit	
			£	p	£	p
	The Account(s) to be Debited					
	The Account(s) to be Credited					
	Supporting Details					

Unlike the ledger, where the details column tells us where the double-entry is to be found, here the details tell us the name of the account (or accounts) where the debit has to go, and where the credit has to go. Notice that there is an imaginary margin before the accounts to be credited, and there is a line ruled across the details column after the entry has been completed.

We can now look at some examples. Below is part of a page from the journal illustrating typical entries:

The Journal

Date	Details	Folio	Debit	Credit
			£	£
19–3				
Jan 1	Bank Motor vehicles Capital account Being assets introduced at start of business	CB1 GL3 GL1	800.00 1500.00	2300.00
Jan 10	Office Machinery Suppliers Ltd Being purchase of cash register per Order No. 2564 dated 31 October 19–2	GL7 PL5	100.00	100.00
Jan 23	W. Bennett A. Clark Being correction of error of commission on 15 December 19–2	SL10 SL25	35.50	35.50

Note The figures do not need to be totalled or balanced.

The Journal is a **day book** (a book of original entry). The ledger is posted from the above entries, the folios indicating that this has been done. In the ledger the folio will be 'J' followed by the page number, as shown on the next pages. Remember that the folios are entered only *after* each posting has been made in the Ledger account.

The actual double-entry postings would be as follows:

Cash Book

Cash Book

				£					
19–3									
Jan 1	Capital	J1		800					

General Ledger

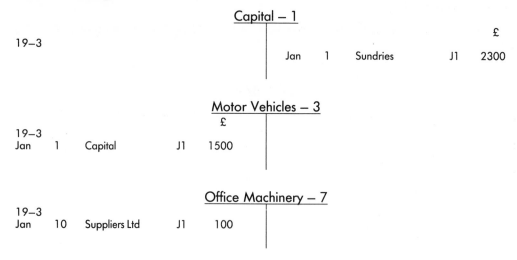

Capital – 1

19–3							£
			Jan	1	Sundries	J1	2300

Motor Vehicles – 3

19–3					£
Jan	1	Capital	J1	1500

Office Machinery – 7

19–3					
Jan	10	Suppliers Ltd	J1	100

Purchases Ledger

Suppliers Ltd – 5

19–3							£
			Jan	10	Office machinery	J1	100

Sales Ledger

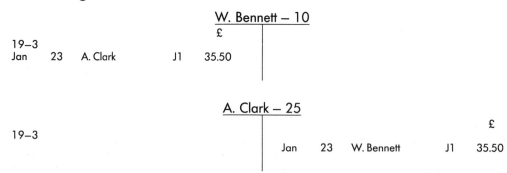

W. Bennett – 10

19–3					£
Jan	23	A. Clark	J1	35.50

A. Clark – 25

19–3							£
			Jan	23	W. Bennett	J1	35.50

Note the use of 'Sundries' on the capital account. This can be done whenever there is a posting to more than one other account (e.g. bank *and* motor vehicles) or when we do not know for certain where the posting should be shown.

Remember that this is not a complete set of books, only a selection of postings to illustrate certain points.

Correction of Errors

A trial balance, you will remember, is a list of balances extracted from the ledger. If it balances, it proves that the arithmetic is correct; that is, all the debits equal all the credits.

However, it does *not* prove that our entries are correct. If an error affects the debit side and the credit side of our double-entry to the same extent, then the trial balance will still balance. There are, in fact, six types of errors not shown up by the trial balance:

O Omission   Missed out completely.

C Commission   Posted to wrong account, but the right *type* (usually involving personal accounts).

P Principle   Posted to wrong *type* of account (e.g. a revenue account instead of a capital account).

O Original Entry   The wrong figure used for *both* entries (e.g. £125 posted instead of £152 – a transposed figure).

R Reversal   Debit and credit mixed up and posted incorrectly.

C Compensating   One or more errors on both the debit side and credit side, which have nothing whatsoever to do with each other, but just happen to cancel each other out.

An easy way to remember these six is to think – | **OCPORC** |

We can now look at an example of each of these errors and see the journal entries for them.

Examples

Omission   Cash sales £236 on 7 January not entered in the books.

Commission   Credit sale of £175 to J. Clark on 15 January posted to J. Clarkson's account.

Principle   Bill for motor repairs, £78, posted to motor vehicles account on 22 January.

Original Entry   Cash purchases of £245 on 27 January posted as £254.

Reversal   Payment of rent by cheque of £150 paid on 29 January, entries reversed.

Compensating   A posting of £100 to purchases on 30 January, entered as £10; cash sale on 31 January of £90 not entered on sales account.

The Journal

Date	Particulars	Folio	Dr	Cr
			£	£
19–7 Feb 8	Cash Sales Being correction of an error of omission on 7 January		236.00	236.00
	J. Clark J. Clarkson Being correction of an error of commission on 15 January		175.00	175.00
	Motor repairs Motor vehicles Being correction of an error of principle on 22 January		78.00	78.00
	Cash Purchases Being correction of an error of original entry £245 posted as £254 on 27 January		9.00	9.00
	Rent Bank Being correction of an error of reversal of £150 on 29 January		300.00	300.00
	Purchases Sales Being correction of compensating errors £100 posted as £10 on Purchases account on 30 January and sale of £90 on 31 January omitted		90.00	90.00

Note An error of original entry needs the **difference** to correct the mistake; an error of reversal needs **double** the original figure, and a compensating error may need a combination of figures in order to correct the mistake.

Can you think why some mistakes need different figures in order to correct them?

Using the Suspense Account

Here is an example of a trial balance which does not balance:

B. Good's Trial Balance on 31 December 19–9

	£	£
Capital		37 800
Drawings	400	
Premises	33 000	
Fixtures & fittings	1500	
Motor vehicles	600	
Office Equipment	1100	
Stock 1 January	1000	
Sales		7000
Purchases	3535	
Wages	730	
Advertising	105	
Insurance	25	
Stationery	72	
Motor expenses	140	
Debtors	1076	
Creditors		1876
Cash	23	
Bank	2210	
Returns in	150	
Returns out		244
Carriage in	265	
Carriage out	178	
Rates	257	
Heating & lighting	194	
Miscellaneous expenses	76	
	46 636	46 920

In this case, there is a difference of £284, the debits being less than the credits.

If this happens, first of all re-cast the figures in the trial balance, as it may simply be an arithmetical error. Then look for the figure of £284, to see if an entry has been left out, or a balance has not been included. Finally, check for *half* the difference (£142) in case an entry or a balance has been put on the wrong side. Only then, and provided the difference is not material (that is, large in comparison to the rest of the figures), we *add* the difference to the smaller side to make the trial balance agree.

To make the two sides agree, we must add £284 to the debit side:

B. Good's Trial Balance on 31 December 19–9

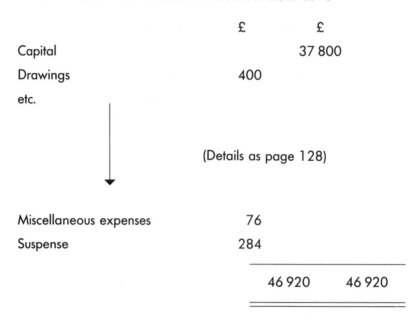

	£	£
Capital		37 800
Drawings	400	
etc.		
	(Details as page 128)	
Miscellaneous expenses	76	
Suspense	284	
	46 920	46 920

This difference must then be posted to a suspense account, in order to keep the double-entry in balance. As we have added £284 to the list of debit balances in this example, then the suspense account will have a *debit* balance:

Suspense a/c

19–9			£	
Dec	31	Difference as per Trial Balance	284	

We can now use the trial balance to draw up the final accounts (Units 10 – 13); the suspense account balance has to be included on the balance sheet.

Now, as soon as any **one-sided** errors are discovered, the suspense account can be used to correct the mistake. The balance on the account may get bigger before it is cleared out, but hopefully, if all the mistakes are found, there will eventually be no balance at all left on this account. By opening such an account we are admitting that there are mistakes somewhere in the books, and we are not trying to hide the fact.

We can now see how one-sided errors can be corrected through the journal, using the suspense account.

Example

- Cash sales of £127 on 30 November have not been posted to the sales account.

- A page in the purchases book has been undercast by £371 (remember that the *total* figure is posted to the purchases account).

- £20 goods returned by a customer on 15 December were posted to the credit of the returns out account.

The entries in the journal will be:

The Journal

19–9			£	£
Jan 28	Suspense Sales Being correction of posting omitted on 30 November		127.00	127.00
30	Purchases Suspense Being correction of undercasting in the Purchases Book		371.00	371.00
Feb 7	Returns out Returns in Suspense Being correction of wrong posting on 15 December		20.00 20.00	40.00

These will be posted to the suspense account as follows:

<u>Suspense</u>

19–9			£				£
Dec	31	Difference as per trial balance	284				
19–0							£
Jan	28	Sales	127	Jan	30	Purchases	371
				Feb	7	Returns	40
			411				411

As this account is now cleared out, it can be assumed that there are no more one-sided errors to be found.

Effect of Corrections on Profits

Since a suspense account is only opened if the trial balance does not balance, then it follows that final accounts drawn up from such a trial balance are not entirely correct. Once all the mistakes have been found, and the suspense account cleared out, it will be necessary to re-calculate the correct net profit.

A simple example is shown below.

Statement to Show Corrected Net Profit		£
Net Profit as Reported		2560
Add	£	
Sales understated	150	
Rent overstated	10	160
		2720

Less		
Purchases understated	600	
Discounts allowed omitted	50	<650>

Corrected net profit   2070

Questions

1 What are the main uses of the journal?

2 Name the errors which are not revealed by a trial balance.

3 What is an error of transposition?

4 What steps should a book-keeper take if a trial balance does not balance?

5 Where does the suspense account balance go in the final accounts?

6 Prepare the journal entries to correct the following errors:
a) £78 vehicle repairs bill posted to motor vehicles account.
b) Wages paid in cash £169 posted to the accounts as £196.
c) Credit purchases from P. Axon Ltd for £185 posted to credit side of purchases account and debit side of the personal account.
d) Rent receivable £82 paid to us by cheque not entered in the books.
e) Discounts allowed £97 posted to the drawings account.

7 On 30 June 19—4 the trial balance of P. Williams does not balance, and a thorough check is made of all the ledger postings. The errors shown below are discovered:
a) A sales invoice for £20 for goods supplied to R. Farmer had been completely omitted from the books.
b) A payment of £12 for stationery had been entered on the credit side of the stationery account.
c) In T. Hamilton's account (a debtor) an invoice had been posted short by £10.
d) £16 paid for vehicle repairs had been posted to the vehicles account.
e) Cash sales of £185 had been entered in the sales account as £155.
f) The credit side of V. Mason's account (a creditor) totals £31·8 and debit side £102. The balance has been entered in the trial balance as £218.
  (i) Which of the errors would not make any difference to the trial balance balancing, though still needing corrections?
  (ii) Show the journal entries necessary to correct the above errors.

8 Open up the books for E. Fisher using the journal for those entries which will not appear in one of the day books. Record the daily transactions for the month of April in the ledger and extract a trial balance at the end of the month.

19—8
April 1 **Assets**: premises £12 000; motor vehicles £1450; fixtures £2600; stock £1583; Debtors: R. Hardy £25; A. Hamilton £89; bank £1234; cash £45
Liabilities: Creditors: R. Reagan £275; H. Cassidy £99
3 Paid for purchases by cheque £248

    5 Goods bought on credit H. Cassidy £108; B. Green £72
    9 Credit sales £126 to R. Hardy; £63 to P. Jones
  11 Motor expenses paid in cash £29
  13 Drawings made from bank £50
  17 Goods returned to H. Cassidy £9
  19 Purchased another vehicle on credit from A B Motors Ltd £2175 paying a deposit by cheque of £500
  27 Settled the outstanding accounts for Reagan and Cassidy
  28 Received cheques to settle the accounts of Hardy and Jones
  30 Negotiated a bank loan from Natpro Bank plc for £2000

Note • What **types** or entries are made through the journal?
       • How much capital does Fisher have. How can it be calculated?

9 Jo Verrons' trial balance fails to agree. Subsequently the following errors come to light. Draw up Jo's suspense account to show the extent of the original difference.

a) A credit sale to Bear was posted in the sales ledger as £128 instead of £281.
b) A payment for motor repairs £160 was posted to purchases.
c) The purchases book was overcast by £100.
d) A cheque received from J. Bee for £58 was posted to the credit side of the cash book.
e) Goods taken by Jo for her own use £35 not recorded in the books.
f) £100 withdrawn from the bank not shown in the cash account.
g) Goods returned to U. Rogers £75 not recorded in the personal account.
h) Discount allowed totalling £47 recorded in the cash book but not posted to the general ledger.

10 Sid Richards' sales ledger control account does not agree with his list of debtors. The errors detailed below are subsequently discovered. Draw up a statement to show the effect of each of these errors on the control account balance and/or debtors list to reconcile the two figures.

      Sales ledger control accounts balance   £10 000
      Total debtors as per sales ledger   £10 369

a) A page total of £620 had not been included in sales for the month.
b) £35 returns made by F. Dew were posted to F. Door's account.
c) Discount allowed of £35 was not carried forward in the cash book totals for the month.
d) An R/D cheque for £146 was not posted to the personal account.
e) Bad debts of £395 were written off, but had not been recorded in the control account.
f) A settlement of £175 by direct debit had not been recorded in the sales ledger.
g) Interest totalling £23 charged on overdue accounts was omitted from the control account.
h) A contra set-off of £127 against a purchases ledger account was not included in the personal account.

11 Paul Kruger calculates that his net profit for the year comes to £12 500. He subsequently discovers that the following errors have been made. You are asked to draw up a statement to show his corrected net profit after taking into account the effect of each of these errors.

a) A page total from the sales day book of £540 has not been included.

b) Rent receivable £150 has not been shown in the trial balance.

c) An electricity bill of £210 has been paid but was not recorded in the heating and lighting account.

d) Purchases included £100 of stock taken by Paul for his own use.

e) An invoice sent out to K. Bolt for £78 has not been entered anywhere in the books.

f) Cash discount received by Paul amounting to £64 was not listed in the trial balance.

g) The cost of a new motor vehicle £5000 was included in the purchases account. Depreciation is ignored.

h) £140 paid out for insurance was posted to the wages account.

Note The net profit is calculated by deducting all the expenses of a business from all the income for a period. Therefore, if an expense item has been *overstated*, the original profit figure must now be *increased*.

12 Prepare journal entries with suitable narratives to correct the following errors which were discovered after a trial balance had been prepared. Construct the suspense account to show by how much the original trial balance failed to agree.

a) The purchases returns book was overcast by £110.

b) A payment received from a customer B. Jones for £230 was posted to the debit of P. Jones' account in the purchases ledger.

c) Bank charges of £76 had been posted to motor vehicles.

d) £500 cash taken by the owner for his own use had been posted to the credit of the capital account.

e) An invoice for £327 for goods received from J. Black had not been entered at all.

f) The balance of £620 cash at the bank had been carried down and listed as an overdraft.

g) A page total of £580 had not been included in the sales book figures.

h) £410 received for commission had been posted to the credit of the cash book and treated as commission payable.

13 Pierre Duchamp has tried to draw up his trial balance. You are asked to re-draft it in correct form after taking into account the effect of errors which were found later. Show also how the suspense account will be cleared.

Trial Balance on 29 February 19–8

	£	£
Capital		45 000
Cash in hand		100
Bank overdraft	1 400	
Office machinery	6 000	
Debtors		2 600
Creditors	3 800	
Motor vehicles	8 700	
Salaries and wages	10 850	
Rent and insurance	2 570	
Heating and lighting	1 780	
Stock		2 700
Purchases	27 650	
Sales		49 990
Purchases returns	480	

Sales returns		200
Commission receivable	820	
Discount allowed	4200	
Discount received	3600	
Premises	40 000	
Suspense		11 260
	111 850	111 850

a) Bank charges of £200 were not posted to a ledger account although the cash book had been adjusted accordingly.
b) A sales book page total of £2100 had not been included in the sales figure.
c) Office machinery costing £600 bought on credit on 28 February had not been included in the accounts.
d) The general expenses figure of £540 was omitted from the trial balance.
e) The balance on motor vehicles has been transposed. The figure should be £7800.

Note If a trial balance is correct there is no suspense account.

14 Brian Wyse — Newsagent

On 19 September B. Wyse purchases some new shop fittings on credit from Eezee Shopfitters Ltd for £2700, paying a deposit of £270. Show the journal entry to record this transaction.

After extracting a trial balance, Brian discovers that it does not balance — there is a difference of £270 short on the debit side. Subsequently, the following mistakes were discovered:
a) An invoice received from A. Black for £175 had been mislaid, so no entries were made.
b) Cash sales had been shown in the sales account as £365 instead of £536.
c) Cash drawings of £75 had been entered in the motor expenses account.
d) The amount for a customer F. Wolf had been balanced correctly, but the balance of £441 had not been brought down, so was not included in the debtors' total.
e) Cash paid for sundry expenses £32 was shown on the debit side of the cash book and the credit side of the ledger account.

Show the journal entries necessary to correct these errors and the suspense account.

What is the advantage of keeping a journal?

Answers

8 E. Fisher:

Capital	£18 652		
Cash book balances		Cash	£16 DR
		Bank	£2177 DR
Trial balance totals			£22 597

---

14 Brian Wyse – Newsagent

19–8			£	£
Sept 19	Fixtures and fittings		2700	
	Eezee Shopfitters Ltd		270	
	Bank			270
	Eezee Shopfitters Ltd			2700
	Being acquisition of shop fittings on credit 10% deposit paid			

Note This can be posted in a different way showing the *net* amount due on the credit of the personal account.

			£	£
a)	Purchases		175	
	A. Black			175
	Being correction of an error of omission			
b)	Suspense		171	
	Sales			171
	Being correction of posting of £536 entered as £365			
c)	Drawings		75	
	Motor expenses			75
	Being correction of an error of principle			
d)	Debtors		441	
	Suspense			441
	Being balance omitted from trial balance			

e)	Sundry expenses	64	
	Cash		64
	Being correction of an error		
	of reversal of £32		

Suspense account

19–8	£		£
Balance as per trial balance	270	Debtors balance omitted	441
Sales (transferred)	171		
	——		——
	441		441
	══		══

The advantage in keeping a journal is that it acts as an 'aide-mémoire', providing additional information about transactions.

Unit 8

Value Added Tax

At the end of this unit you will be able to:

1 Understand who should register for VAT and when this should be done

2 Understand the various VAT rates and show the difference between VAT Outputs and VAT Inputs

3 Maintain VAT records and complete a VAT return.

Budget Update 1989

Value Added Tax

If the turnover for a calendar year exceeds £23 600, then a business will be required to be registered for VAT purposes. If turnover exceeds £8000 in any one quarter but total turnover for the year will not exceed £23 600, registration is not necessary, although **notification** of liability is compulsory. Late registration can incur heavy penalties. The limit for cancellation of registration is £1000 less than the registration level i.e. £22 600. Incorrect declarations of VAT can also incur heavy penalties.

The scope of VAT is being extended to cover business use: fuel, power, water and construction of non-residential buildings. After August 1989, landlords may charge VAT on rent. Charities are now exempt on fund-raising activities (including advertising).

Income Tax

No change to current rates of 25% basic and 40% higher. Personal allowances raised in line with inflation to: Single person £2785, Married £4375
Basic rate limit raised to £20 700.
Retirement pension earnings rule scrapped.
Age allowances raised, and extended to over 75's.
Company car scales increased by a third.

National Insurance Contributions

Simplified structure:
Lower limit raised to £43 per week.
Employee's contributions on earnings above £43:
    2% of first £43
    9% on all other earnings to upper limit of £325 per week.

Corporation Tax

Small companies with profits up to £150 000 per annum pay at the lower rate of income tax (25%).
Top rate of 35% applied to companies with annual profits over £750000.
A sliding scale operates for companies between these two limits.

VAT Registration

With certain exceptions, every person, partnership or company supplying 'taxable goods or services' is:
1 a taxable person
2 liable to register with Customs and Excise
3 liable to account for the VAT on his own transactions.

His invoices must clearly state his VAT registration number and show the tax as a separate amount. Small traders whose business *turnover* (not profit) is less than a certain limit need not register. This limit is reviewed each year in the Budget.

It is the duty of every trader to notify the VAT office within one month of the date that he expects his turnover to exceed the registration limit if he is not yet registered. Failure to do this may result in the VAT registration being backdated and VAT will become due on all sales made since that date even if no VAT has been charged to the customer. In addition, there could be heavy penalties for late registration.

When forms have been sent to the local VAT office, and provided the trader is liable to be registered, the local VAT office will send a preliminary advice of registration. This will give the trader's registration number and show the effective date from which he is registered.

If the trader has applied for voluntary registration, or for registration before he starts making taxable supplies, he will normally get his registration number as soon as the written acceptance of any conditions imposed on the registration has been received. He will also be sent Notice No. 700 *VAT General Guide*, which explains fully the basic operation of the tax, Notice No. 701 *VAT Scope and Coverage*, and any other notices or leaflets which he has requested, such as Notice 727 *Retail Schemes*.

Charging VAT

The trader will have to account for VAT from the date on which he was first required to be registered. This date will not necessarily be the date he notified his liability to be registered or the date he received his certificate of registration. This applies whether or not he has included VAT on his prices. So he should start keeping VAT records and charging VAT to his customers as soon as he knows he is required to be registered. He must *not* show VAT as a separate item on any invoice that he issues until he knows his registration number. However, he can adjust his price to include VAT and explain to any of his customers who are registered that he will send them VAT invoices later. Once he has his registration number, he should issue the necessary invoices showing VAT, within 30 days.

If you are in business and not registered for VAT, or about to start in business, you should obtain the pamphlet called *Should I Be Registered For VAT?* from your local VAT office.

VAT Procedures

The theory of VAT is that it is a **tax on sales**. When a taxable person sells goods or services which are liable to VAT, the VAT must be charged to the customer. If the customer uses these goods or services in his business, then the VAT can be claimed back. The VAT charged on the sales invoice is called **output tax** and the VAT claimed back is called **input tax**.

In Unit 5, we saw how credit transactions are entered in the day books before being posted to the ledger. One important aspect of invoices and information found in the day books relates to Value Added Tax (VAT).

When VAT was introduced in 1973, most existing book-keeping procedures required some adjustment. An extra VAT column in the cash books, purchases and sales day book is one example, in addition to an amended and freshly designed invoice, and a VAT account in the ledger to record tax inputs (debits) and tax outputs (credits). In practice an extra column is needed in each of the various books, as we saw in the sales and purchases day books in Unit 5.

Invoices

In addition to recording VAT separately from copies of the invoices he issues to his customers, the trader must also record in his books the VAT invoiced to him by his suppliers. Copy sales invoices and purchase invoices are required by law to be kept for six years and must be produced to the Customs and Excise officers on demand. This has serious implications for the way in which invoices are filed.

Once the trader has his registration number, he must issue tax invoices to other registered traders for all supplies which are taxable, including zero-rated items.

The tax invoice must show:

- an identifying number and the date;

- name, address and VAT registration number

- the time of the supply (i.e. tax point)

- the customer's name and address

- a description and the quantity of the goods or extent of the services supplied

- the charge made, before tax

- the rate of tax

- the total tax payable.

This information is required by Customs & Excise as a step towards the prevention of fraud. Retailers do not normally issue tax invoices, but must do so if asked. A simplified tax invoice, showing the VAT-inclusive price and the tax rate, may be issued if the value of the goods is not more than £50 including VAT.

VAT and Settlement Discounts

Where a cash discount is offered (i.e. freely available to anyone) VAT should be calculated on the basis that the discount will be taken. If it is not taken no adjustment is made to the VAT calculation on the invoice. If a trader is offered a cash discount in terms of a percentage, say 5%, the VAT must be deducted from the total amount before calculating the cash discount.

Example:

	£
Cash discount offered 10%	
List price of goods supplied	100.00
VAT @ 15% on (100 – 10) £90	13.50
	———
	113.50
	———
So, if discount is taken, payment will actually be	103.50
	———

VAT Records

The traders' records of purchases and sales must be designed to enable him, every three months, to complete a Return (VAT Form 100). This shows his **total output tax** (i.e. on sales) as charged to his customers *less* **total input tax** (as paid by him on purchases). The difference is paid to the Customs and Excise VAT Central Unit at Southend-on-Sea or received back, as is the case with some firms (particularly those supplying zero-rated goods or services).

Goods and services can, for VAT purposes, be described by one of the following terms:

Positive rated goods or services are taxable at the current rate (15% at the moment).
Zero-rated goods or services are taxable at a positive rate, but the rate is zero, e.g. electricity, gas, most food, children's clothing.
Exempt goods or services are free from tax by law, e.g. banking, insurance and medical services, or because they are supplied by a person whose taxable turnover is below the limit.

Notice No. 700 gives information about the records and accounts the trader needs to keep, and can be obtained from your local VAT office. It also contains other helpful information for a person starting in business as a taxable trader. If he is already in business, he may find that normal accounts need only to be modified.
The trader must keep:

- copies of all invoices and credit notes issued

- invoices and credit notes received for business purchases

- copies of customers' entries for imported goods

- evidence of the export of goods sent abroad.

The trader must be sure to keep a record of:

Output tax
Tax charged and due to be paid to Customs and Excise. If he is a retailer, (i.e. he runs a shop or provides services directly to the public) Notice No. 727, obtainable from H M

Customs & Excise, will help him to choose one of the special schemes tailored to different types of business. These schemes allow output tax to be calculated from takings.

Input tax

Tax paid on purchases for the business. Tax cannot be reclaimed on cars, even if they are used for business, or on business entertainments. Neither can tax be reclaimed on any goods or services bought for personal or private use, or other non-business purposes.

Totals of Output and Input Tax in each Tax Period

These are summarised in a VAT account so that a VAT return can be completed. Keeping a VAT account is mandatory, as it can be kept as a personal account of H M Customs & Excise, as shown below.

Golden Rules for VAT

The VAT account in the ledger should be written up as follows:

> - **Debit it with Input Tax on Purchases (less Purchases returns).**
> - **Credit it with Output Tax on Sales (less Sales returns).**

Whether the transactions are for cash or credit makes no difference. A debit balance on this account is in our favour, i.e. a repayment from Customs & Excise. A credit balance indicates tax payable by us to Customs & Excise.

Customs & Excise
Value Added Tax a/c

Input	**Output**
Postings from:	Postings from:
Purchases day book	Sales day book
Purchases returns book (minus)	Sales returns book (minus)
Cash book	Cash book
Petty cash book	

Some organisations treat this as the personal account of H M Customs and Excise, as either a debtor or creditor, as appropriate.

How to Complete Value Added Tax Returns

The current rate of Value Added Tax is 15%. Accordingly, this should be added to all standard-rated goods and services.

As previously discussed, VAT is generally entered into the accounting books separately and would be entered in the VAT account from the cash book and other day books.

Some retailers have special schemes whereby, because of the burden of keeping detailed VAT records in respect of many small transactions, they are able to enter their sales gross and take a fraction of $\frac{3}{23}$ as the VAT on sales. This is equivalent to adding 15% on to sales prices to cover VAT.

Value Added Tax Return

For the period

01 05 86 **to** 31 07 86

Due to reach the VAT Central Unit by 31 08 86
These dates must not be altered.

H M Customs and Excise

For Official Use

Registration No	Period
123 4567 89	07 86

Before you fill in this form please read the notes on the other side. You must complete all boxes — writing "none" where necessary.
If you need to show an exact amount of pounds, please write "00" in the pence column. Don't put a dash or leave the column blank. Please write clearly in ink.
You must ensure that the completed form and any VAT payable are received no later than the due date by the Controller, VAT Central Unit, H M Customs and Excise, 21 Victoria Avenue, SOUTHEND-ON-SEA X

An envelope is enclosed for your use.

	For Official Use	£	p
VAT DUE in this period on OUTPUTS (sales, etc), certain postal imports and services received from abroad	1		
Underdeclarations of VAT made on previous returns (but not those notified in writing by Customs and Excise)	2		
TOTAL VAT DUE (box 1 + box 2)	3		
VAT DEDUCTIBLE in this period on INPUTS (purchases, etc)	4		
Overdeclarations of VAT made on previous returns (but not those notified in writing by Customs and Excise)	5		
TOTAL VAT DEDUCTIBLE (box 4 + box 5)	6		
NET VAT PAYABLE OR REPAYABLE (Difference between boxes 3 and 6)	7		

FOR OFFICIAL USE

Please tick only ONE of these boxes:

box 3 greater than box 6 — payment by credit transfer ☐   payment enclosed ☐

box 6 greater than box 3 — repayment due ☐

		£	p
Value of Outputs (excluding any VAT)	8		00
Value of Inputs (excluding any VAT)	9		00

How to pay the VAT due

Cross all cheques and postal orders "A/C Payee only" and make them payable to "H M Customs and Excise". Make credit transfers through account 3078027 at National Girobank or 10-70-50 52055000 for Bank Giros and keep your payment slip. You can order pre-printed booklets of credit transfer slips from your local VAT office. In your own interest do not send notes, coins, or uncrossed postal orders through the post.
Please write your VAT registration number on the back of all cheques and credit transfer slips.

Please tick box(es) if the statement(s) apply:

box 5 includes bad debt relief ☐   box 8 includes exempt outputs ☐   box 8 includes exports ☐

Retail schemes If you have used any of the schemes in the period covered by this return please tick the box(es) to show all the schemes used

A	B	C	D	E	F	G	H	J

Remember, you could be liable to a financial penalty if your return and all the VAT payable are not received by the due date.
DECLARATION by the signatory to be completed by or on behalf of the person named above.

I, ... declare that the
(full name of signatory in BLOCK LETTERS)
information given above is true and complete.

Signed .... Date.. 19......
*(Proprietor, partner, director, secretary, responsible officer, committee member of club or association, duly authorised person)   *Delete as necessary

FOR OFFICIAL USE

VAT 100   F3790 (JULY 1986)

VAT Form 100

The VAT form usually covers three months but it can be for some other period, e.g. one month. VAT tax periods can normally be arranged to fit in with a trader's financial year if details are sent to the local VAT office with Registration Form VAT 1. The actual period covered is stated at the top of the form. You also get one month to complete the form. The VAT 100 must be received by Customs & Excise with payment by the date shown, otherwise a penalty may be issued.

Box 1 Shows output VAT for the period (from the VAT account in the general ledger). This is equivalent to VAT charged on the period's sales and other income, e.g. sale of a fixed asset.

Box 2 If there has been an error on previous returns, an adjustment can be made here.

Box 3 Is the total of Boxes 1 and 2.

Box 4 Is the total of input VAT from the VAT account in the general ledger. This is the tax paid on purchases and other expenses.

Box 5 Here again errors on previous returns can be adjusted.

Box 6 Is the total of Boxes 4 and 5.

The total of Box 3 is deducted from the total of Box 6 to give the amount of VAT payable, entered in Box 7.

Sometimes there is more input than output VAT (for example zero-rated companies) so the difference is refunded by Customs and Excise.

Box 8 This is the value of your sales which you will get from the sales account in the general ledger and the journal.

Box 9 This is the value of your purchases and expenses which you will get from your purchases account, an analysis of your cash book and petty cash and the journal.

Recent Changes in VAT Regulations

Small Businesses

- Threshold for registration raised to £23 600

- Businesses with annual turnover of *less* than £250 000 (more than half of all those registered) can choose:

  to make *annual* returns (instead of quarterly),

  to make their returns based on cash receipts, instead of *invoiced* accounts – so overcoming problems of cash flow and bad debts

- Simpler schemes introduced for small to medium-sized firms.

Charities

- Some charities are now able to claim relief for:

  welfare vehicles (e.g. transport for hospices)
  adaptations to homes for the disabled
  drugs used in research
  equipment used for first-aid and mountain rescue

  These concessions are in addition to those already allowed for transport used for the blind, deaf and mentally handicapped. Vehicles used by organisations for the elderly and disabled are not included.

Income from covenants is affected by changes in basic rate of income tax.

Example

Here is a worked example of how to post VAT entries from various day books to the VAT account.

A. Poly   Cash Book

Date	Details		Output Tax	Cash	Bank	Date	Details		Input Tax	Cash	Bank
			£	£	£				£	£	£
19–8											
Aug 1	Balances	b/d		300	450	Aug 1	Purchases		39.13		300
2	Cash sale		78.26	600		2	J. Quicks Ltd				414
3	Cash sale		58.69	450		4	W. Cookston				368
4	B. Good				230	5	Purchases		32.61		250
5	J. Soap				460	6	Purchases		13.04	100	
5	Cash sale		65.22	500		7	Balances	c/d		1750	153
6	N. Brown				345						
			202.17	1850	1485				84.78	1850	1485
Aug 8	Balances	b/d		1750	153						

Post to VAT a/c   Post to VAT a/c

Note
- When posting from the cash book to the VAT account, only the *totals* of the output and input tax need be posted.
- The output and input tax columns are memorandum only and are totalled but not brought down.
- The output and input tax for credit transactions are not shown in the cash book but would appear in their respective day books.
- If cash discounts are received or allowed, then a fourth column would be needed to record this.

A. Poly   Purchase Day Book

Date	Details	Net	VAT	Total
		£	£	£
19–8				
Aug 1	J. Quicks Ltd	360	54.00	414
4	W. Cookston	320	48.00	368
		680	102.00	782
			To VAT a/c	

Purchase Returns Book

Date	Details	Net	VAT	Total
		£	£	£
Aug 2	R. Ralph	25	3.75	28.75
			To VAT a/c	

A. Poly   Sales Day Book

Date	Details	Net	VAT	Total
		£	£	£
19—8				
Aug 1	B. Good	200	30	230
2	J. Soap	400	60	460
3	N. Brown	300	45	345
		900	135	1035
			To VAT a/c	

A. Poly   Sales Return Book

Date	Details	Net	VAT	Total
		£	£	£
19—8				
Aug 5	J. Soap	20	3	23
			To VAT a/c	

A. Poly   Petty Cash Book

Float	Date	Details	PCV	Total	Petrol	Stationery	Cleaning	Misc. VAT
				£	£	£	£	£
100.00	19–8 Aug 1	Cash	CB					
	1	Stationery	1	28.75		21.25		3.75
	2	Petrol	2	23.00	17.00			3.00
	2	Overalls	3	40.25			29.75	5.25
				92.00	17.00	21.25	29.75	12.00
		Balance	c/d	8.00				
100.00				100.00				↓
								To VAT a/c
8.00	8	Balance	b/d					
92.00	8	Cash Re-imbursed	CB					

Value Added Tax (Input) A/C

Aug	Purchase Day Book			£ 102.00	Aug "	Purchase Returns			£ 3.75
	Cash Book			84.78		Balance	c/d		195.03
	Petty Cash			12.00					
				198.78					198.78
Sept	Balance	b/d		195.03					

Value Added Tax (Output) A/C

Aug	Sales Returns			£ 3.00	Aug "	Sales Day Book			£ 135.00
	Balance	c/d		334.17		Cash Book			202.17
				337.17					337.17
					Sept	Balance	b/d		334.17

Some businesses combine the input and output tax into one account as shown on the next page, but this is not good accounting practice. As you can see, returns and other adjustments have to be deducted from either side and this can be confusing.

Example

Value Added Tax a/c

	Input	£		Output	£
Aug 31	Purchases day book *Less* Purchase returns	102.00 < 3.75>	Aug 31	Sales day book *Less* Sales returns	135.00 < 3.00>
		98.25			132.00
	Cash book Petty cash Balance	84.78 12.00 c/d 139.14		Cash book	202.17
		334.17			334.17
			Sept 1	Balance	b/d 139.14

The total payable to Customs and Excise would be £139.14 made up of:

Output tax	334.17
Less Input tax	195.03
Net payable	139.14

Remember that a cheque (or some other form of payment) for this amount has to be sent to Customs and Excise with the return within one month of the end of the period. This may need to be taken into account when budgeting for cash flow!

Questions

1   What is meant by a) Exempt?
                    b) Positive rated?
                    c) Zero-rated?

2   Where do we get the information to prepare the VAT account?

3   What are the source documents which must be kept to back up the VAT return, and how long should they be kept?

4   Define Input Tax and Output Tax.

5   What period of time does a VAT Form 100 usually cover, and are there any exceptions to this?

6 You are required to prepare the VAT account for the first quarter of 19–8 from the following information:

19–8	VAT Inclusive	£
Jan 1 to Mar 31	Credit sales	10750
	Cash sales	2125
	Sales returns	460
	Purchases	7690
	Purchase returns	230
	Petty cash	55

Balance off the account and bring down the balance.

Remember to use the VAT fraction $\frac{3}{23}$.

7 The following credit sales were made by D. Bird Ltd during Jan 19–8. You are required to prepare a sales day book and post the items to the ledger accounts. All sales are inclusive of VAT.

19–8		£
Jan 2	J. Anstey Ltd	120
4	R. Dennis & Co.	210
5	S. Whitaker Ltd	64
10	K. Tanner Ltd	430
16	H. Smith & Co.	315
20	T. Baker Ltd	165
25	R. Trodd & Co.	218
26	B. Wells Ltd	102

8 The credit sales and purchases of N. Wood Ltd for August 19–8 were as follows:

19–8		Inclusive of VAT £
Aug 3	Sold to R. Clark & Co.	345
5	Bought from D. Smith Ltd	483
7	Sold to F. Bloore Ltd	690
9	Sold to J. Sullivan & Co.	138
11	Bought from B. Croy & Co.	460
12	Sold to C. Crowe Ltd	230
14	Sold to E. Cram & Co.	92
15	Sold to D. Mate Ltd	161
17	Goods returned by F. Bloore Ltd	23
20	Goods returned by D. Mate Ltd	46
25	Goods sold to G. Gold Ltd	276
30	Bought from A. Bartlett & Co.	253

You are required to enter up the day books and post the items to the ledger accounts and VAT account.

9 Mr Ross is a wholesaler and a retailer. From the following information prepare a four column cashbook with columns for VAT, sales, cash and bank. Write up the necessary day books, VAT a/c and other ledger accounts.

19–8

Aug 1 Balances in the cash book are £300 Cash £800 Bank
1 Sold goods on credit to J. Smith for £700 plus VAT
2 Bought goods on credit from R. Rose £500 plus VAT
3 Cash takings £460 including VAT
4 Returned goods to R. Rose £23 including VAT
5 Bought goods from T. Top on credit for £800 plus VAT
6 Sold goods on credit for £600 plus VAT to B. Good
7 Paid wages by cheque £250 (exempt VAT)
8 Received cheque from J. Smith £805
  Paid cheque to T. Top £920
9 Cash sales £750 (including VAT)
10 Goods returned from B. Good £100 plus VAT
11 Bought goods for cash £100 plus VAT
  Cash sales of £345 (including VAT)
12 Sold goods on credit to B. James for £200 plus VAT.
  Bought goods from K. Bull for £400 plus VAT and paid him £460 cash
13 The VAT from the petty cash book amounted to £15.00 paid out

10 Using as much of the following information as required, draw up the VAT account(s) at the end of August and balance off.

Sales Day Book

	Net £	VAT £	Total £
Aug 3	40	6	46
Aug 9	120	18	138
Aug 21	200	30	230
Aug 28	240	36	276

Sales Returns Book

	Net £	VAT £	Total £
Aug 7	20	3	23
Aug 11	60	9	69

Purchases Day Book

	Net £	VAT £	Total £
Aug 2	80	12	92
10	280	42	322
14	140	21	161
20	420	63	483

Purchases Returns Book

	Net £	VAT £	Total £
Aug 12	40	6	46
Aug 27	100	15	115

Petty Cash Summary

		Total	Travel	Stationery	Misc	VAT
		£	£	£	£	£
Totals		164	35	54	61	14
Balance	c/d	36				
		200				

Cash Book Summary

			Disc	VAT	Bank		Disc	VAT	Bank
			£	£	£		£	£	£
Aug 31	Balance	c/d	–	–	547		–	–	–
	Totals		51	1,146	8,321	Totals	36	221	8,321

Note It is presumed that all VAT paid can be re-claimed.

11 Draw up a table as shown and fill in the missing figures.

	Net		VAT		
Stage	Purchase Price	Sales Price	Input	Output	Payable to C & E
		£			
Prime Producer	–	80			
1st Manufacturer		120			
2nd Manufacturer		260			
Wholesaler		320			
Retailer		480			
Customer					

What is the amount collected by Customs and Excise?
Calculate VAT at 15%.
Ignore all other inputs and outputs for this exercise.

12 Construct a suitable invoice to record the following information. If the account is settled within 14 days, what will be the value of the cheque?

On 1 May 19–3 S. Peters of 205 Hague Bar, Manchester (VAT registration number 123 456 7890) sends 200 bone china tea sets and 100 pottery coffee mugs to B. Baggins, The Croft, Burnley. The invoice is numbered 001234. Each tea-set is priced at £3.60; coffee mugs at £1.20.
Sue offers Bill 20% trade discount, but charges an additional £10 for carriage. Terms are Net 30 days, 2% for 14 days. VAT is charged at 15%.

Who will record the VAT as input tax?

13 Post the following details to the appropriate day books, including cash book and journal. There is no need to complete the double-entry. The cash book should show three columns for VAT, cash and bank. Balance it off at 30 September. Show the entries in the VAT account with the balance carried down.

19–1

Sept 1 Balances brought forward: Cash in hand £75
                                    Bank overdraft £540

2 Credit purchases net of VAT: P. Cox £420, J. Little £370

4 Cash sales £598 banked after paying £55.20 for car repairs and £96.60 for stationery. These items are all VAT inclusive

7 More purchases made on credit net of VAT: P. Cox £250; F. Grey £310 and W. Blow £530

9 Faulty goods returned to Blow £38 and Grey £18 both net

12 An amount of £276 owed by R. Roy is written off. The VAT element of this debt can be reclaimed

14 Casual wages paid in cash £43

17 Cash sales £736 VAT inclusive paid into the bank

19 Credit sales net of VAT made to S. Jenkins £340; Z. Day £164

20 £100 cash withdrawn from the bank, £50 of which is used by the proprietor for personal expenses

23 Further sales made on credit: £390 to Day; £618 to F. Lowe

24 Received a cheque from Jenkins in full settlement including £923 brought forward from August

27 Banked cash sales of £701.50, including VAT

29 Sent out cheques to Cox and Little £1500 and £425 respectively

14 Using the following information, draw up the VAT account for Jean Morel for the months of July, August and September using the appropriate folios. Balance off at the end of each month.

At the end of the quarter will Jean send or receive a cheque from Customs and Excise? What is the sum involved?

19–1

July 1 Balance brought forward £2100.15 credit, being the amount due for the quarter

3 VAT element of a bad debt written off £36.10

10 Cheque forwarded to Customs and Excise for sum due

Aug 15 VAT on a bad debt recovered £225.50

21 VAT included in a bad debt written off £72.85

Sept 11 Further bad debts written off included £192.40 VAT

Totals posted from the day books for the period:

	July £	August £	September £
Cash book: Sales	2120.18	2845.60	2568.48
Expenses	542.54	638.79	326.90
Petty cash book	21.36	15.43	19.95
Purchases day book	4465.76	1234.12	1645.19
Sales day book	1140.62	845.20	967.46
Purchases returns book	283.44	88.80	119.91

On 10 August Jean received a letter from Customs and Excise informing her that VAT of £36.20 included in her claim for the previous quarter has been disallowed as this was for goods she had taken for her own use.

---

15 Brian Wyse — Newsagent

During June, Brian Wyse's total sales (all of which carry VAT) amount to £3450 (including VAT). How much of this is tax? Show the entry in the VAT account for the output tax and balance off. Remember that there are already entries on this account from Unit 5 where we have input tax of £279.30.

Would he have to send a cheque to Customs and Excise, or is he entitled to a refund? How much is it for?

At this level of sales, does he have to be registered?

Answers

6 VAT Control Balance: £639.13CR

7

	Cost	VAT	Total
Sales day book totals	£1412.16	£211.84	£1624.00

8

	Cost £	VAT £	Total £
Sales day book	1680	252	1932
Sales returns book	60	9	69
Purchases day book	1040	156	1196

VAT a/c Balance = £87

9

	£
Cash balance	1280.00
Bank balance	435.00
VAT a/c balance	130.83

---

15 Brian Wyse — Newsagent

Cash Sales £3450 including VAT

VAT $\frac{3}{23}$ £450

VAT

19–8	Inputs		£				£
June 30	Total	PB	279.30		June 30	Sales	450.00
	Balance c/d		170.70				
			450.00				
					July 1	Balance b/d	170.70

A credit balance means that Brian Wyse *owes* £170.70 to Customs and Excise.

Presuming his sales continue at this sort of level he *will* have to be registered.

Unit 9

Wages, Income Tax and National Insurance

At the end of this unit you will be able to:

1 Prepare wages

2 Understand PAYE (Pay as you Earn) income tax calculations

3 Understand the accounting transactions to record wages, income tax, national insurance and other deductions.

Wages

One of the key accounting tasks is to make sure that all employees are properly paid. Accordingly, the preparation of wages and all of the accompanying tasks of paying out money are important functions for the accounts department.

The systems involved in paying wages can differ in various organisations. For instance, some employees fill in time cards or a time sheet; for others, there is no specific record of actual attendance. Wages are prepared by different methods, from the very simplest manual system up to the most advanced computer. However, all of the procedures are basically the same.

A pictorial representation of a wages system is shown overleaf.

Wages Book

A wages book may be maintained in which details of weekly wages paid are shown. It may look like this:

No	Name of Employee	Earnings					Tax Details to Date				Deductions				Net Pay
		Basic	Over-Time	Gross Pay	Gross To Date	Tax Free	Taxable Pay	Tax Due	Tax Paid	Tax	NI	Subs	Nat. Savs.	Total Deducts	
		£	£	£	£	£	£	£	£	£	£	£	£	£	£
1	A. Smith	110.80	51.00	193.80	513.40	138.99	374.41	93.50	56.50	37.00	17.41	2.50	1.00	57.91	135.89
2	T. Pope	117.60	12.60	130.20	386.40	245.16	141.24	35.25	23.00	12.25	11.74	2.50	1.50	27.99	102.21
3	L. Kaye	100.80	16.20	117.00	337.60	150.54	187.06	46.75	30.00	16.75	10.57	2.50	2.00	31.82	85.18
4	M. Jones	142.80	47.60	190.40	518.20	211.11	307.09	76.75	46.75	30.00	17.14	2.50	6.00	55.64	134.76
5	A. Brown	117.60	25.20	142.80	411.60	179.37	232.23	58.00	37.25	20.75	12.82	2.50		36.07	106.73
6	A. James	159.60	8.55	168.15	487.35	248.61	238.74	59.50	38.25	21.25	15.16	2.50		38.91	129.24
		781.20	161.15	942.35						138.00	84.84	15.00	10.50	248.34	694.01

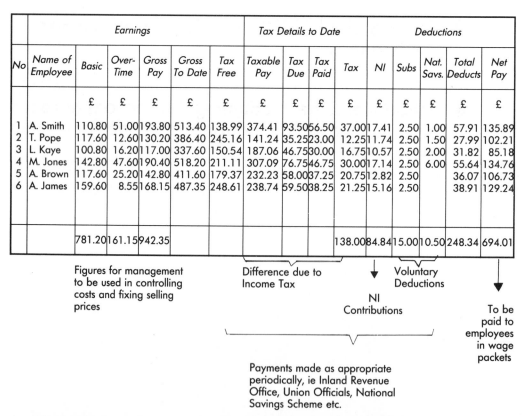

Figures for management to be used in controlling costs and fixing selling prices

Difference due to Income Tax

NI Contributions

Voluntary Deductions

To be paid to employees in wage packets

Payments made as appropriate periodically, ie Inland Revenue Office, Union Officials, National Savings Scheme etc.

A wages book is normally kept in a small business with few employees. In such circumstances we maintain the P11 personal record card provided by the Inland Revenue as illustrated on page 154.

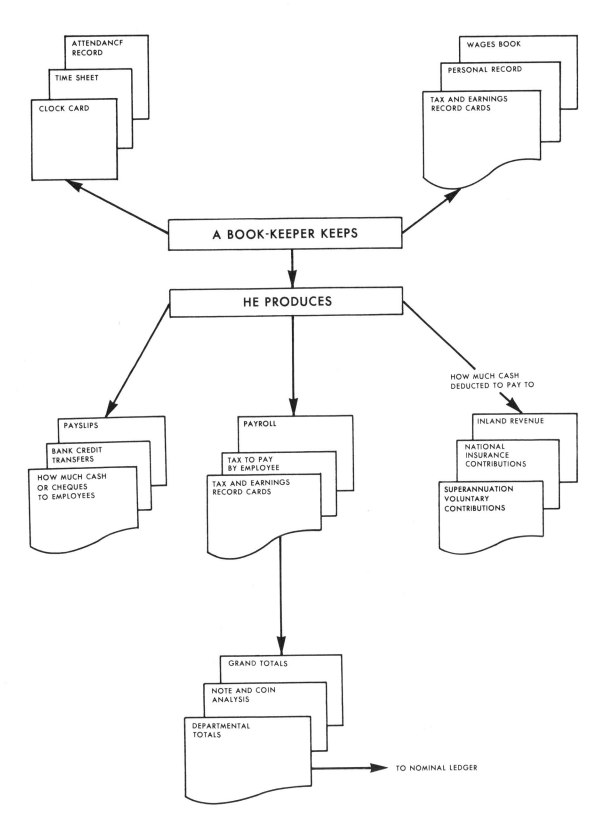

Wages Records

Wages Record Card

For each employee we keep a Wages Record Card (or Earnings Record Card) which states:

- Name and address
- Date of birth
- Tax code number
- Weekly gross pay
- Tax deducted
- National Health Insurance contribution
- Any other deductions
- Net pay.

An example of a personal record card is shown overleaf.

Form P11

For smaller firms the personal record sheet Form P11 (see top of page 154) provided by the Inland Revenue can be used. Larger firms usually use their own design of form, a P11 substitute.

This tax deduction sheet is used to record an employee's total pay, tax and National Insurance contributions paid. They are issued to all firms at the beginning of each year for existing employees.

At the end of the tax year an end of year return (P14) is submitted to the Inland Revenue for each employee. The end of year return must show the employee's pay, tax, National Insurance contributions, SSP and SMP. The employee is also given a form (P60, see page 154) showing this information. In addition an end of year summary (P35) must be submitted to the Inland Revenue listing all employees.

18162 (Front) Individual Pay Record

Rate of Pay			Nat. Ins. No. Ym SO SS 33 D	Surname MILLER	No. 26
Date 6/4	Amount 105 —		Date of Birth / Married/Single	Forenames KEITH EDWARD	
			Position	Address 42 SOUTH STREET	
			Trade	ANYTOWN	

Notes

	Date	Code	Date	N.I. letter
	6/4	321H	6/4	A

Wk. or Month No.		1	Date 7/6		2	Date 14/6
Details	per					
Earnings A	wk	105	00		105	00
B		9	00		9	00
C		6	00		6	00
D						
E Gross Pay		120	00		120	00
Superannuation		6	00		6	00
Gross Pay for Tax Purpose		114	00		114	00
G.P. to Date for Tax Purposes		114	00		228	00
Tax Free Pay		61	91		123	82
Taxable Pay to Date		52	09		104	18
Tax Due to Date		13	00		26	00
Tax Refund						
Deductions Tax		13	00		13	00
N.I. Contribution		10	84		10	84
1						
3						
4						
5						
6						
Total Ded'ns		23	84		23	84
Net Pay						
F						
G						
Employer Total Amount Payable		90	16		90	16
N.I. Contribution		10	84		10	84
H						

Payment Details | Employee | Total N.I. Conf's Incl Employer

153

Form P11

Form P60

Sent out by an employer to all employees at the end of the tax year to confirm the total amount of pay for tax purposes and the total tax deducted.

P60 Certificate of Pay, Income Tax and National Insurance contributions — Do not destroy

Income Tax and PAYE

What is PAYE?

The letters PAYE stand for *Pay As You Earn*. The PAYE system was devised in the UK during the 1939/45 World War when the Government wanted to obtain finance from the working population. An employer takes tax from weekly or monthly pay before paying it out. He then pays over the tax for all his employees to the Inland Revenue. This saves the employee from getting a bill, which would have to be paid in a lump sum at the end of the tax year, which runs from 6 April to the following 5 April. This still happens for Schedule 'D' taxpayers (self-employed). Employees who are subject to PAYE pay under tax Schedule 'E'.

How does PAYE work?

Everybody is allowed to earn or receive a certain amount of income in each tax year before paying tax. This amount is known as **personal allowances** and varies according to personal circumstances (explained in the leaflet IR22 *Income Tax: Personal Allowances*). Under PAYE these allowances are divided equally over the year. For weekly paid, 1/52nd of the allowance or for monthly paid, 1/12th of the allowance is made each pay day. Allowances for weeks of sickness or absence are not lost, but are carried forward to the next pay day.

By using the official tables each pay day, the employer is able to work out the amount of tax to be deducted. These tables ensure that the right amount of personal allowances are given. By the end of the year, all the allowances will have been given as the system is cumulative over the tax year.

What is a PAYE code?

Each employee receives a code number and this is an indication of the amount of tax that he or she should pay. The code number reflects the amount of personal allowances to which an employee is entitled and this is used when compiling the net wages to be paid.

A PAYE code is normally a number followed by a letter. The number is the total amount of personal allowances without the last figure. For example, allowances of £2587 = 258. There are several letters which can appear with the number:

L   (Lower)   shows the code including a single person's allowance or the wife's earned income allowance.

H   (Higher)   shows the code including a married man's allowance or a single person's allowance with the additional personal allowance.

P   shows the code including the age allowance for a single person.

V   shows the code including the age allowance for a married couple.

T   is for all other cases in which the number represents the allowances, or where L, H, P or V would follow the number but for some reason you do not wish one of those letters to be used.

There are three special codes which either do not include numbers, or have numbers that do not represent allowances. They mean that tax is to be deducted from total pay at a single rate (as shown on the coding notice). The first two are mainly used for second jobs:

BR   means that tax is to be deducted at the basic rate.

D   *followed by a number* means that tax is to be deducted at a higher rate.

F   *followed by a number* means that tax due on a National Insurance pension or benefit is to be collected from your earnings, or your pension from a previous employment.

There is also a code **NT** which means that no tax is to be deducted.

The most usual letters are L and H (Lower/Higher) and these will let your employer change your tax quickly if there is a change in the amount of the personal allowances. With the letters T or F, there may be a short delay in adjusting the tax because the tax office will have to work out the new code. Codes BR and D will only be affected if there is a change in the tax rates or bands.

New Employers or Employees Leaving

Form P45

When an employee leaves, his employer gives him this form duly completed to pass on to his next employer. The new employer will then use this form from the previous employer which will advise him of the new employee's tax code, details of previous pay to date and tax paid to date.

This is used as authority to make future tax deducations.

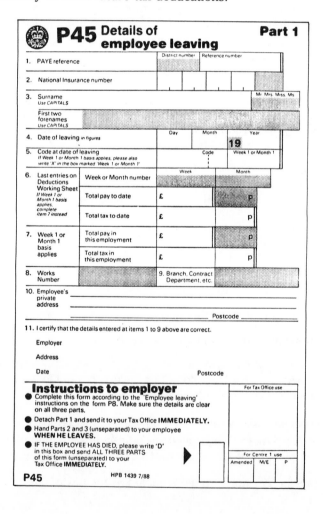

P45 New employee — Part 3
Details of previous employment

1. Previous PAYE reference
2. National Insurance number
3. Surname — Mr. Mrs. Miss. Ms.
   First two forenames
4. Date of leaving — Day / Month / Year 19
5. Code at date of leaving
   'X' means Week 1 or Month 1 basis — Code
6. Last entries on Deductions Working Sheet
   If there is an 'X' at item 5, there will be no entries here.
   Week or Month number — Week / Month / Week 1 or Month 1
   Total pay to date £ — p
   Total tax to date £ — p

New employer
Please complete items 7 to 14 below and send this form to your Tax Office IMMEDIATELY. Please also read the 'New Employee' instructions on the form P8.

7. New PAYE reference
8. Date employment commenced (in figures) — Day / Month / Year 19
9. Tick '✓' here if you want these details to be shown on code notifications — Works number / Branch, Dept.
10. Write 'P' here if this employee will not be paid by you between the date shown at item 8 and the next 5 April. — 'P' / N/D / P47 / M/E / DOM
11. If tax entered at item 6 does not agree with tax entered on Deductions Working Sheet from the Tax Tables, write the Tax Table figure here. £
12. Employee's private address — Postcode
13. Nature of employment
14. Declaration
    I have prepared a Deductions Working Sheet in accordance with the above details.
    Employer
    Address — Postcode ___ Date ___

For Centre 1 use — Ind Cd / T

P45

P45 Employee leaving — Part 2
Copy of employer's certificate

1. Previous PAYE reference
2. National Insurance number
3. Surname — Mr. Mrs. Miss. Ms.
   First two forenames
4. Date of leaving — Day / Month / Year 19
5. Code at date of leaving
   'X' means Week 1 or Month 1 basis — Code
6. Last entries on Deductions Working Sheet
   If there is an 'X' at item 5, there will be no entries here.
   Week or Month number — Week / Month / Week 1 or Month 1
   Total pay to date £ — p
   Total tax to date £ — p

For Centre 1 use

Employee – This form is important. Do not lose it. You cannot get a duplicate. Do not separate the two parts

● **Going to a new job?**
Give this form to your new employer, otherwise he will have to tax you under the emergency code. If for some special reason you do not want your new employer to know the details entered on this form send it to your Tax Office with a letter saving so BEFORE you start your new job, and give the name and address of your new employer. The Tax Office can make special arrangements, but you may pay too much tax for a time as a result.

● **Claiming unemployment benefit*?**
Take this form to the benefit office so that they can pay you any tax refund to which you may be entitled when your claim ends (or at 5 April if earlier).

● **Not working and not claiming unemployment benefit*?**
If you wish to claim a tax refund, get form P50 from any Tax Office or PAYE Enquiry Office. The form tells you what to do.

*(including supplementary benefit paid by reason of unemployment)

Instructions to new employer
● Check and complete this form and prepare a Deductions Working Sheet according to the 'New Employee' instructions on the form. P8.
● Detach Part 3 and send it to your Tax Office IMMEDIATELY. Keep Part 2.

P45

Compiling Wages

Procedure

Complete the personal record card as follows:

Step 1
Calculate the **gross** amount to be paid from the clock card/time sheet or from the pay details shown at the top of the personal wages record.

Step 2
Enter this on the gross wages line; add to the total gross pay to date from the previous pay day to give the **total gross pay to date**.

Step 3
Refer to Table A on pages 160–4, using the appropriate week/month number. The code number gives **tax free pay to date**.

Step 4
Deduct the tax free pay from the gross pay to date (Step 3) to give **taxable pay to date**.

Step 5
Refer to Table B on page 165. Find the total tax due to date for the taxable pay calculated in Step 4.

Step 6
Enter this figure on the appropriate line. Deduct last week's tax to date. This gives the amount of tax to be deducted this week. If the tax due to date in the current week is **less** than the tax due last week, the difference will be **a refund**.

Step 7
National Insurance deductions can be obtained from the appropriate DSS tables, based on gross pay (and the status of the individual). Enter the **employee's** contribution.

Step 8
Any voluntary deductions will need to be inserted. The employee must give written agreement for such deductions to be made.

Step 9
Total the deductions (including tax) and take away from the gross pay to complete the **net pay**. (A **refund** must be **added** to gross pay.)

Step 10
If there are any non-taxable allowances to be paid, they are entered after net pay to give the total amount payable.

Finally
Enter the **employer's** contribution for National Insurance. Show the appropriate amounts in accordance with gross pay.

Example

PAY ADVICE

	WEEK OR MONTH NO.	DATE	1	7/4
EARNINGS	DETAILS			
	A		105	00
	B		9	00
	C		6	00
	D			
	E			
	GROSS PAY		120	00
	PENSION/SUPERANNUATION		6	00
	GROSS PAY FOR TAX PURPOSES		114	00
	GROSS PAY TO DATE FOR TAX PURPOSES		114	00
	TAX FREE PAY		61	91
	TAXABLE PAY TO DATE		52	09
	TAX DUE TO DATE		13	00
	TAX REFUND			
DEDUCTIONS	TAX		13	00
	N.I. CONTRIBUTION		10	84
	1			
	2			
	3			
	4			
	5			
	6			
	TOTAL DEDUCTIONS		23	84
	NET PAY			
	F			
	G			
	TOTAL AMOUNT PAYABLE		90	16
EMPLOYER'S CONTRIBUTIONS	NATIONAL INSURANCE		10	84
	H			
	J			

From Table A → (TAX FREE PAY)

from Table B → (TAX DUE TO DATE)

YOUR PAY IS MADE UP AS SHOWN ABOVE

K.E. Miller

Compare this with individual Pay Record shown on page 160.

TABLE A – Free Pay

Code	Total free pay to date	Code	Total free pay to date	Code	Total free pay to date	Code	Total free pay to date	Code	Total free pay to date	Code	Total free pay to date	Code	Total free pay to date	Code	Total free pay to date
	£		£		£		£		£		£		£		£
0	NIL	61	11.91	121	23.45	181	34.99	241	46.52	301	58.06	361	69.60	421	81.14
1	0.37	62	12.10	122	23.64	182	35.18	242	46.72	302	58.25	362	69.79	422	81.33
2	0.56	63	12.29	123	23.83	183	35.37	243	46.91	303	58.45	363	69.99	423	81.52
3	0.75	64	12.49	124	24.02	184	35.56	244	47.10	304	58.64	364	70.18	424	81.72
4	0.95	65	12.68	125	24.22	185	35.75	245	47.29	305	58.83	365	70.37	425	81.91
5	1.14	66	12.87	126	24.41	186	35.95	246	47.49	306	59.02	366	70.56	426	82.10
6	1.33	67	13.06	127	24.60	187	36.14	247	47.68	307	59.22	367	70.75	427	82.29
7	1.52	68	13.25	128	24.79	188	36.33	248	47.87	308	59.41	368	70.95	428	82.49
8	1.72	69	13.45	129	24.99	189	36.52	249	48.06	309	59.60	369	71.14	429	82.68
9	1.91	70	13.64	130	25.18	190	36.72	250	48.25	310	59.79	370	71.33	430	82.87
10	2.10	71	13.83	131	25.37	191	36.91	251	48.45	311	59.99	371	71.52	431	83.06
11	2.29	72	14.02	132	25.56	192	37.10	252	48.64	312	60.18	372	71.72	432	83.25
12	2.49	73	14.22	133	25.75	193	37.29	253	48.83	313	60.37	373	71.91	433	83.45
13	2.68	74	14.41	134	25.95	194	37.49	254	49.02	314	60.56	374	72.10	434	83.64
14	2.87	75	14.60	135	26.14	195	37.68	255	49.22	315	60.75	375	72.29	435	83.83
15	3.06	76	14.79	136	26.33	196	37.87	256	49.41	316	60.95	376	72.49	436	84.02
16	3.25	77	14.99	137	26.52	197	38.06	257	49.60	317	61.14	377	72.68	437	84.22
17	3.45	78	15.18	138	26.72	198	38.25	258	49.79	318	61.33	378	72.87	438	84.41
18	3.64	79	15.37	139	26.91	199	38.45	259	149.99	319	61.52	379	73.06	439	84.60
19	3.83	80	15.56	140	27.10	200	38.64	260	50.18	320	61.72	380	73.25	440	84.79
20	4.02	81	15.75	141	27.29	201	38.83	261	50.37	321	61.91	381	73.45	441	84.99
21	4.22	82	15.95	142	27.49	202	39.02	262	50.56	322	62.10	382	73.64	442	85.18
22	4.41	83	16.14	143	27.68	203	39.22	263	50.75	323	62.29	383	73.83	443	85.37
23	4.60	84	16.33	144	27.87	204	39.41	264	50.95	324	62.49	384	74.02	444	85.56
24	4.79	85	16.52	145	28.06	205	39.60	265	51.14	325	62.68	385	74.22	445	85.75
25	4.99	86	16.72	146	28.25	206	39.79	266	51.33	326	62.87	386	74.41	446	85.95
26	5.18	87	16.91	147	28.45	207	39.99	367	51.52	327	63.06	387	74.60	447	86.14
27	5.37	88	17.10	148	28.64	208	40.18	268	51.72	328	63.25	388	74.79	448	86.33
28	5.56	89	17.29	149	28.83	209	40.37	369	51.91	329	63.45	389	74.99	449	86.52
29	5.75	90	17.49	150	29.02	210	40.56	270	52.10	330	63.64	390	75.18	450	86.72
30	5.95	91	17.68	151	29.22	211	40.75	271	52.29	331	63.83	391	75.37	451	86.91
31	6.14	92	17.87	152	29.41	212	40.95	272	52.49	332	64.02	392	75.56	452	87.10
32	6.33	93	18.06	153	29.60	213	41.14	273	52.68	333	64.22	393	75.75	453	87.29
33	6.52	94	18.25	154	29.79	214	41.33	274	52.87	334	64.41	394	75.95	454	87.49
34	6.72	95	18.45	155	29.99	215	41.52	275	53.06	335	64.60	395	76.14	455	87.68
35	6.91	96	18.64	156	30.18	216	41.72	276	53.25	336	64.79	396	76.33	456	87.87
36	7.10	97	18.83	157	30.37	217	41.91	277	53.45	337	64.99	397	76.52	457	88.06
37	7.29	98	19.02	158	30.56	218	42.10	278	53.64	338	65.18	398	76.72	458	88.25
38	7.49	99	19.22	159	30.75	219	42.29	279	53.83	339	65.37	399	76.91	459	88.45
39	7.68	100	19.41	160	30.95	220	42.49	280	54.02	340	65.56	400	77.10	460	88.64
40	7.87	101	19.60	161	31.14	221	42.68	281	54.22	341	65.75	401	77.29	461	88.83
41	8.06	102	19.79	162	31.33	222	42.87	282	54.41	342	65.95	402	77.49	624	89.02
42	8.25	103	19.99	163	31.52	223	43.06	283	54.60	343	66.14	403	77.68	463	89.22
43	8.45	104	20.18	164	31.72	224	43.25	284	54.79	344	66.33	404	77.87	464	89.41
44	8.64	105	20.37	165	31.91	225	43.45	385	54.99	345	66.52	405	78.06	465	89.60
45	8.83	106	20.56	166	32.10	226	43.64	286	55.18	346	66.72	406	78.25	466	89.79
46	9.02	107	20.75	167	32.29	227	43.83	287	55.37	347	66.91	407	78.45	467	89.99
47	9.22	108	20.95	168	32.49	228	44.02	288	55.56	348	67.10	408	78.64	468	90.18
48	9.41	109	21.14	169	32.68	229	44.22	289	55.75	349	67.29	409	78.83	469	90.37
49	9.60	110	21.33	170	32.87	230	44.41	209	55.95	350	67.49	410	79.02	470	90.56
50	9.79	111	21.52	171	33.06	231	44.60	291	56.14	351	67.68	411	79.22	471	90.75
51	9.99	112	21.72	172	33.25	232	44.79	292	56.33	352	67.87	412	79.41	472	90.95
52	10.18	113	21.91	173	33.45	233	44.99	293	56.52	353	68.06	413	79.60	473	91.14
53	10.37	114	22.10	174	33.64	234	45.18	294	56.72	354	68.25	414	79.79	474	91.33
54	10.56	115	22.29	175	33.83	235	45.37	295	56.91	355	68.45	415	79.99	475	91.52
55	10.75	116	22.49	176	34.02	236	45.56	296	57.10	356	68.64	416	80.18	476	91.72
56	10.95	117	22.68	177	34.22	237	45.75	297	57.29	357	68.83	417	80.37	477	91.91
57	11.14	118	22.87	178	34.41	238	45.95	298	57.49	358	69.02	418	80.56	478	92.10
58	11.33	119	23.06	179	34.60	239	46.14	299	57.68	359	69.22	419	80.75	479	92.29
59	11.52	120	23.25	180	34.79	240	46.33	300	57.87	360	69.41	420	80.95	480	92.49
60	11.72														

WEEK 2
Apr 13 to Apr 19

TABLE A – Free Pay

Code	Total free pay to date	Code	Total free pay to date	Code	Total free pay to date	Code	Total free pay to date	Code	Total free pay to date	Code	Total free pay to date	Code	Total free pay to date	Code	Total free pay to date
	£		£		£		£		£		£		£		£
0	NIL														
1	0.74	61	23.82	121	46.90	181	69.98	241	93.04	301	116.12	361	139.20	421	162.28
2	1.12	62	24.20	122	47.28	182	70.36	242	93.44	302	116.50	362	139.58	422	162.66
3	1.50	63	24.58	123	47.66	183	70.74	243	93.82	303	116.90	363	139.98	423	163.04
4	1.90	64	24.98	124	48.04	184	71.12	244	94.20	304	117.28	364	140.36	424	163.44
5	2.28	65	25.36	125	48.44	185	71.50	245	94.58	305	117.66	365	140.74	425	163.82
6	2.66	66	25.74	126	48.82	186	71.90	246	94.98	306	118.04	366	141.12	426	164.20
7	3.04	67	26.12	127	49.20	187	72.28	247	95.36	307	118.44	367	141.50	427	164.58
8	3.44	68	26.50	128	49.58	188	72.66	248	95.74	308	118.82	368	141.90	428	164.98
9	3.82	69	26.90	129	49.98	189	73.04	249	96.12	309	119.20	369	142.28	429	165.36
10	4.20	70	27.28	130	50.36	190	73.44	250	96.50	310	119.50	370	142.66	430	165.74
11	4.58	71	27.66	131	50.74	191	73.82	251	96.90	311	119.98	371	143.04	431	166.12
12	4.98	72	28.04	132	51.12	192	74.20	252	97.28	312	120.36	372	143.44	432	166.50
13	5.36	73	28.44	133	51.50	193	74.58	253	97.66	313	120.74	373	143.82	433	166.90
14	5.74	74	28.82	134	51.90	194	74.98	254	98.04	314	121.12	374	144.20	434	167.28
15	6.12	75	29.20	135	52.28	195	75.36	255	98.44	315	121.50	375	144.58	435	167.66
16	6.50	76	29.58	136	52.66	196	75.74	256	98.82	316	121.90	376	144.98	436	168.04
17	6.90	77	29.98	137	53.04	197	76.12	257	99.20	317	122.28	377	145.36	437	168.44
18	7.28	78	30.36	138	53.44	198	76.50	258	99.58	318	122.66	378	145.74	438	168.82
19	7.66	79	30.74	139	53.82	199	76.90	259	99.98	319	123.04	379	146.12	439	169.20
20	8.04	80	31.12	140	54.20	200	77.28	260	100.36	320	123.44	380	146.50	440	169.58
21	8.44	81	31.50	141	54.58	201	77.66	261	100.74	321	123.82	381	146.90	441	169.98
22	8.82	82	31.90	142	54.98	202	78.04	262	101.12	322	124.20	382	147.28	442	170.36
23	9.20	83	32.28	143	55.36	203	78.44	263	101.50	323	124.58	383	147.66	443	170.74
24	9.58	84	32.66	144	55.74	204	78.82	264	101.90	324	124.98	384	148.04	444	171.12
25	9.98	85	33.04	145	56.12	205	79.20	265	102.28	325	125.36	385	148.44	445	171.50
26	10.36	86	33.44	146	56.50	206	79.58	266	102.66	326	125.74	386	148.82	446	171.90
27	10.74	87	33.82	147	56.90	207	79.98	267	103.04	327	126.12	387	149.20	447	172.28
28	11.12	88	34.20	148	57.28	208	80.36	268	103.44	328	126.50	388	149.58	448	172.66
29	11.50	89	34.58	149	57.66	209	80.74	269	103.82	329	126.90	389	149.98	449	173.04
30	11.90	90	34.98	150	58.04	210	81.12	270	104.20	330	127.28	390	150.36	450	173.44
31	12.28	91	35.36	151	58.44	211	81.50	271	104.58	331	127.66	391	150.74	451	173.82
32	12.66	92	35.74	152	58.82	212	81.90	272	104.98	332	128.04	392	151.12	452	174.20
33	13.04	93	36.12	153	59.20	213	82.28	273	105.36	333	128.44	393	151.50	453	174.58
34	13.44	94	36.50	154	59.58	214	82.66	274	105.74	334	128.82	394	151.90	454	174.98
35	13.82	95	36.90	155	59.98	215	83.04	275	106.12	335	129.20	395	152.28	455	175.36
36	14.20	96	37.28	156	60.36	216	83.44	276	106.50	336	129.58	396	152.66	456	175.74
37	14.58	97	37.66	157	60.74	217	83.82	277	106.90	337	129.98	397	153.04	457	176.12
38	14.98	98	38.04	158	61.12	218	84.20	278	107.28	338	130.36	398	153.44	458	176.50
39	15.36	99	38.44	159	61.50	219	84.58	279	107.66	339	130.74	399	153.82	459	176.90
40	15.74	100	38.82	160	61.90	220	84.98	280	108.04	340	131.12	400	154.20	460	177.28
41	16.12	101	39.20	161	62.28	221	85.36	281	108.44	341	131.50	401	154.58	461	177.66
42	16.50	102	39.58	162	62.66	222	85.74	282	108.82	342	131.90	402	154.98	462	178.04
43	16.90	103	39.98	163	63.04	223	86.12	283	109.20	343	132.28	403	155.36	463	178.44
44	17.28	104	40.36	164	63.44	224	86.50	284	109.58	344	132.66	404	155.74	464	178.82
45	17.66	105	40.74	165	63.82	225	86.90	285	109.98	345	133.04	405	156.12	465	179.20
46	18.04	106	41.12	166	64.20	226	87.28	286	110.36	346	133.44	406	156.50	466	179.58
47	18.44	107	41.50	167	64.58	227	87.66	287	110.74	347	133.82	407	156.90	467	179.98
48	18.82	108	41.90	168	64.98	228	88.04	288	111.12	348	134.20	408	157.28	468	180.36
49	19.20	109	42.28	169	65.36	229	88.44	289	111.50	349	134.58	409	157.66	469	180.74
50	19.58	110	42.66	170	65.74	230	88.82	290	111.90	350	134.98	410	158.04	470	181.12
51	19.98	111	43.04	171	66.12	231	89.20	291	112.28	351	135.36	411	158.44	471	181.50
52	20.36	112	43.44	172	66.50	232	89.58	292	112.66	352	135.74	412	158.82	472	181.90
53	20.74	113	43.82	173	66.90	233	89.98	293	113.04	353	136.12	413	159.20	473	182.28
54	21.12	114	44.20	174	67.28	234	90.36	294	113.44	354	136.50	414	159.58	474	182.66
55	21.50	115	44.58	175	67.66	235	90.74	295	113.82	355	136.90	415	159.98	475	183.04
56	21.90	116	44.98	176	68.04	236	91.12	296	114.20	356	137.28	416	160.36	476	183.44
57	22.28	117	45.36	177	68.44	237	91.50	297	114.58	357	137.66	417	160.74	477	183.82
58	22.66	118	45.74	178	68.82	238	91.90	298	114.98	358	138.04	418	161.12	478	184.20
59	23.04	119	46.12	179	69.20	239	92.28	299	115.36	359	138.44	419	161.50	479	184.58
60	23.44	120	46.50	180	69.58	240	92.66	300	115.74	360	138.82	420	161.90	480	184.98

TABLE A – Free Pay

WEEK 3
Apr 20 to Apr 26

Code	Total free pay to date £	Code	Total free pay to date £	Code	Total free pay to date £	Code	Total free pay to date £	Code	Total free pay to date £	Code	Total free pay to date £	Code	Total free pay to date £	Code	Total free pay to date £
0	NIL														
1	1.11	61	35.73	121	70.35	181	104.97	241	139.56	301	174.18	361	208.80	421	243.42
2	1.68	62	36.30	122	70.92	182	105.54	242	140.16	302	174.75	362	209.37	422	243.99
3	2.25	63	36.87	123	71.49	183	106.11	243	140.73	303	175.35	363	209.97	423	244.56
4	2.85	64	37.47	124	72.06	184	106.68	244	141.30	304	175.92	364	210.54	424	245.16
5	3.42	65	38.04	125	72.66	185	107.25	245	141.87	305	179.49	365	211.11	425	245.73
6	3.99	66	38.61	126	73.23	186	107.85	246	142.47	306	177.06	366	211.68	426	246.30
7	4.56	67	39.18	127	73.80	187	108.42	247	143.04	307	177.66	367	212.25	427	246.87
8	5.16	68	39.75	128	74.37	188	108.99	248	143.61	308	178.23	368	212.85	428	247.47
9	5.73	69	40.35	129	74.97	189	109.56	249	144.18	309	178.80	369	213.42	429	248.04
10	6.30	70	40.92	130	75.54	190	110.16	250	144.75	310	179.37	370	213.99	430	248.61
11	6.87	71	41.49	131	76.11	191	110.73	251	145.35	311	179.97	371	214.56	431	249.18
12	7.47	72	42.06	132	76.68	192	111.30	252	145.92	312	180.54	372	215.16	532	249.75
13	8.04	73	42.66	133	77.25	193	111.87	253	146.49	313	181.11	373	215.73	433	250.35
14	8.61	74	43.23	134	77.85	194	112.47	254	147.06	314	181.68	374	216.30	434	250.92
15	9.18	75	43.80	135	78.42	195	113.04	255	147.66	315	182.25	375	216.87	435	251.49
16	9.75	76	44.37	136	78.99	196	113.61	256	148.23	316	182.85	376	217.47	436	252.06
17	10.35	77	44.97	137	79.56	197	114.18	257	148.80	317	183.42	377	218.04	437	252.66
18	10.92	78	45.54	138	80.16	198	114.75	258	149.37	318	183.99	378	218.61	438	253.23
19	11.49	79	46.11	139	80.73	199	115.35	259	149.97	319	184.56	379	219.18	439	253.80
20	12.06	80	46.68	140	81.30	200	115.92	260	150.54	320	185.16	380	219.75	440	254.37
21	12.66	81	47.25	141	81.87	201	116.49	261	151.11	321	185.73	381	220.35	441	254.97
22	13.23	82	47.85	142	82.47	202	117.06	262	151.68	322	186.30	382	220.92	442	255.54
23	13.80	83	48.42	143	83.04	203	117.66	263	152.25	323	186.87	383	221.49	443	256.11
24	14.37	84	48.99	144	83.61	204	118.23	264	152.85	324	187.47	384	222.06	444	256.68
25	14.97	85	49.56	145	84.18	205	118.80	265	153.42	325	188.04	385	222.66	445	257.25
26	15.54	86	50.16	146	84.75	206	119.37	266	153.99	326	188.61	386	223.33	446	257.85
27	16.11	87	50.73	147	85.35	207	119.97	367	154.56	327	189.18	387	223.80	447	258.42
28	16.68	88	51.30	148	85.92	208	120.54	268	155.16	328	189.75	388	224.37	448	258.99
29	17.25	89	51.87	149	86.49	209	121.11	269	155.73	329	190.35	389	224.97	449	259.56
30	17.85	90	52.47	150	87.06	210	121.68	270	156.30	330	190.92	390	225.54	450	260.16
31	18.42	91	53.04	151	87.66	211	122.25	271	156.87	331	191.49	391	226.11	451	260.73
32	18.99	92	53.61	152	88.23	212	122.85	272	157.47	332	192.06	392	226.68	452	261.30
33	19.56	93	54.18	153	88.80	213	123.42	273	158.04	333	192.66	393	227.25	453	261.87
34	20.16	94	54.75	154	89.37	214	123.99	274	158.61	334	193.23	394	227.85	454	262.47
35	20.73	95	55.35	155	89.97	215	124.56	275	159.18	335	193.80	395	228.42	455	263.04
36	21.30	96	55.92	156	90.54	216	125.16	276	159.75	336	194.37	396	228.99	456	263.61
37	21.87	97	56.49	157	91.11	217	125.73	277	160.35	337	194.97	397	229.56	457	264.18
38	22.47	98	57.06	158	91.68	218	126.30	278	160.92	338	195.54	398	230.16	458	264.75
39	23.04	99	57.66	159	92.25	219	126.87	279	161.49	339	196.11	399	230.73	459	265.35
40	23.61	100	58.23	160	92.85	220	127.47	280	162.06	340	196.68	400	231.30	460	265.92
41	24.18	101	58.80	161	93.42	221	128.04	281	162.66	341	197.25	401	231.87	461	266.49
42	24.75	102	59.37	162	93.99	222	128.61	282	163.23	342	197.85	402	232.47	462	267.06
43	25.35	103	59.97	163	94.56	223	129.18	283	163.80	343	198.42	403	233.04	463	267.66
44	25.92	104	60.54	164	95.16	224	129.75	284	164.37	344	198.99	404	233.61	464	268.23
45	26.49	105	61.11	165	95.73	225	130.35	285	164.97	345	199.56	405	234.18	465	268.80
46	27.06	106	61.68	166	96.30	226	130.92	286	165.54	346	200.16	406	234.75	466	269.37
47	27.66	107	62.25	167	96.87	227	131.49	287	166.11	347	200.73	407	235.35	467	269.97
48	28.23	108	62.85	168	97.47	228	132.06	288	166.68	348	201.30	408	235.92	468	270.54
49	28.80	109	63.42	169	98.04	229	132.66	289	167.25	349	201.87	409	236.49	469	271.11
50	29.37	110	63.99	170	98.61	230	133.23	290	167.85	350	202.47	410	237.06	470	271.68
51	29.97	111	64.56	171	99.18	231	133.80	291	168.42	351	203.04	411	237.66	471	272.25
52	30.54	112	65.16	172	99.75	232	134.37	292	168.99	352	203.61	412	238.23	472	272.85
53	31.11	113	65.73	173	100.35	233	134.97	293	169.56	353	204.18	413	238.80	473	273.42
54	31.68	114	66.30	174	100.92	234	135.54	294	170.16	354	204.75	414	239.37	474	273.99
55	32.25	115	66.87	175	101.49	235	136.11	295	170.73	355	205.35	415	239.97	475	274.56
56	32.85	116	67.47	176	102.06	236	136.68	296	171.30	356	205.92	416	240.54	476	275.16
57	33.42	117	68.04	177	102.66	237	137.25	297	171.87	357	206.49	417	241.11	477	275.73
58	33.99	118	68.61	178	103.23	238	137.85	298	172.47	358	207.06	418	241.68	478	276.30
59	34.56	119	69.18	179	103.80	239	138.42	299	173.04	359	207.66	419	242.25	479	276.87
60	35.16	120	69.75	180	104.37	240	138.99	300	173.61	360	208.23	420	242.85	480	277.47

TABLE A – Free Pay

WEEK 4
Apr 27 to May 3

Code	Total free pay to date	Code	Total free pay to date	Code	Total free pay to date	Code	Total free pay to date	Code	Total free pay to date	Code	Total free pay to date	Code	Total free pay to date	Code	Total free pay to date
	£		£		£		£		£		£		£		£
0	NIL														
1	1.48	61	47.64	121	93.80	181	139.96	241	186.08	301	232.24	361	278.40	421	324.56
2	2.24	62	48.40	122	94.56	182	140.72	242	186.88	302	233.00	362	279.16	422	325.32
3	3.00	63	49.16	123	95.32	183	141.48	243	187.64	303	233.80	363	279.96	423	326.08
4	3.80	64	49.96	124	96.08	184	142.24	244	188.40	304	234.56	364	280.72	424	326.88
5	4.56	65	50.72	125	96.88	185	143.00	245	189.16	305	235.32	365	281.48	425	327.64
6	5.32	66	51.48	126	97.64	186	143.80	246	189.96	306	236.08	366	282.24	426	328.40
7	6.08	67	52.24	127	98.40	187	144.56	247	190.72	307	236.88	367	283.00	427	329.16
8	6.88	68	53.00	128	99.16	188	145.32	248	191.48	308	237.64	368	283.80	428	329.96
9	7.64	69	53.80	129	99.96	189	146.08	249	192.24	309	238.40	369	284.56	429	330.72
10	8.40	70	54.56	130	100.72	190	146.88	250	193.00	310	239.16	370	285.32	430	331.48
11	9.16	71	55.32	131	101.48	191	147.64	251	193.80	311	239.96	371	286.08	431	332.24
12	9.96	72	56.08	132	102.24	192	148.40	252	194.56	312	240.72	372	286.88	432	333.00
13	10.72	73	56.88	133	103.00	193	149.16	253	195.32	313	241.48	373	287.64	433	333.80
14	11.48	74	57.64	134	103.80	194	149.96	254	196.08	314	242.24	374	288.40	434	334.56
15	12.24	75	58.40	135	104.56	195	150.72	255	196.88	315	243.00	375	289.16	435	335.32
16	13.00	76	59.16	136	105.32	196	151.48	256	197.64	316	242.80	376	289.96	436	336.08
17	13.80	77	59.96	137	106.08	197	152.24	257	198.40	317	244.56	377	290.72	437	336.88
18	14.56	78	60.72	138	106.88	198	153.00	258	199.16	318	245.32	378	291.48	438	337.64
19	15.32	79	61.48	139	107.64	199	153.80	259	199.96	319	246.08	379	292.24	439	338.40
20	16.08	80	62.24	140	108.40	200	154.56	260	200.72	320	246.88	380	293.00	440	339.15
21	16.88	81	63.00	141	109.16	201	155.32	261	201.48	321	247.64	381	293.80	441	339.96
22	17.64	82	63.80	142	109.96	202	156.08	262	202.24	322	248.40	382	294.56	442	340.72
23	18.40	83	64.56	143	110.72	203	156.88	263	203.00	323	249.16	383	295.32	443	341.48
24	19.16	84	65.32	144	111.48	204	157.64	264	203.80	324	249.96	384	296.08	444	342.24
25	19.96	85	66.08	145	112.24	205	158.40	265	204.56	325	250.72	385	296.88	445	343.00
26	20.72	86	66.88	146	113.00	206	159.16	266	205.32	326	251.48	386	297.64	446	343.80
27	21.48	87	67.64	147	113.80	207	159.96	267	206.08	327	252.24	387	298.40	447	344.56
28	22.24	88	68.40	148	114.56	208	160.72	268	206.88	328	253.00	388	299.16	448	345.32
29	23.00	89	69.16	149	115.32	209	161.48	269	207.64	329	253.80	389	299.96	449	346.08
30	23.80	90	69.96	150	116.08	210	162.24	270	208.40	330	254.56	390	300.72	450	346.88
31	24.56	91	70.72	151	116.88	211	163.00	271	209.16	331	255.32	391	301.48	451	347.64
32	25.32	92	71.48	152	117.64	212	163.80	272	209.96	332	256.08	392	302.24	452	348.40
33	26.08	93	72.24	153	118.40	213	164.56	273	210.72	333	256.88	393	303.00	453	349.16
34	26.88	94	73.00	154	119.16	214	165.32	274	211.48	334	257.64	394	303.80	454	349.96
35	27.64	95	73.80	155	119.96	215	166.08	275	212.24	335	258.40	395	304.56	455	350.72
36	28.40	96	74.56	156	120.72	216	166.88	276	213.00	336	259.16	396	305.32	456	351.48
37	29.16	97	75.32	157	121.48	217	167.64	277	213.80	337	259.96	397	306.08	457	352.24
38	29.96	98	76.08	158	122.24	218	168.40	278	214.56	338	260.72	398	306.88	458	353.00
39	30.72	99	76.88	159	123.00	219	169.16	279	215.32	339	261.48	399	307.64	459	353.80
40	31.48	100	77.64	160	123.80	220	169.96	280	216.08	340	262.24	400	308.40	460	354.56
41	32.24	101	78.40	161	124.56	221	170.72	281	216.88	341	263.00	401	309.16	461	355.32
42	33.00	102	79.16	162	125.32	222	171.48	282	217.64	342	263.80	402	309.96	462	356.08
43	33.80	103	79.96	163	126.08	223	172.24	283	218.40	343	264.56	403	310.72	463	356.88
44	34.56	104	80.72	164	126.88	224	173.00	284	219.16	344	265.32	404	311.48	464	357.64
45	35.32	105	81.48	165	127.64	225	173.80	285	219.96	345	266.08	405	312.24	465	358.40
46	36.08	106	82.24	166	128.40	226	174.56	286	220.72	346	266.88	406	313.00	466	359.16
47	36.88	107	83.00	167	129.16	227	175.32	287	221.48	347	267.64	407	313.80	467	359.96
48	37.64	108	83.80	168	129.96	228	176.08	288	222.24	348	268.40	408	314.56	468	360.72
49	38.40	109	84.56	169	130.72	229	176.88	289	223.00	349	269.16	409	315.32	469	361.48
50	39.16	110	85.32	170	131.48	230	177.64	290	223.80	350	269.96	410	316.08	470	362.24
51	39.96	111	86.08	171	132.24	231	178.40	291	224.56	351	270.72	441	316.88	471	363.00
52	40.72	112	86.88	172	133.00	232	176.16	292	225.32	352	271.48	412	317.64	472	363.80
53	41.48	113	87.64	173	133.80	233	179.96	293	226.08	353	272.24	413	318.40	473	364.56
54	42.24	114	88.40	174	134.56	234	180.72	294	226.88	354	273.00	414	319.16	474	365.32
55	43.00	115	89.16	175	135.32	235	181.48	295	227.64	355	273.80	415	319.96	475	366.08
56	43.80	116	89.96	176	136.08	236	182.24	296	228.40	356	274.56	416	320.72	476	366.88
57	44.56	117	90.72	177	136.88	237	183.00	297	229.16	357	275.32	417	321.48	477	367.64
58	45.32	118	91.48	178	137.64	238	183.80	298	229.96	358	276.08	418	322.24	478	368.40
59	46.08	119	92.24	179	138.40	239	184.56	299	230.72	359	276.88	419	323.00	479	369.16
60	46.88	120	93.00	180	139.16	240	185.32	300	231.48	360	277.64	420	323.80	480	369.96

TABLE A – Free Pay

Code	Total free pay to date £	Code	Total free pay to date £	Code	Total free pay to date £	Code	Total free pay to date £	Code	Total free pay to date £	Code	Total free pay to date £	Code	Total free pay to date £	Code	Total free pay to date £
0	NIL														
1	1.85	61	59.55	121	117.25	181	174.95	241	232.60	301	290.30	361	348.00	421	405.70
2	2.80	62	60.50	122	118.20	182	175.90	242	233.60	302	291.25	362	348.95	422	406.65
3	3.75	63	61.45	123	119.15	183	176.85	243	234.55	303	292.25	363	349.95	423	407.60
4	4.75	64	62.45	124	120.10	184	177.80	244	235.50	304	293.20	364	350.90	424	408.60
5	5.70	65	63.40	125	121.10	185	178.75	245	236.45	305	294.15	365	351.85	425	409.55
6	6.65	66	64.35	126	122.05	186	179.75	246	237.45	306	295.10	366	352.80	426	410.50
7	7.60	67	65.30	127	123.00	187	180.70	247	238.40	307	296.10	367	353.75	427	411.45
8	8.60	68	66.25	128	123.95	188	181.65	248	239.35	308	297.05	368	354.75	428	412.45
9	9.55	69	67.25	129	124.95	189	182.60	249	240.30	309	298.00	369	355.70	429	413.40
10	10.50	70	68.20	130	125.90	190	183.60	250	241.25	310	298.95	370	356.65	430	414.35
11	11.45	71	69.15	131	126.85	191	184.55	251	242.25	311	299.95	371	357.60	431	415.30
12	12.45	72	70.10	132	127.80	192	185.50	252	243.20	312	300.90	372	358.60	432	416.25
13	13.40	73	71.10	133	128.75	193	186.45	253	244.15	313	301.85	373	359.55	433	417.25
14	14.35	74	72.05	134	129.75	194	187.45	254	245.10	314	302.80	374	360.50	434	418.20
15	15.30	75	73.00	135	130.70	195	188.40	255	246.10	315	303.75	375	361.45	435	419.15
16	16.25	76	73.95	136	131.65	196	189.35	256	247.05	316	304.75	376	362.45	436	420.10
17	17.25	77	74.95	137	132.60	197	190.30	257	248.00	317	305.70	377	363.40	437	421.10
18	18.20	78	75.90	138	133.60	198	191.25	258	248.95	318	306.65	378	364.35	438	422.05
19	19.15	79	76.85	139	134.55	199	192.25	259	249.95	319	307.60	379	365.30	439	423.00
20	20.10	80	77.80	140	135.50	200	193.20	260	250.90	320	308.60	380	366.25	440	423.95
21	21.10	81	78.75	141	136.45	201	194.15	261	251.85	321	309.55	381	367.25	441	424.95
22	22.05	82	79.75	142	137.45	202	195.10	262	252.80	322	310.50	382	368.20	442	425.90
23	23.00	83	80.70	143	138.40	203	196.10	263	253.75	323	311.45	383	369.15	443	426.85
24	23.95	84	81.65	144	139.35	204	197.05	264	254.75	324	312.45	384	370.10	444	427.80
25	24.95	85	82.60	145	140.30	205	198.00	265	255.70	325	313.40	285	371.10	445	428.75
26	25.90	86	83.60	146	141.25	206	198.95	266	256.65	326	314.35	386	372.05	446	429.75
27	26.85	87	84.55	147	142.25	207	199.95	267	257.60	327	315.30	387	373.00	447	430.70
28	27.80	88	85.50	148	143.20	208	200.90	268	258.60	328	316.25	388	373.95	448	431.65
29	28.75	89	86.45	149	144.15	209	201.85	269	259.55	329	317.25	389	374.95	449	432.60
30	29.75	90	87.45	150	145.10	210	202.80	270	260.50	330	318.20	390	375.90	450	433.60
31	30.70	91	88.40	151	146.10	211	203.75	271	261.45	331	319.15	391	376.85	451	434.55
32	31.65	92	89.35	152	147.05	212	204.75	272	262.45	332	320.10	392	377.80	452	435.50
33	32.60	93	90.30	153	148.00	213	205.70	273	263.40	333	321.10	393	378.75	453	436.45
34	33.60	94	91.25	154	148.95	214	206.65	274	264.35	334	322.05	394	379.75	454	437.45
35	34.55	95	92.25	155	149.95	215	207.60	275	265.30	335	323.00	395	380.70	455	438.40
36	35.50	96	93.20	156	150.90	216	208.60	276	266.25	336	323.95	396	381.65	456	439.35
37	36.45	97	94.15	157	151.85	217	209.55	277	267.25	337	324.95	397	382.60	457	440.30
38	37.45	98	95.10	158	152.80	218	210.50	278	268.20	338	325.90	398	383.60	458	441.25
39	38.40	99	96.10	159	153.75	219	211.45	279	269.15	339	326.85	399	384.55	459	442.25
40	39.35	100	97.05	160	154.75	220	212.45	280	270.10	340	327.80	400	385.50	460	443.20
41	40.30	101	98.00	161	155.70	221	213.40	281	271.10	341	328.75	401	386.45	461	444.15
42	41.25	102	98.95	162	156.65	222	214.35	282	272.05	342	329.75	402	387.45	462	445.10
43	42.25	103	99.95	163	157.60	223	215.30	283	273.00	343	330.70	403	388.40	463	446.10
44	43.20	104	100.90	164	158.60	224	216.25	284	273.95	344	331.65	404	389.35	464	447.05
45	44.15	105	101.85	165	159.55	225	217.25	285	274.95	345	332.60	405	390.30	465	448.00
46	45.10	106	102.80	166	160.50	226	218.20	286	275.90	346	336.60	406	391.25	466	448.95
47	46.10	107	103.75	167	161.45	227	219.15	287	276.85	347	334.55	407	392.25	467	449.95
48	47.05	108	104.75	168	162.45	228	220.10	288	277.80	348	335.50	408	393.20	468	450.90
49	48.00	109	105.70	169	163.40	229	221.10	289	278.75	349	336.45	409	394.15	469	451.85
50	48.95	110	106.65	170	164.35	230	222.05	290	279.75	350	337.45	410	395.10	470	452.80
51	49.95	111	107.60	171	165.30	231	223.00	291	280.70	351	338.40	441	396.10	471	453.75
52	50.90	112	108.60	172	166.25	232	223.95	292	281.65	352	339.35	412	397.05	472	454.75
53	51.85	113	109.55	173	167.25	233	224.95	293	282.60	353	340.30	413	398.00	473	455.70
54	52.80	114	110.50	174	168.20	234	225.90	294	283.60	354	341.25	414	398.95	474	456.65
55	53.75	115	111.45	175	169.15	235	226.85	295	284.55	355	342.25	415	399.95	475	457.60
56	54.75	116	112.45	176	170.10	236	227.80	296	285.50	356	343.20	416	400.90	476	458.60
57	55.70	117	113.40	177	171.10	237	228.75	297	286.45	357	344.15	417	401.85	477	459.55
58	56.65	118	114.35	178	172.05	238	229.75	298	287.45	358	345.10	418	402.80	478	460.50
59	57.60	119	115.30	179	173.00	239	230.70	299	288.40	359	346.10	419	403.75	479	461.45
60	58.60	120	116.25	180	173.95	240	213.65	300	289.35	360	347.05	420	404.75	480	462.45

TABLE B

TAX DUE ON TAXABLE PAY FROM £1 TO £360

Total TAXABLE PAY to date	Total TAX DUE to date	Total TAXABLE PAY to date	Total TAX DUE to date	Total TAXABLE PAY to date	Total TAX DUE to date	Total TAXABLE PAY to date	Total TAX DUE to date	Total TAXABLE PAY to date	Total TAX DUE to date	Total TAXABLE PAY to date	Total TAX DUE to date
£	£	£	£	£	£	£	£	£	£	£	£
1	0.25	61	15.25	121	30.25	181	45.25	241	60.25	301	75.25
2	0.50	62	15.50	122	30.50	182	45.50	242	60.50	302	75.50
3	0.75	63	15.75	123	30.75	183	45.75	243	60.75	303	75.75
4	1.00	64	16.00	124	31.00	184	46.00	244	61.00	304	76.00
5	1.25	65	16.25	125	31.25	185	46.25	245	61.25	305	76.25
6	1.50	66	16.50	126	31.50	186	46.50	246	61.50	306	76.50
7	1.75	67	16.75	127	31.75	187	46.75	247	61.75	307	76.75
8	2.00	68	17.00	128	32.00	188	47.00	248	62.00	308	77.00
9	2.25	69	17.25	129	32.25	189	47.25	249	62.25	309	77.25
10	2.50	70	17.50	130	32.50	190	47.50	250	62.50	310	77.50
11	2.75	71	17.75	131	32.75	191	47.75	251	62.75	311	77.75
12	3.00	72	18.00	132	33.00	192	48.00	252	63.00	312	78.00
13	3.25	73	18.25	133	33.25	193	48.25	253	63.25	313	78.25
14	3.50	74	18.50	134	33.50	194	48.50	254	63.50	314	78.50
15	3.75	75	18.75	135	33.75	195	48.75	255	63.75	315	78.75
16	4.00	76	19.00	136	34.00	196	49.00	256	64.00	316	79.00
17	4.25	77	19.25	137	34.25	197	49.25	257	64.25	317	79.25
18	4.50	78	19.50	138	34.50	198	49.50	258	64.50	318	79.50
19	4.75	79	19.75	139	34.75	199	49.75	259	64.75	319	79.75
20	5.00	80	20.00	140	35.00	200	50.00	260	65.00	320	80.00
21	5.25	81	20.25	141	35.25	201	50.25	261	65.25	321	80.25
22	5.50	82	20.50	142	35.50	202	50.50	262	65.50	322	80.50
23	5.75	83	20.75	143	35.75	203	50.75	263	65.75	323	80.75
24	6.00	84	21.00	144	36.00	204	51.00	264	66.00	324	81.00
25	6.25	85	21.25	145	36.25	205	51.25	265	66.25	325	81.25
26	6.50	86	21.50	146	36.50	206	51.50	266	66.50	326	81.50
27	6.75	87	21.75	147	36.75	207	51.75	267	66.75	327	81.75
28	7.00	88	22.00	148	37.00	208	52.00	268	67.00	328	82.00
29	7.25	89	22.25	149	37.25	209	52.25	269	67.25	329	82.25
30	7.50	90	22.50	150	37.50	210	52.50	270	67.50	330	82.50
31	7.75	91	22.75	151	37.75	211	52.75	271	67.75	331	82.75
32	8.00	92	23.00	152	38.00	212	53.00	272	68.00	332	83.00
33	8.25	93	23.25	153	38.25	213	53.25	273	68.25	333	83.25
34	8.50	94	23.50	154	38.50	214	53.50	274	68.50	334	83.50
35	8.75	95	23.75	155	38.75	215	53.75	275	68.75	335	83.75
36	9.00	96	24.00	156	39.00	216	54.00	276	69.00	336	84.00
37	9.25	97	24.25	157	39.25	217	54.25	277	69.25	337	84.25
38	9.50	98	24.50	158	39.50	218	54.50	278	69.50	338	84.50
39	9.75	99	24.75	159	39.75	219	54.75	279	69.75	339	84.75
40	10.00	100	25.00	160	40.00	220	55.00	280	70.00	340	85.00
41	10.25	101	25.25	161	40.25	221	55.25	281	70.25	341	85.25
42	10.50	102	25.50	162	40.50	222	55.50	282	70.50	342	85.50
43	10.75	103	25.75	163	40.75	223	55.75	283	70.75	343	85.75
44	11.00	104	26.00	164	41.00	224	56.00	284	71.00	344	86.00
45	11.25	105	26.25	165	41.25	225	56.25	285	71.25	345	86.25
46	11.50	106	26.50	166	41.50	226	56.50	286	71.50	346	86.50
47	11.75	107	26.75	167	41.75	227	56.75	287	71.75	347	86.75
48	12.00	108	27.00	168	42.00	228	57.00	288	72.00	348	87.00
49	12.25	109	27.25	169	42.25	229	57.25	289	72.25	349	87.25
50	12.50	110	27.50	170	42.50	230	57.50	290	72.50	350	87.50
51	12.75	111	27.75	171	42.75	231	57.75	291	72.75	351	87.75
52	13.00	112	28.00	172	43.00	232	58.00	292	73.00	352	88.00
53	13.25	113	28.25	173	43.25	233	58.25	293	73.25	353	88.25
54	13.50	114	28.50	174	43.50	234	58.50	294	73.50	354	88.50
55	13.75	115	28.75	175	43.75	235	58.75	295	73.75	355	88.75
56	14.00	116	29.00	176	44.00	236	59.00	296	74.00	356	89.00
57	14.25	117	29.25	177	44.25	237	59.25	297	74.25	357	89.25
58	14.50	118	29.50	178	44.50	238	59.50	298	74.50	358	89.50
59	14.75	119	29.75	179	44.75	239	59.75	299	74.75	359	89.75
60	15.00	120	30.00	180	45.00	240	60.00	300	75.00	360	90.00

National Insurance Contributions

These are payable by employees and employers to meet the cost of medical services, pension schemes and unemployment benefits. At the present time the employee's contribution is between 5% and 9% of the gross wage, depending on the amount earned, and the employer's contribution is between 5% and 10.45% of the gross wage.

Contracting-out

Until April 1988, contracting-out of the State Earnings Related Pension Scheme (SERPS) was only possible with an appropriate 'salary-related' occupational pension scheme. Such schemes had to satisfy a minimum benefit test which ensured that they provided their members with benefits which were at least as good as those provided by the state scheme. From April 6 1988 onwards, occupational pension schemes may contract-out of the state scheme by satisfying a minimum contribution test instead. The benefits arising from the minimum contribution depend not only on the contribution itself but also on the investment income which it generates. The benefits may in the event be worse than, equal to or better than those provided by SERPS.

From July 1 1988 another method of contracting-out was introduced. From that date, it became possible for individual employees to contract-out of the state pension scheme by taking out appropriate 'personal pensions'. In the context of personal pensions it should be noted that 'appropriate' means 'contracted-out'.

Statutory Sick Pay

Employers are responsible for paying Statutory Sick Pay for up to eight weeks' absence due to sickness in any tax year. It is treated as any other pay for tax and National Insurance purposes. Any money paid out for SSP is recovered from the monthly payment made over to the Collector of Taxes.

The actual rate to be paid depends on earnings during the eight weeks preceding the 'period of incapacity for work' (PIW). Depending on the level of pay, SSP is payable at standard or lower rates. These are detailed at the back of the National Insurance tables.

Statutory Maternity Pay

This is payable by an employer for up to 18 weeks. The rates depend on length of employment with the particular employer, but the first six weeks receive a maximum of 90% of earnings and the remaining 12 weeks are paid at the lower flat rate.

To receive either SSP or SMP an employee must be in receipt of earnings above the lower limit for National Insurance purposes. Separate leaflets are available which give details of Statutory Sick Pay, Statutory Maternity Pay and the regulations for people who are either self-employed, unemployed or not receiving SSP and SMP benefit.

Any queries about National Insurance, SSP or SMP regulations should be referred to your local DSS Office.

Deductions Working Sheet

The employer must record details of National Insurance contributions and Income Tax (PAYE) deductions or refunds for each person he employs. This information is shown on the Deduction Sheet in the following way:

Total of employee's and employer's contributions		Employee's contribution		Wk No	Pay in the week or month		Total pay to date		Total free pay to date as shown by Table A		Total taxable pay to date		Total tax due to date as shown by Taxable Pay Tables		Tax deducted or refunded in the week or month (mark refunds 'R')	
(1a)		(1b)			(2)		(3)		(4)		(5)		(6)		(7)	
				1												
				2												
				3												
				4												

- Contributions for National Insurance and income tax calculations are based on gross pay.
- The figures for columns 1(a) and 1(b) will be found in the National Insurance contribution table. (The exercises use Standard-Rate Contributions Weekly Table A.)
- The details entered in columns (2) and (3) refer to the employee's gross pay: earnings in the current week or month (2), and total earnings in the tax year (3).
- The employee's Code Number, used in conjunction with Tax Table A, provides the figures shown in columns (4) and (5).
- Tax Table B gives the figures in columns (6) and (7).

Note The individual pay record (page 153) shows the same information in a different format, and is acceptable to the Inland Revenue.

An example of National Insurance Deduction Tables is shown on the following pages:

Weekly

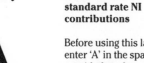

	Not contracted-out standard rate NI contributions	**Use this table**	• for employees who are aged 16 and under pension age (65 men, 60 women)
	Before using this label enter 'A' in the space provided on the Deductions Working Sheet P11 or substitute (see Instructions)		• for employees who have their own personal pension (from July 1988).
		Do not use this table	• for married women and widows who pay NI contributions at the reduced rate – see Table B.
			• for employees over pension age or for whom form RD950 is held – see Table C.

6 April 1989 to 5 April 1990

Entries to be made on P11 • copy the figures from columns 1a, 1b and 1c to columns 1a, 1b and 1c of the P11.

If the exact gross pay is not shown in the table, use the next smaller figure shown.

Earnings on which employee's contributions payable 1a	Total of employees and employer's contributions payable 1b	Employee's contribution payable 1c	Employer's contributions*	Earnings on which employee's contributions payable 1a	Total of employees and employer's contributions payable 1b	Employee's contribution payable 1c	Employer's contributions*
£	£	£	£	83	11.68	5.84	5.84
43	4.30	2.15	2.15	84	11.82	5.91	5.91
44	4.44	2.22	2.22	85	11.96	5.98	5.98
45	4.54	2.27	2.27	86	12.10	6.05	6.05
46	4.64	2.32	2.32	87	12.24	6.12	6.12
47	4.74	2.37	2.37	88	12.38	6.19	6.19
48	4.84	2.42	2.42	89	12.52	6.26	6.26
49	4.94	2.47	2.47	90	12.66	6.33	6.33
50	5.04	2.52	2.52	91	12.80	6.40	6.40
51	5.14	2.57	2.57	92	12.94	6.47	6.47
52	5.24	2.62	2.62				
				£	£	£	£
53	5.34	2.67	2.67	93	13.08	6.54	6.54
54	5.44	2.72	2.72	94	13.22	6.61	6.61
55	5.54	2.77	2.77	95	13.36	6.68	6.68
56	5.64	2.82	2.82	96	13.50	6.75	6.75
57	5.74	2.87	2.87	97	13.64	6.82	6.82
58	5.84	2.92	2.92	98	13.78	6.89	6.89
59	5.94	2.97	2.97	99	13.92	6.96	6.96
60	6.04	3.02	3.02	100	14.06	7.03	7.03
61	6.14	3.07	3.07	101	14.20	7.10	7.10
62	6.24	3.12	3.12	102	14.34	7.17	1.17
63	6.34	3.17	3.17	103	14.48	7.24	7.24
64	6.44	3.22	3.22	104	14.62	7.31	7.31
65	6.54	3.27	3.27	105	14.76	7.38	7.38
66	6.64	3.32	3.32	106	14.90	7.45	7.45
67	6.74	3.37	3.37	107	15.04	7.52	7.52
68	6.84	3.42	3.42	108	15.18	7.59	7.59
69	6.94	3.47	3.47	109	15.32	7.66	7.66
70	7.04	3.52	3.52	110	15.46	7.73	7.73
71	7.14	3.57	3.57	111	15.60	7.80	7.80
72	7.24	3.62	3.62	112	15.74	7.87	7.87
73	7.34	3.67	3.67	113	15.88	7.94	7.94
74	7.44	3.72	3.72	114	16.02	8.01	8.01
75	10.56	5.28	5.28	115	20.78	10.39	10.39
76	10.70	5.35	5.35	116	20.96	10.48	10.48
77	10.84	5.42	5.42	117	21.14	10.57	10.57
78	10.98	5.49	5.49	118	21.32	10.66	10.66
79	11.12	5.56	5.56	119	21.50	10.75	10.75
80	11.26	5.63	5.63	120	21.68	10.84	10.84
81	11.40	5.70	5.70	121	21.86	10.93	10.93
82	11.54	5.77	5.77	122	22.04	11.02	11.02

Weekly Table A continued
6 April 1989 to 5 April 1990

Earnings on which employee's contributions payable 1a	Total of employee's and employer's contributions payable 1b	Employee's contribution payable 1c	Employer's contributions*	Earnings on which employee's contributions payable 1a	Total of employee's and employer's contributions payable 1b	Employee's contribution payable 1c	Employer's contributions*
£	£	£	£	£	£	£	£
123	22.22	11.11	11.11	173	33.74	15.61	18.13
124	22.40	11.20	11.20	174	33.94	15.70	18.24
125	22.58	11.29	11.29	175	34.13	15.79	18.34
126	22.76	11.38	11.38	176	34.32	15.88	18.44
127	22.94	11.47	11.47	177	34.52	15.97	18.55
128	23.12	11.56	11.56	178	34.71	16.06	18.65
129	23.30	11.65	11.65	179	34.91	16.15	18.76
130	23.48	11.74	11.74	180	35.10	16.24	18.86
131	23.66	11.83	11.83	181	35.30	16.33	18.97
132	23.84	11.92	11.92	182	35.49	16.42	19.07
133	24.02	12.01	12.01	183	35.69	16.51	19.18
134	24.20	12.10	12.10	184	35.88	16.60	19.28
135	24.38	12.19	12.19	185	36.07	16.69	19.38
136	24.56	12.28	12.28	186	36.27	16.78	19.49
137	24.74	12.37	12.37	187	36.46	16.87	19.59
138	24.92	12.46	12.46	188	36.66	16.96	19.70
139	25.10	12.55	12.55	189	36.85	17.05	19.80
140	25.28	12.64	12.64	190	37.05	17.14	19.91
141	25.46	12.73	12.73	191	37.24	17.23	20.01
142	25.64	12.82	12.82	192	37.44	17.32	20.12
143	25.82	12.91	12.91	193	37.63	17.41	20.22
144	26.00	13.00	13.00	194	37.83	17.50	20.33
145	26.18	13.09	13.09	195	38.02	17.59	20.43
146	26.36	13.18	13.18	196	38.21	17.68	20.53
147	26.54	13.27	13.27	197	38.41	17.77	20.64
148	26.72	13.36	13.36	198	38.60	17.86	20.74
149	26.90	13.45	13.45	199	38.80	17.95	20.85
150	27.08	13.54	13.54	200	38.99	18.04	20.95
151	27.26	13.63	13.63	201	39.19	18.13	21.06
152	27.44	13.72	13.72	202	39.38	18.22	21.16
153	27.62	13.81	13.81	203	39.58	18.31	21.27
154	27.80	13.90	13.90	204	39.77	18.40	21.37
155	27.98	13.99	13.99	205	39.96	18.49	21.47
156	28.16	14.08	14.08	206	40.16	18.58	21.58
157	28.34	14.17	14.17	207	40.35	18.67	21.68
158	28.52	14.26	14.26	208	40.55	18.76	21.79
159	28.70	14.35	14.35	209	40.74	18.85	21.89
160	28.88	14.44	14.44	210	40.94	18.94	22.00
161	29.06	14.53	14.53	211	41.13	19.03	22.10
162	29.24	14.62	14.62	212	41.33	19.12	22.21
163	29.42	14.71	14.71	213	41.52	19.21	22.31
164	29.60	14.80	14.80	214	41.72	19.30	22.42
165	32.18	14.89	17.29	215	41.91	19.39	22.52
166	32.38	14.98	17.40	216	42.10	19.48	22.62
167	32.57	15.07	17.50	217	42.30	19.57	22.73
168	32.77	15.16	17.61	218	42.49	19.66	22.83
169	32.96	15.25	17.71	219	42.69	19.75	22.94
170	33.16	15.34	17.82	220	42.88	19.84	23.04
171	33.35	15.43	17.92	221	43.08	19.93	23.15
172	33.55	15.52	18.03	222	43.27	20.02	23.25

169

Weekly Table A continued
6 April 1989 to 5 April 1990

Earnings on which employee's contributions payable 1a	Total of employee's and employer's contributions payable 1b	Employee's contribution payable 1c	Employer's contributions*	Earnings on which employee's contributions payable 1a	Total of employee's and employer's contributions payable 1b	Employee's contribution payable 1c	Employer's contributions*
£	£	£	£	£	£	£	£
223	43.47	20.11	23.36	243	47.36	21.91	25.45
224	43.66	20.20	23.46	244	47.55	22.00	25.55
225	43.85	20.29	23.56	245	47.74	22.09	25.65
226	44.05	20.38	23.67	246	47.94	22.18	25.76
227	44.24	20.47	23.77	247	48.13	22.27	25.86
228	44.44	20.56	23.88	248	48.33	22.36	25.97
229	44.63	20.65	23.98	249	48.52	22.45	26.07
230	44.83	20.74	24.09	250	48.72	22.54	26.18
231	45.02	20.83	24.19	251	48.91	22.63	26.28
232	45.22	20.90	24.30	252	49.11	22.72	26.39
233	45.41	21.01	24.40	253	49.30	22.81	26.49
234	45.61	21.10	24.51	254	49.50	22.90	26.60
235	45.80	21.19	24.61	255	49.69	22.99	26.70
236	45.99	21.28	24.71	256	49.88	23.08	26.80
237	46.19	21.37	24.82	257	50.08	23.17	26.91
238	46.38	21.46	24.92	258	50.27	23.26	27.01
239	46.58	21.55	25.03	259	50.47	23.35	27.12
240	46.77	21.64	25.13	260	50.66	23.44	27.22
241	46.97	21.73	25.24	261	50.86	23.53	27.33
242	47.16	21.82	25.34	262	51.05	23.62	27.43

* for information only – Do not enter on P11

Alternative Methods of Payment

- Wages and salaries may be paid by cheque. This helps security and saves time.

- If we prepare wages monthly rather than weekly it saves time and effort, and only involves work once a month rather than four or five times.

- Wages can also be paid by bankers orders, if the employees agree. This is the safest way of paying wages and salaries.

- Some useful publications can be obtained from your local Tax Office: *IR34 Income Tax: PAYE; P7 Employers Guide to PAYE*. If you are involved with wages calculations, it will help to have copies available for reference.

Summary

As we compile the wages for the various employees at the end of the week, we total up the amount of tax deducted together with other deductions and prepare a Wages Summary, as follows:

Gross Pay	PAYE Tax & NHI Deducted	Other Deductions	Net Pay
£1000	£250	£50 (e.g. Savings Fund)	£700

Note and Coinage Analysis

To facilitate making up pay packets we prepare a note and coinage analysis, going through each employee's net cash requirements and summarising how much is to be paid in various notes and denominations of coins.

Example

Employee	Net Pay	£10	£5	£1	50p	20p	10p	5p	2p	1p
A. Axon B. Bray C. Cooper	£127.35 99.78 63.12	12 9 6	1 1 –	2 4 3	– 1 –	1 1 –	1 – 1	1 1 –	– 1 1	– 1 –
Total	£290.25	27	2	9	1	2	2	2	2	1

This can be checked:

$$
\begin{array}{rcl}
£10 \times 27 & = & 270.00 \\
£5 \times 2 & = & 10.00 \\
£1 \times 9 & = & 9.00 \\
50p \times 1 & = & 0.50 \\
20p \times 2 & = & 0.40 \\
10p \times 2 & = & 0.20 \\
5p \times 2 & = & 0.10 \\
2p \times 2 & = & 0.04 \\
1p \times 1 & = & 0.01 \\
\hline
& & £290.25 \\
\end{array}
$$

The breakdown is given to the bank so that the correct amounts are included. When the pay packets are made up this acts as a double-check on the accuracy, because when you come to the last packet you should have *exactly* the right amount left.

Accounting Of Wages

When money is paid out, we **credit** the **cash book** and **debit** the **ledger account**. When we pay out money for *wages* we **credit** the **cash book** and **debit** the **wages account**.

Wages Account

	£
Cash: Net Pay	500
Bank: Tax/NI	180
Savings	20

Cash Book

	£
Wages	500
Tax/NI	180
Savings	20

See example of Wages Book on page 150.

Control Account

Some firms use a Control Account. This reflects the **gross** wages, so acts as a check to ensure that all deductions are paid over to the appropriate authorities and is used in modern accounting systems for management purposes in larger organisations.

Wages Control Account

	£		£
Net Pay	3425	Gross pay	5000
Tax/NI	1200	(to profit and	
Union Dues	175	loss account)	
National Savings	200		
(from cash book)			

Summary

Preparing wages is quite a straightforward task. Once a routine is established it is a job that can be tackled by almost anyone. Use commonsense and good organisation. If in doubt regarding tax matters, refer to the local Tax Office for advice.

Questions

1 What is a P45?

2 Are wages best paid by cash, bankers orders, or cheques?

3 State what action you would take if you were having difficulty with the operation of PAYE.

4 State and explain the various tax forms and tables you may encounter in the operation of a wages system.

5 Calculate the following gross wages:

  a) 35 hours @ £2.10 per hour
      5 hours @ double time

  b) 40 hours @ £4.60 per hour
      7 hours @ time and a quarter

  c) 32 hours @ £3.80 per hour
      6 hours @ time and a half.

6 The following is an example of a Clock Card showing that A. Green worked a five day week:

No. **306**		**NAME**	GREEN A				
WEEK ENDING		30/3		HRS	RATE	£	p
ORDINARY TIME				40	3-50		
OVERTIME				6			
TOTAL WAGES							
LESS INCOME TAX							
NAT. INSURANCE							
PENSION							
TOTAL DEDUCTIONS							
AMOUNT PAID							

SIGNATURE:-

	MON.	TUES.	WED.	THURS.	FRI.	SAT.	SUN.	TOTAL
In	7.53	7.59	7.58	7.56	7.58			
Out	12.02	12.00	12.00	12.00	12.02			
In	12.59	12.58	12.59	1.00	12.58			
Out	5.03	7.03	7.05	7.00	5.02			
In								
Out								
In								
Out								
LOST TIME								
OVER TIME		2	2	2				
DAILY HRS	8	8	8	8	8			

Assume that this employee works a 40 hour basic week, and all additional hours are counted as overtime, at time and a half.

Check the figures so far calculated by the wages section and calculate the amount due for basic hours and overtime hours, giving the total gross pay.

7 Deduction Card: PAYE

This is an extract from a Deduction Card. The National Insurance contribution has been omitted, as this exercise is concerned only with PAYE.
Weeks 1 and 2 have been completed. Using Tax Tables A and B, calculate the deductions for Weeks 3, 4 and 5.
This employee's Code Number is: 260L.

Week No.	Pay in the week or month	Total pay to date	Total free pay to date as shown by Table A	Total taxable pay to date	Total tax due to date as shown by Taxable Pay Tables	Tax deducted or refunded in the week or month (mark refunds 'R')
	(2)	(3)	(4)	(5)	(6)	(7)
1	104 00	104 00	50 18	53 82	13 25	13 25
2	101 40	205 40	100 36	105 04	26 25	13 00
3	111 80	317 20				
4	106 60					
5	104 00					
6						

Note Column 6: if the exact amount of taxable pay is now shown in Table B, use the next smaller figure shown.

8 Deduction Card: National Insurance Contribution

The following is an example of the entries made for NI contributions. Entries have been made for Weeks 1 and 2. Using Standard Contributions Weekly Table A, calculate the deductions for Weeks 3, 4 and 5.

Total of employee's and employer's contributions	Employee's contribution	Wk. No.	Pay in the week or month
(1a)	(1b)		(2)
14 62	7 31	1	104 00
14 20	7 10	2	101 40
		3	111 80
		4	106 60
		5	104 00
		6	

Note: If the exact gross pay figure is not shown in the Contribution Table, use the next smaller figure shown.

9 As the wages clerk in a small firm, it is your responsibility to prepare the payroll in respect of five weekly-paid employees. Complete the following tasks using the information provided for Tax Week 3 on the following pages.
   a) Calculate the gross pay for each employee from the clockcards.
   b) Using Tax Tables A and B on pages 160–5, and NI Standard-Rate Contribution Table A on pages 168–70, calculate the statutory deductions.
   c) Make the necessary entries for PAYE and NI tax deduction cards.
   d) Note voluntary deductions, where applicable (as shown on payroll, page 180).
   e) Prepare a Pay Advice for each employee, using voluntary deduction where applicable.

The employees of the company work a 42-hour week, over five days, as follows:

Monday to Thursday 8.30am – 12.30pm and 1.30pm – 6.00pm = 8½ hrs
Friday 8.30am – 12.30pm and 1.30pm – 5.30pm = 8 hrs

Overtime Monday to Friday (paid at time-and-a-half)
          Saturday (paid at time-and-a-half)
          Sunday (to be shown as 'Additional Overtime'.
                  Paid at double-time. See Clockcard for A. Cox)

The employees are all paid in cash. The Pay Advice Slip is enclosed in their pay envelopes.

Hourly rates for the basic working week are as follows and extra deductions indicated in brackets:

Walsh B.	Stores	£2.70 per hour
Jones F.	Machine Shop	£3.70 per hour (Savings £4.00)
Cox A.	Machine Shop	£3.50 per hour (Savings £4.00)
Marshall D.	Machine Shop	£3.00 per hour (Subscription 10p)
Perry T.	Despatch	£2.70 per hour (Subscription 10p)

Note: The cards and forms shown on the following pages are for information only.

Clock Cards

A No. 49   NAME WALSH R.

WEEK ENDING 23/4

	HRS RATE £	p
ORDINARY TIME		
OVERTIME		
TOTAL WAGES		

LESS		
INCOME TAX		
NAT. INSURANCE		
PENSION		
TOTAL DEDUCTIONS		
AMOUNT PAID		

SIGNATURE:-

	MON.	TUES.	WED.	THURS.	FRI.	SAT.	SUN.	TOTAL
In	8.30	8.28	8.25	8.32	8.20	8.30		
Out	12.31	12.34	12.30	12.32	12.32	12.30		
In	1.29	1.30	1.28	1.27	1.28			
Out	6.02	7.03	8.05	6.01	5.32			
In								
Out								
In								
Out								
LOST TIME								
OVER TIME								
DAILY HRS								

B No. 21   NAME JONES F.

WEEK ENDING 23/4

	HRS RATE £	p
ORDINARY TIME		
OVERTIME		
TOTAL WAGES		

LESS		
INCOME TAX		
NAT. INSURANCE		
PENSION		
TOTAL DEDUCTIONS		
AMOUNT PAID		

SIGNATURE:-

	MON.	TUES.	WED.	THURS.	FRI.	SAT.	SUN.	TOTAL
In	8.32	8.26	8.25	8.30	8.28	8.30		
Out	12.32	12.34	12.31	12.32	12.34	12.30		
In	1.30	1.31	1.27	1.28	1.27			
Out	6.04	6.06	8.06	8.07	5.31			
In								
Out								
In								
Out								
LOST TIME								
OVER TIME								
DAILY HRS								

C No. 28 | NAME Cox A.

WEEK ENDING 23/4	HRS	RATE £	p
ORDINARY TIME			
OVERTIME			
TOTAL WAGES			
LESS INCOME TAX			
NAT. INSURANCE			
PENSION			
TOTAL DEDUCTIONS			
AMOUNT PAID			

SIGNATURE:-

	MON.	TUES.	WED.	THURS.	FRI.	SAT.	SUN.	TOTAL
In	8.25	8.26	8.27	8.29	8.32	8.30	8.30	
Out	12.32	12.30	12.32	12.35	12.32	12.30	12.31	
In	1.25	1.30	1.27	1.29	1.27			
Out	6.04	7.05	6.06	8.06	5.31			
In								
Out								
In								
Out								
LOST TIME								
OVER TIME								
DAILY HRS								

D No. 30 | NAME MARSHALL D.

WEEK ENDING 23/4	HRS	RATE £	p
ORDINARY TIME			
OVERTIME			
TOTAL WAGES			
LESS INCOME TAX			
NAT. INSURANCE			
PENSION			
TOTAL DEDUCTIONS			
AMOUNT PAID			

SIGNATURE:-

	MON.	TUES.	WED.	THURS.	FRI.	SAT.	SUN.	TOTAL
In	8.30	8.25	8.22	8.31	8.26	8.31		
Out	12.33	12.34	12.33	12.36	12.32	12.32		
In	1.26	1.27	1.28	1.27	1.29			
Out	8.02	8.03	8.01	8.02	5.31			
In								
Out								
In								
Out								
LOST TIME								
OVER TIME								
DAILY HRS								

		HRS RATE £	HRS RATE p								MON.	TUES.	WED.	THURS.	FRI.	SAT.	SUN.	TOTAL
E No. 42 NAME Perry T.	WEEK ENDING 23/4	ORDINARY TIME	OVERTIME	TOTAL WAGES	LESS INCOME TAX / NAT. INSURANCE / PENSION	TOTAL DEDUCTIONS	AMOUNT PAID	SIGNATURE:-	In		8.33	8.30	8.31	8.29	8.28			
									Out		12.31	12.33	12.30	12.32	12.33			
									In		1.27	1.28	1.26	1.28	1.29			
									Out		6.03	6.01	6.04	6.05	5.32			
									LOST TIME / OVER TIME / DAILY HRS									

PAYE and NI Tax Deduction Cards

A

NATIONAL INSURANCE CONTR				MONTH NO.	WEEK NO.	Pay in the week or month		Total pay to date		Total free pay to date as shown by Table A		Total taxable pay to date		Total tax due to date as shown by taxable pay tables		Tax deducted or refunded in week or month (mark refunds 'R')	
Total of employee's & employer's contributions (1a)		Employers basic contributions (1b)				(2)		(3)		(4)		(5)		(6)		(7)	

CODE 224L	Amended Code	Wk/Mnth No. in which applied		Employee's Surname WALSH		First Two Forenames BARRY											
(1a)		(1b)		6 APR TO 5 MAY		(2)		(3)		(4)		(5)		(6)		(7)	
24	74	12	37		1	137	70	137	70	43	25	94	45	23	50	23	50
25	10	12	55		2	139	82	277	52	86	50	191	02	47	75	24	25
					3												

B

CODE 396H					Employee's Surname JONES		First Two Forenames FRASER						
(1a)		(1b)		6 APR TO 5 MAY		(2)		(3)		(4)		(5)		(6)		(7)	

(1a)		(1b)		6 A P R T O 5 M A Y	#	(2)		(3)		(4)		(5)		(6)		(7)	
35	69	16	51		1	183	15	183	15	76	33	106	82	26	50	26	50
36	66	16	96		2	188	70	371	85	152	66	219	19	54	75	28	25
					3												

C

CODE 399H					Employee's Surname COX		First Two Forenames ADAM						

(1a)		(1b)		6 A P R T O 5 M A Y	#	(2)		(3)		(4)		(5)		(6)		(7)	
34	71	16	06		1	178	50	179	50	76	91	101	59	25	25	25	25
35	69	16	51		2	183	75	362	25	153	82	208	43	52	00	26	75
					3												

D

CODE 409H					Employee's Surname MARSHALL		First Two Forenames DAVID						

(1a)		(1b)		6 A P R T O 5 M A Y	#	(2)		(3)		(4)		(5)		(6)		(7)	
27	08	13	54		1	150	75	150	75	78	83	71	92	17	75	17	75
35	10	16	24		2	180	00	330	75	157	66	173	09	43	25	25	50
					3												

E

CODE 420V					Employee's Surname PERRY		First Two Forenames TREVOR						

(1a)		(1b)		6 A P R T O 5 M A Y	#	(2)		(3)		(4)		(5)		(6)		(7)	
21	14	10	57		1	117	45	117	45	80	95	36	50	9	00	9	00
21	86	10	93		2	121	50	238	95	161	90	77	05	19	25	10	25
					3												

Payroll

Week ending 25 April 19—   Tax Week No. 3

| Wks No | Name | Earnings | | | | | | GROSS PAY | Deductions | | | | | Additions | | | NET PAY | Employers NI Contrib |
		Basic Hours	Rate	O/T Hrs	Rate	Addnl O/T Hrs	Rate		PAYE	NI Contr	Savings	Subs	TOTAL DEDNS	Tax Refund	Allcs &/or Expns	TOTAL ADDNS		
49	WALSH B.																	
21	JONES F.										4 00							
28	COX A.										4 00							
30	MARSHALL D.											10						
42	PERRY T.											10						
	TOTAL																	

Pay Advice

A

PAY ADVICE

WEEK OR MONTH NO.	DATE		
DETAILS			
EARNINGS A			
B			
C			
D			
E			
GROSS PAY			
GROSS PAY TO DATE			
TAX FREE PAY			
TAXABLE PAY TO DATE			
TAX DUE TO DATE			
TAX REFUND			
TAX			
N.I. CONTRIBUTION			
DEDUCTIONS 1			
2			
3			
4			
5			
6			
TOTAL DEDUCTIONS			
NET PAY			
F			
G			
TOTAL AMOUNT PAYABLE			
EMPLOYER'S CONTRIBUTIONS	NATIONAL INSURANCE		
	H		
	J		
YOUR PAY IS MADE UP AS SHOWN ABOVE			B. WALSH

B

PAY ADVICE

WEEK OR MONTH NO.	DATE		
DETAILS			
EARNINGS A			
B			
C			
D			
E			
GROSS PAY			
GROSS PAY TO DATE			
TAX FREE PAY			
TAXABLE PAY TO DATE			
TAX DUE TO DATE			
TAX REFUND			
TAX			
N.I. CONTRIBUTION			
DEDUCTIONS 1			
2			
3			
4			
5			
6			
TOTAL DEDUCTIONS			
NET PAY			
F			
G			
TOTAL AMOUNT PAYABLE			
EMPLOYER'S CONTRIBUTIONS	NATIONAL INSURANCE		
	H		
	J		
YOUR PAY IS MADE UP AS SHOWN ABOVE			F. JONES

C

PAY ADVICE

WEEK OR MONTH NO.	DATE			
DETAILS				
EARNINGS	A			
	B			
	C			
	D			
	E			
	GROSS PAY			
GROSS PAY TO DATE				
TAX FREE PAY				
TAXABLE PAY TO DATE				
TAX DUE TO DATE				
TAX REFUND				
DEDUCTIONS	TAX			
	N.I. CONTRIBUTION			
	1			
	2			
	3			
	4			
	5			
	6			
	TOTAL DEDUCTIONS			
NET PAY				
F				
G				
TOTAL AMOUNT PAYABLE				
EMPLOYER'S CONTRIBUTIONS	NATIONAL INSURANCE			
	H			
	J			
YOUR PAY IS MADE UP AS SHOWN ABOVE		A. Cox		

D

PAY ADVICE

WEEK OR MONTH NO.	DATE			
DETAILS				
EARNINGS	A			
	B			
	C			
	D			
	E			
	GROSS PAY			
GROSS PAY TO DATE				
TAX FREE PAY				
TAXABLE PAY TO DATE				
TAX DUE TO DATE				
TAX REFUND				
DEDUCTIONS	TAX			
	N.I. CONTRIBUTION			
	1			
	2			
	3			
	4			
	5			
	6			
	TOTAL DEDUCTIONS			
NET PAY				
F				
G				
TOTAL AMOUNT PAYABLE				
EMPLOYER'S CONTRIBUTIONS	NATIONAL INSURANCE			
	H			
	J			
YOUR PAY IS MADE UP AS SHOWN ABOVE		D. MARSHALL		

E

PAY ADVICE

WEEK OR MONTH NO.	DATE		
DETAILS			

EARNINGS	A			
	B			
	C			
	D			
	E			
	GROSS PAY			

GROSS PAY TO DATE		
TAX FREE PAY		
TAXABLE PAY TO DATE		
TAX DUE TO DATE		
TAX REFUND		

DEDUCTIONS	TAX		
	N.I. CONTRIBUTION		
	1		
	2		
	3		
	4		
	5		
	6		
	TOTAL DEDUCTIONS		

NET PAY		
F		
G		
TOTAL AMOUNT PAYABLE		

EMPLOYER'S CONTRIBUTIONS	NATIONAL INSURANCE		
	H		
	J		

YOUR PAY IS
MADE UP AS
SHOWN ABOVE

T. Perry

10 Phil O'Hara works in a factory. His current rate of pay is £3.20 per hour for a 36 hour week, additional hours are paid at time-and-a-half, double-time for weekends.
Phil pays tax at the rate of 25% of earnings over £44 per week, National Insurance at 9% on gross pay, and union dues at £1 per week.
In one week Phil works a total of 44 hours, including 4 hours on the Saturday. Calculate how much his net pay will be, showing all your calculations.

The company is considering paying on piece-rates at 50p per unit for standard output and a bonus of an additional 20p for every extra unit completed. The standard proposed is 250 per week. Phil's normal level of output is 310 per week.

Based purely on financial considerations, should Phil agree to the proposal for piece rates? Show the workings to support your answer.

11 Fred Clarke Ltd pay some of their employees in cash, using the minimum number of notes and coins for each pay packet. They do not use notes above £20 in value, nor do they issue a pay-packet without at least one £5 note or a £1 coin.

From the following details of net pay you are asked to prepare the coin and note analysis to show how the total payroll should be made up.

Employee	Net Pay £
W. Brett	127.45
I. Duncan	70.29
P. Eyres	165.88
S. Norman	211.16
J. Salmon	83.77
V. Wells	99.90

12 Jan Skoda takes on three new members of staff on 2 May. The information taken from the P45 forms is as shown:

Name	Tax Code	Earnings £	Tax £
R. Walker	270	305.25	24.00
M. Greenstreet	115	221.80	33.00
J. Hall	425	350.40	5.50

In the week to 7 May, Jan calculates the gross pay for each of the new employees as:

	£
R. Walker	154.20
M. Greenstreet	88.25
J. Hall	110.40

Jan has also been informed that Jes Hall's tax code has been changed to 395.

You are asked to calculate the amount to be deducted from each employee in respect of tax and National Insurance and show their net pay for the week.

13 Alison Joyce is paid £2.50 per hour as a shop assistant. From the following information calculate her deductions and net pay for Weeks 1–3.

Tax Code:		260L
Hours worked:	Week 1	35 hours
	Week 2	15 hours
	Week 3	15 hours

14 J. Mason's wages bill for the month of April was made up as follows:

	£
Total net pay	2675
Tax deductions	548
Employee's NI Contributions	310
Employer's NI Contributions	325

The wages were paid by cheque on 28 April. The deductions were paid to the Inland Revenue by cheque on 14 May.

Write up the appropriate ledger entries in J. Mason's ledger. A wages control account is not required.

15 Brian Wyse – Newsagent

Brian Wyse interviews Shirley Davies who starts working with him on 1 May (week 5), on a weekly wage of £85. She brings along her P45 which shows that her earnings to date were £325, total tax paid to date was £31, and her tax code was 260L.
Calculate her net pay for her first week in the shop, presuming there are no voluntary deductions.
Show the breakdown of notes and coins in Shirley's wage packet.

Answers

5 a) £94.50
b) £224.25
c) £155.80

6 £171.50

7
Week 3	Tax deducted	£15.25
Week 4	Tax deducted	£14.25
Week 5	Tax deducted	£13.25

8
Total contributions		Employee's contributions
Week 3	£15.60	£7.80
Week 4	£14.90	£7.45
Week 5	£14.62	£7.31

9

Name	Gross	Tax	NI	Savings	Subs	Net
	£	£	£	£	£	£
Walsh	141.75	24.50	12.73	–	–	104.52
Jones	199.80	30.75	17.95	4.00	–	147.10
Cox	211.75	33.75	19.03	4.00	–	154.97
Marshall	180.00	25.25	16.24	–	0.10	138.41
Perry	113.40	8.00	7.94	–	0.10	97.36
Total	846.70	122.25	73.89	8.00	0.20	642.36

15   Brian Wyse – Newsagent

		£
Shirley Davies	Gross pay for week	85.00
	Total pay to date	410.00 (+ 325)
(Table A, Week 5)	Tax free pay to date	250.90 (Code 260L)
	Taxable pay to date	159.10
(Table B)	Tax due to date	39.75
	Tax due this week	8.75 (−31)
(Table A)	National Insurance	5.98
	Total deductions	14.73
	Net pay	70.27

Coin Analysis

		£
£10 notes	× 7	70.00
20p	× 1	0.20
5p	× 1	0.05
2p	× 1	0.02
Total		70.27

Unit 10

Trading and Profit and Loss Accounts

Year End Adjustments (Part 1)

At the end of this unit you will be able to:

1 Prepare final accounts

2 Understand accounting concepts

3 Prepare a trading account and a profit and loss account

4 Understand the format and the compilation of the figures

5 Make various adjustments before accounts are finalised in order to cover all events during the accounting period.

Guidelines for the Preparation of Final Accounts

Every limited company is required by the Companies Acts to produce a set of Annual Accounts. These accounts inform the shareholders and others about the company's financial position and copies also have to be sent to the Registrar of Companies and to the Inland Revenue for tax purposes. Tax law is a highly specialised area and the profits shown in the Annual Report will not necessarily be the basis for calculation of tax due.

Other businesses are not legally compelled to produce annual accounts but have to in practice in order to satisfy the requirements of the Inland Revenue, if for no other reason.

The annual accounts consist of a **Trading Account** and **Profit and Loss Account** which summarise the firm's income and expenditure over the year and show whether the firm is making a profit or a loss, and a **Balance Sheet** which summarises the firm's assets and liabilities at the year end and shows the net worth of the business.

The firm's history can therefore be summarised in a series of Final Accounts as follows:

	BS		BS	
19–1		19–2		19–3
P & L a/c		P & L a/c		P & L a/c

It is a common misconception to think about the Profit and Loss Account as being a summary of cash flowing in to and out of the business, leaving either an increase in cash (profit) or decrease in cash (loss) at the year end. The real situation is more complex than that, as we shall see.

Capital and Revenue Expenditure

Cash flowing **in** to a business may be grouped into two main categories:
- Cash received from customers (sales) and other sources (e.g. discounts and interest) which are not repayable. These cash in-flows are classified as **income** and appear in the **trading and profit and loss account.**
- Cash received as loans to the company or as investments by shareholders which are repayable at some time in the future or when the company is wound up. These cash in-flows are classified as **liabilities** invested in the business and appear in the **balance sheet.**

Cash flowing **out** of the business may similarly be divided into:
- Cash spent on wages, materials and other things which have been used up during the year. These cash out-flows are classified as **expenses** and are shown in the **trading and profit and loss account.**
- Cash spent on plant and machinery and other things which are still in use at the year end. These cash out-flows are classified as **assets** and are shown in the **balance sheet.**

Cash flows affecting the profit and loss account are generally referred to as **Revenue,** and cash flows affecting the balance sheet as **Capital.**

Although in most cases it will be fairly obvious whether a cash flow should appear in the profit and loss account or in the balance sheet, this is not always the case. For example, it may be difficult to decide whether certain types of expenditure on plant are repairs (profit and loss account) or replacements (balance sheet).

The situation is further complicated by cash flows which initially affect the profit and loss account and subsequently the balance sheet or vice versa. For example:

Expenditure on purchases is normally classed as revenue and appears in the trading account. If stocks exist at the year-end (as is usually the case) this is treated as an *asset* in the balance sheet and *deducted* from the purchases figure in the trading account.

Income is defined as what is *earned* during the year and not just what is *received* during the year. Any money owing to the business at the year-end (debtors) is included in the sales figures and shown in the balance sheet as an asset. Similarly, the amounts owing *by* the business at the year-end (creditors) are shown as liabilities.

The following table may help you to decide which items are 'Capital' and which are 'Revenue' expenditure.

Item	Capital	Revenue
Vehicles	original cost	replacement of spares maintenance depreciation running costs
Buildings	original cost extensions improvements	re-decorating repairs maintenance
Machinery	original cost improvements	maintenance replacements of parts depreciation
Office Equipment	original cost	repairs depreciation

Accounting Concepts

When an accountant draws up the final accounts of a business – the trading and profit and loss account and the balance sheet – he takes into consideration certain assumptions and conventions which require adjustments to the figures. These are:

1 The Monetary Measurement Concept

Money is not always a good measure of value, nor a good store of value. In times of inflation it has certain disadvantages. Therefore, some organisations measure in terms of the number of units produced or passengers carried, as well as in financial terms. However, money is a good way of comparing different aspects of a business.

2 The Cost Concept

Generally, the value of assets, expenses and liabilities are recorded at the time they were incurred. This is known as the cost concept. However, because of inflation some organisations revalue their assets every year in line with the current market value.

3 The Business Entity Concept

The business is separate from the proprietor, who lends money (or other assets – capital) to it. The capital is shown as a liability and reflects that the organisation and its proprietor are different. From a legal point of view, if a sole trader or partnership becomes bankrupt, the court can go behind the business to settle any claims because the owner does not have limited liability.

4 The Going Concern Concept

When an accountant draws up the figures and the auditor certifies them as correct, it must be assumed that the business will continue. Any values placed upon the assets are on this basis.

5 The Accruals (or Realisation) Concept

This is most important and recognises that all revenue (income) earned in a specific accounting period has to be matched against the expenditure of that period. This expenditure is measured at the time the liability is incurred and *not* when it is actually paid. Conversely, revenue (income) is measured from the date it is due, *not* when the amount has been paid.

All income and expenditure is measured in the year to which it relates, and *not* when it is actually received or paid.

This is an illustration to show how final accounts are prepared.

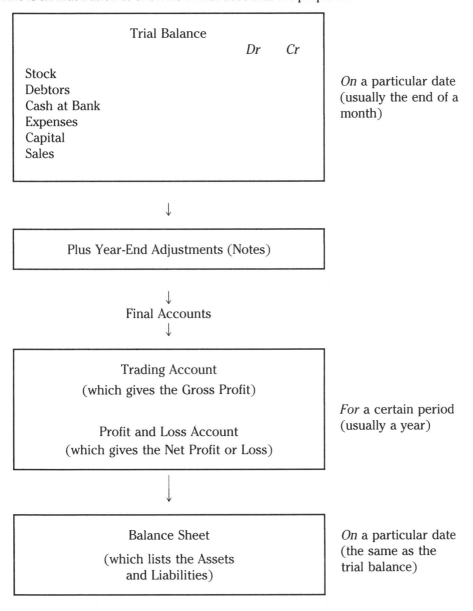

So: J. Smith's trial balance on 31 December 19–7

leads to: J. Smith's trading and profit and loss accounts for year ending 31 December 19–7

and   J. Smith's balance sheet on 31 December 19–7.

The Trading and Profit and Loss Accounts

Accounting

Accounting is the language of business and all our efforts must eventually be measured in terms of financial results. To enable us to understand that language, it is necessary that we know about the final accounts.

Accounting is essential because it provides:

- A measurement to evaluate performance

- A picture of the financial standing

- A statement of the net worth

- A means of controlling the business.

Accounting helps with decision-making and is an important way of providing information so that we can make the best decisions, exercise judgements and take action.

The profit and loss account is essentially a 'results' statement. It shows the revenue from sales and then deducts how much it has cost to achieve those sales to produce a **Gross Profit**. We then deduct expenses so as to arrive at a **Net Profit.** This is a **Revenue** account.

A profit statement should be prepared for every business and for every activity within that business.

How to Prepare Final Accounts

At the end of the accounting period we prepare the trial balance. We must first decide which items in the trial balance appear in the balance sheet *or* the trading and profit and loss account.

In the presentation of the trading and profit and loss account the Income is placed at the top of the list and then we deduct:

- The cost of the goods sold, to give **gross** profit
- The expenses of running the business, to give **net** profit.

Vertical Presentation

Note that we will be using the modern 'vertical presentation' of final accounts as shown in published annual reports.

Although it may not appear so at first, this still conforms with basic double-entry principles. Instead of straightforward debits and credits, this layout uses additions and subtractions to give meaningful figures. Sub-totals are calculated in order to provide useful information for management purposes.

Larger organisations use accounting information to provide statistical analyses and comparisons as a basis of improving profitability.

Trading Account

The object of this account is to arrive at *Gross* profit, as shown below:

		£	£
Sales			100
Less Cost of goods sold			
	Stock at start	90	
	Add Purchases	70	
		160	
	Less Stock at end	(100)	(60)
	Gross Profit (Difference)		40

From the trial balance we have inserted figures as follows:

The Sales (exclusive of VAT)

and Cost of sales, using the following formula:

Stock at start	(from the trial balance)
add Purchases	(from the trial balance)
deduct Stock at end	(from the notes)
= Cost of goods sold	(or cost of sales)

The cost of goods sold is an important figure to calculate. The difference between this and sales is *Gross Profit.*

Pictorially we could show it this way:

Returns/Carriage In

If these appear on the trial balance they must be shown in the trading account, as they are concerned with stocks. Returns will *reduce* the sales or purchases figure, Carriage In *increases* the purchases figure.

Other Trading Items

If a trial balance figure (or note) affects the cost of sales it should also be included in the trading account. Such items may include customs duty on imported goods or goods taken by the owner (Drawings) if not already shown in the books.

Profit and Loss Account

The gross profit is carried to the profit and loss account where we deduct the general expenses of running the business. These are normally put down in a logical order, either under sub-headings or some order such as: Employee costs (Wages, Salaries etc.); Premises (Rent, Rates etc.); Others (largest first). The profit and loss account shows the general expenses or **overheads**, as they are often described.

From the trial balance and notes we use all of the items of a revenue nature. Remember, in the trial balance a debit balance indicates expenses or losses, and this is a fair guide as to what goes into the profit and loss account as an expense. Income items (e.g. rent receivable) have credit balances, and are added to the gross profit before the expenses are deducted.

In the example below we have shown administration, selling and distribution and financial expenses.

J. Smith's Trading and Profit and Loss Account
for the year ending 31 December 19–2

		£
Sales		1000
less Returns		(100)
		——
Turnover		900
less Cost of Sales		
		£
Opening stock	£	900
add Purchases	800	
Less Returns	(200)	600
		1500
less Stock at end	(1000)	(500)
Gross profit		400
Rent receivable		50
		450
less Overheads		
Administration	100	
Selling and Distribution	60	
Financial	140	(300)
Net profit		150

Note 3-column cash paper is useful for this style of account.

Adjustments in Final Accounts

So far, all our book-keeping has been concerned with recording events after they have actually happened. Once we start adjustments to these figures we are in the realms of accounting. The purpose of adjustments is to ensure that the accounts reflect a true and fair view, and therefore we must include everything that has happened since the last set of final accounts. These adjustments have not been recorded so we need to take some action in order to reflect their existence in the final accounts.

At the end of an accounting period, the following matters may still be incomplete:

Accruals or Accrued Expenses

These are expenses for which we have had the benefit, but not yet received a bill, or not yet paid. When we have had the benefit of some services or goods but the expense has not yet been entered in the books, it has to be reflected in our accounts.

The treatment is to increase the expense, so as to reflect the actual cost for the year. Such expenses could be wages, lighting and heating or motor expenses.

In order to make sure that the actual cost is charged to the profit and loss account, we must show a closing balance on the debit side of the appropriate expense account, which is carried forward to the start of the next period as a **Credit Balance**.

Example

Rent payable £10 per week; actual payment made on 3 January £130; 7 April £120; 10 June £100 and £120 on 20 September. The account will look like this:

Rent a/c

19–			£				£
Jan	3	Bank	130	Dec	31	Profit & loss	520
Apr	7	"	120				
June	10	"	100				
Sept	20	"	120				
Dec	31	Accrual c/d	50				
			520				520
19–2				Jan	1	Balance b/d	50

Alternatively, for a small business, this adjustment can be made in the profit and loss account itself.

Payments in Advance

These are payments made in advance and therefore relating to the next accounting period. It follows, therefore, that an amount paid in respect of the next accounting period will be deducted from our expenses in this period. Such items may be rates or insurance. The entry in respect of the adjustment above would be to:

> ### Credit the Rates Account

and **decrease** the cost shown in the profit and loss account.

Similarly, any income (such as rent receivable) can be either in arrears or in advance. If an account is in **arrears**:

> ### Credit the Income Account

and **increase** the amount shown in the profit and loss account. Alternatively, if an income account is in **advance**:

Debit the Income Account

---

and **decrease** the amount in the profit and loss account.

Depreciation

This is the reduction in value of assets because of wear and tear or obsolescence (becoming out-dated). It is the value consumed during the life of a fixed asset. The 'life' of an asset means the number of years it is used in the business.

When we described a fixed asset, you may remember from Unit 2, we indicated that it was a piece of equipment or other asset used in the business for the purpose of producing profits. These assets usually decrease in value as they are used. In order to recognise this in accounting we 'depreciate' assets and show the effect of this in the accounts. This is often known as a Depreciation Provision.

The aim is to set aside from profits each year during the life of an asset sufficient funds to cover the loss in value. Unless a specific amount of cash is actually set aside for this purpose, it does not provide for the replacement of an asset.
Depreciation has three functions:

- To show against profit the extent of the wearing out of the assets in money terms.

- To discourage the owner from taking too much cash out of the business.

- To help provide finance for expansion by leaving cash in the business.

When each new asset is purchased, three things should be determined:

- Its cost

- Its expected life

- Its scrap or residual value.

One way to arrive at the amount for depreciation each year is to deduct the scrap value from the original cost and then divide the balance over the life of the asset. This is known as the **Straight Line Method**. The same effect can be achieved by applying a set percentage or fraction to the original cost. Essentially, it gives the same amount of depreciation for each year of the life of a particular asset.
Alternatively, a pre-determined percentage can be applied to the reduced value of the asset at the end of each year. This is the **Diminishing Balance Method**. This gives a smaller charge for depreciation as the asset gets older.

Example

	£
Cost of Asset	1000
Year 1 Depreciation at 10%	(100)
Net Book Value	900
Year 2 Depreciation at 10%	(90)

Net Book Value	810
Year 3 Depreciation at 10%	(81)
Net Book Value	729

Simply by charging this **notional expense** to our profit and loss account does not guarantee enough funds to replace the asset when the time comes. However, by showing a reduced profit figure the owner is discouraged from taking too much out of the business.

Unfortunately, in times of high inflation, the amounts set aside do not usually cover the increased cost of replacement. Accordingly it makes sense to put aside extra cash: if a business does not do this it may weaken its position and also reduce its competitiveness and profitability in later years.

Entries in the accounts:

Debit the Profit and Loss Account (as an Expense)

Credit the Provision for Depreciation Account

Profit and Loss			Provision for Depreciation		
Depreciation: Motor vehicles	£ 100			Profit and loss	£ 100

Note The asset accounts themselves should always show the value of the assets *at cost.*

Stock Valuation

Stock should always be valued at the end of each accounting period, and this subject will be discussed in Unit 14. Closing stock is deducted from purchases expenditure in *this* period because it will be used in the *next* accounting period.

Bad Debts

These are debts that have to be written off when a customer cannot pay. Provision for Bad Debts is an amount set aside from the profits in case other debtors cannot pay. These will be discussed in the next unit.

Questions

1 How do we arrive at gross profit?

2 Smith buys £8000 worth of goods and sells three-quarters of them for £10 000. What is his gross profit?

3 Cross out the wrong word in the following sentences:

   a) A trading account shows sales plus/minus the cost of the sales.
   b) To calculate cost of sales: stock at the beginning, add/less the purchases, and add/less the stock at the end.
   c) the profit and loss statement shows the gross profit plus/minus expenses incurred/paid for in the accounting period.

4 Profit is the difference between .... and ....

5 Why are accruals and prepayments used in year end adjustments?

6 What do you understand by depreciation?

7 Show the entries in the books if we provide depreciation on a computer which we bought for £10 000 and depreciated by 20% in the first year.

8 Ted King started a travelling greengrocery business on 1 April 19–0 with £2000 he had saved. He used this to buy a van which cost £1600 and the remaining £400 he kept to buy his daily stock. Every weekday he went to the wholesale market and bought enough for his day's sales. All these sales were for cash. His only expenses were for motoring which he paid for as necessary, and on the basis of this used to take the excess over £400 at the weekend as his profit.

   However, 4 years later, the van was not roadworthy and a garage offered him £200 for it in part-exchange for one costing £2200. Ted was upset to find that he hadn't got that much money and his business was threatened.

   Explain what he should have done from the start of the business in order to be able to buy a replacement van. If you were his adviser, what would you have suggested?

9 From the following trial balance prepare a trading and profit and loss account for R. Taylor for the year ended 30 November 19–9.

	£	£
Stock 1 December 19–8	4000	
Cash	60	
Bank	1385	
Capital		30 000
Premises	20 000	
Fittings	2500	
Purchases	10 000	
Office stationery	20	
Car (at cost)	2500	
Sales		12 000
Car expenses	15	
F. Browning (debtor)	1500	
Miscellaneous	20	
	42 000	42 000

Stock 30 November 19–9 £5000
Depreciation on the car at 20% and fittings at 10% on cost.

10 From B. Fenton's trial balance prepare a trading and profit and loss account for the year ended 30 September 19−2.

	£	£
Capital		30 000
Loan (J. Goodman)		1000
Stock	1000	
Bank	5163	
Buildings	15 000	
Van	4000	
Fittings	5200	
Equipment	1000	
Cash	195	
Purchases	4500	
Sales		5150
Stationery	15	
General expenses	40	
Lighting and heating	35	
Van expenses	152	
B. Stone (creditor)		300
D. Hughes	150	
	36 450	36 450

Stock £1380
Van expenses pre-paid £42
Depreciation on van at 25% per annum.

11 T. Bear has started trading in a toy shop. Record the following transactions in the appropriate accounts and then prepare a trial balance and trading and profit and loss account for the month.

19−3
March 1 Paid £20 000 into bank account.
            Bought fittings £2000 and a van £3200
            Paid both by cheque
        3 Paid rent £200 by cheque. Bought goods on credit for resale from
            I. Adams £2500
        5 Cash sales £260
        8 Paid wages £35 cash
       10 Paid insurance £12 by cheque
       12 Cash sales £400
       15 Paid wages £35 cash.
            Returned goods to I. Adams £480
       17 Paid I. Adams by cheque £1500
       18 Bought goods on credit for re-sale from S. Wales £1400
       19 Cash sales £480
       22 Paid wages £35 cash
       24 Bought office stationery £25 cash
       25 Cash sales £600

27   Paid S. Wales by cheque £700
29   Paid wages £35 cash
31   Paid into bank by cash £1375

Note   Stock in hand at 31 March £2715

Monthly depreciation at the rate of 1% on fittings and 2% on the van.
It is estimated that electricity used so far has cost £75.

12   Wendy Johnson-Bratt presents you with her trial balance on 31 August 19–7.
Using that and the additional notes draw up a trading and profit and loss
account for the year.

Trial Balance on 31 August 19–7

	£	£
Bank	1200	
Cash	250	
Debtors	4680	
Creditors		6100
Loan		5000
Stock	2720	
Sales		29 680
Purchases	14 370	
Wages	3400	
Rent receivable		750
Import duty	240	
Administration	4700	
Selling distribution	2090	
Premises	21 600	
Motor vehicles at cost	5000	
Capital		20 000
Drawings	2280	
Provision for depreciation M.V		1000
	62 530	62 530

Note   Rent receivable owing £50
Stock at end of period £3150
Motor vehicles to be depreciated at 20% on cost
Salesmen's commission owing £210

13   Hugh Wood maintains a heating and lighting account. During the year ended
30 September 19–8 he has paid out the following amounts:

	£
Electricity	2480
Coal	560
Oil	1290

At the end of the year Hugh has an unpaid bill for oil amounting to £340 and
he also estimates that he owes another £120 for electricity. In addition he has
calculated that his stocks of oil and coal on hand on 30 September are worth
£210. Hugh also estimates that he has taken £50 worth of coal for his own use.

Calculate, either in the form of the ledger account or as a statement, the amount which should be charged to the profit and loss account for heating and lighting for the year.

14 Draw up Barry Kay's trading account from the figures given below:

	£		£
Sales	183 475	Purchases	89 143
Returns out	1191	Returns in	2671
Carriage out	357	Carriage in	648
Royalties on		Customs Duty	7356
goods sold	2470	Stock at end	4218
Stock at start	5773	Creditors	8849
Debtors	17480		
		Goods taken by Barry	
		for his own use	177

Note It may not be necessary to use all of these figures in this exercise.

15 From the following balances extracted from the ledger of New Dawn Trading Co. on 31 December 19–8, draw up a trading and profit and loss account for the year ended 31 December 19–8.

	£
Sales	75000
Purchases	57500
Returns in	225
Returns out	625
Stock	2500
Carriage in	175
Wages	7500
Motor expenses	2180
Rent and rates	2250
Light and heating	740
Insurance	985
Carriage out	25
Rent receivable	520
Discounts received	1500

Note Stock on 31 December 19–8 £3125

16 L. Miles pays rent of £2160 a year for his premises, payable quarterly on the first day of January, April, July and October. As at 31 December 19–0 the final payment for the year is still outstanding. The other payments were made on the due dates. L. Miles also pays £12 a week rent for some additional storage space and his payments for the year were:

12 January £36, 28 April £48, 2 August £36, 18 December £36.

Draw up the rent account for the year showing any amounts outstanding or prepaid and the amount to be transferred to the profit and loss account.

17 Brian Wyse – Newsagent

At the end of his second year of trading Brian Wyse extracts the following trial balance from his books:

	£	£
Stock	2000	
Capital		5000
Purchases/sales	46 000	60 000
Returns in/out	100	500
Discounts allowed/received	300	1200
Rent/rates	1800	
Motor expenses	1750	
Wages	6000	
Insurances	825	
Drawings	6365	
Loan – S Wyse		2000
General expenses	1350	
Debtors/creditors	150	2100
Carriage in	140	
Carriage out	20	
Motor van	2000	
Bank cash	2000	
	70 800	70 800

Note • Stock on 30 April 19–0 £2500
• Loan interest not paid (agreed rate 5%)
• Insurance prepaid £230
• Depreciation on van at 20% pa
• Goods taken from stock by Brian but not yet recorded in the books £500

From the above information present his trading and profit and loss account.

Answers

2 £4000

7 Debit profit and loss £2000
Credit provision for depreciation £2000

8 Consider the effect of charging for depreciation over the four years and so reducing profit. Set aside an amount each year to provide the necessary funds to purchase a replacement vehicle at the end of the four years.

9   Net profit £2195

10   Net loss £170

11   Net profit £499

---

17   Brian Wyse – Newsagent

Brian Wyse's Trading and Profit and Loss Account
for the year ending 30 April 19–0

				£
Sales				60 000
Less returns				(100)
				————
Net turnover				59 900
Less Cost of sales:				
			£	
Opening stock		£	2000	
Purchases	£	46 000		
Less Returns	500			
Drawings	500	(1000)		
		————		
		45 000		
Carriage in		140	45 140	
			47 140	
Less Closing stock			2500	(44 640)
Gross profit				15 260
Discount received				1200
				————
				16 460
Less Expenses:				
Wages			6000	
Rent/rates			1800	
Motor expenses			1750	
Discounts allowed			300	
Insurances		825		
Pre-paid		(230)	595	
Carriage out			20	
Loan interest accrued			100	
General			1350	
Depreciation on van			400	(12 315)
Net profit				4145
				————

Unit 11

The Balance Sheet

Year End Adjustments (Part 2)

At the end of this unit you will be able to:

1   Prepare a Balance Sheet

2   Understand the terms and items found in a Balance Sheet

3   Appreciate the important function of the Balance Sheet in giving a financial picture of the business

4   Understand further aspects of year end adjustments

5   Deal with Bad Debts.

The Balance Sheet

The Balance Sheet is a statement of the **assets** and **liabilities** of a business enterprise at a certain date, that date being shown on the top of the balance sheet.

It may help you to understand the balance sheet if it is regarded not only as a statement of assets and liablilities but also as a statement of funds showing where the business has obtained its finance and how it has spent those funds.

Example

Balance Sheet of The Village Shop
on 30 September 19–2

	£
Liabilities (credit balances)	4000
Assets (debit balances)	
Shop fixtures and fittings	750
Stock	2000
Bank	1250
	4000

This is a balance sheet at a very straightforward level. In reality, even the smallest business will be more detailed than this.

The balance sheet is a financial **position** statement of the assets and liabilities of a business. It is not actually an account, but a list of balances of capital accounts, and a statement where items of a permanent nature are shown.

One section of the balance sheet shows where the money has come from. In most cases this is from the owner of the business. Once trading, if the business makes a profit, the best way to expand is to plough back that profit into the business. Most successful businesses plough back a substantial proportion of the profits each year.

Another source of funds is to obtain other people's money, by borrowing on a long-term basis (i.e. for more than one year) either as a loan or as a mortgage or HP commitment.

Capital invested by the owner(s) plus long-term liabilities give us the total **capital employed** in the business.

The other section of the balance sheet (the other half of the equation) shows how that funding has been used. This usually consists of fixed assets (premises, vehicles etc.) and **working capital**.

Working capital is the short-term (less than one year) day-to-day finance available to the business. It is the difference between **current assets** (stock, debtors, cash etc) and **current liabilities** (creditors, accruals). The ideal ratio of current assets to current liabilities is 2:1. This prevents a creditor from forcing a business into liquidation because it cannot settle a debt quickly enough and prevents the business from having too much idle capital not actually earning profits.

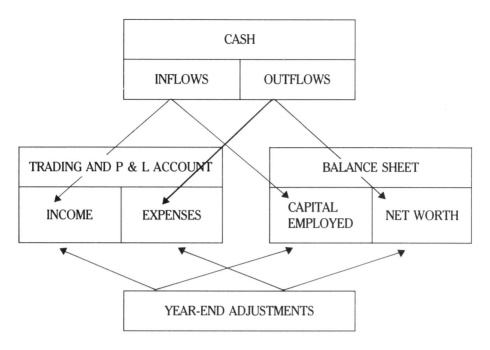

Note Year-end adjustments must be used **twice**.

Example

We can now study the following example of the final accounts of a small business:

B. Fenton
Trial Balance
as at 30 September 19–2

		Dr £	Cr £
(BS)	Capital		30 000
(BS)	Loan (J. Goodman)		1000
(T)	Stock at start	1000	
(BS)	Bank	5163	
(BS)	Buildings	15 000	
(BS)	Van	4000	
(BS)	Fittings	5200	
(BS)	Equipment	1000	
(BS)	Cash	195	
(T)	Purchases	4500	
(T)	Sales		5150
(P&L)	Stationery	15	
(P&L)	Cleaning	40	
(P&L)	Lighting and heating	35	
(P&L)	Van expenses	152	
(BS)	B. Stone (creditor)		300
(BS)	D. Hughes	150	
		36 450	36 450

(T)	(BS)	Stock at end £1380
(P&L)	(BS)	Van expenses prepaid £42
(P&L)	(BS)	Depreciation on van at 25% per annum

From the trial balance, we prepare a trading and profit and loss account as we saw in the previous unit:

B. Fenton's Trading And Profit And Loss Account
For The Year Ended 30 September 19–2

	£	£	£
Sales			5150
Less Cost of sales:			
Stock at start		1000	
Add Purchases		4500	
		5500	
Less Closing stock		<1380>	<4120>
Gross Profit			1030
Less Expenses:			
Stationery		15	
Lighting and heating		35	
Van expenses	152		
Less prepayment	42	110	
Cleaning		40	
Depreciation – van		1000	1200
Net Loss			< 170>

B. Fenton's Balance Sheet on 30 September 19–2

	£
Capital	
Opening balance	30 000
Less Net loss	< 170>
	29 830
Loan	1000
Capital employed	30 830
Represented by:	
Fixed assets	
Buildings	15 000
Van less depreciation	3000
Fittings	5200
Equipment	1000
	24 200

Current assets	£	
Stock	1380	
Debtors	150	
Prepayment	42	
Bank	5163	
Cash	195	
	6930	
Less Current liabilities:		
Creditors	< 300>	6630
Net worth		30 830

Explanation of Terms used in the Final Accounts

The Trading Account

Stock at The Start

This is the stock at the beginning of the trading period and is always shown in the trial balance.

Purchases

Whenever something is bought for resale it is known as a purchase and will be included in the trading account. Purchases are obtained from our creditors.

Closing stock

This is stock at the end of the period and appears in the trading account *and* the balance sheet.

In a manufacturing organisation we also need to prepare a **Manufacturing Account** (See Unit 13) to arrive at cost of goods produced. In this case, opening and closing stocks of raw materials and work in progress will be included, together with all costs associated with the factory.

The trading and profit and loss account contains the income and expenses over a period of time.

The Balance Sheet

Capital

The capital is the amount of finance provided for the business by the owner. It is usually in the form of cash, but could be any asset put into the business by the owner from his own resources. The profit from trading at the end of the year will be added to his original capital.

If a trader takes out cash or stock (or anything else) for his own personal use, this is his **drawings** and is deducted from this original capital plus the profit he has made to date. The drawings are taken out in anticipation of the profits he hopes to make.

Assets

A firm's assets or possessions are normally divided into two main categories: **fixed** (i.e. long-term) assets and **current** (i.e. short-term) assets.

Fixed assets are those which are held for *use* in the business rather than for *resale*. As already indicated, they can be regarded as long-term assets which are owned and kept for a period of years to make profits. Examples of fixed assets are land and buildings, plant and machinery, motor vehicles and fixtures and fittings.

Current assets are those assets which are already cash or which can be converted to cash within a short period of time i.e. they are short-term assets which are readily **realisable** and relatively **liquid**.

Current assets fall under three main headings:
Stock (including raw materials, work in progress and finished goods).
Debtors (including prepayments or income in arrears).
Cash (both at the bank and in hand – including petty cash floats).

Nowadays it is usual to deduct current liabilities from total current assets to show the **net current assets** or **working capital**.

It is not good accounting policy to include employees in balance sheets because we cannot put a fair value on them due to their ability to leave us at any time because we do not own them. **Human asset** accounting is practised by some American companies – they say this helps in making better 'people decisions'. Some British companies would claim that their employees are, in fact, a liability!

Current Liabilities

Current liabilities are liabilities of a relatively short-term nature which the company incurs in the course of carrying on its day-to-day trading activities. Examples are balances owing to suppliers (trade creditors), amounts owing for services (accruals), bank overdraft and so on. They will also include any amounts owing for corporation tax, proposed dividends or VAT.

Year End Adjustments

The purpose of adjustments is to produce an accurate set of final accounts which reflect a 'true and fair view' of the business. In the previous unit, we looked at some of these adjustments and discussed how they were shown in the trading and profit and loss account. We shall now take another look at the adjustments and see how they are shown in the balance sheet:

Accruals or Accrued Expenses

These are amounts for goods or services received during the current accounting period for which no invoice has been received nor any payment made. In order to show the true cost of the expense to the business for the period, an adjustment is made to increase the amount charged to the profit and loss account for that expense.

As the amount is still outstanding, the accrual is shown as a **current liability** in the balance sheet.

Prepayments or Payments in Advance

If payments are made in advance, the amount which relates to the *next* accounting period must be deducted from the expense in *this* period. This amount will be shown as an asset at the accounting year end. This is because if the business were to close down at that date, the money would be repaid to the firm.

A payment in advance is shown under **current assets** in the balance sheet.

Depreciation

Depreciation is charged as a notional expense (i.e. there is no actual movement of cash) to the profit and loss account.

In the balance sheet, the depreciation must always be shown as a deduction from the appropriate asset. The Net Book Value (NBV) of the asset reflects the fact that the asset is reducing in value.

In order to show clearly the effect of depreciation on the fixed assets, a commonly used layout for that section of the balance sheet is as follows:

Example

Fixed Assets	Cost	Depreciation	Net Book Value
	£	£	£
Premises	20 000	–	20 000
Plant & Equipment	15 000	5000	10 000
Motor Vehicles	8000	2000	6000
	43 000	7000	36 000

Notice how there is still an entry under 'Cost' for the premises, even though there is no depreciation; the 'Cost' and 'Depreciation' columns are ruled off because they are there for additional information but are not actually a part of the balance sheet totals.

Disposal of Fixed Assets

When we decide to dispose of an asset, we will know how much it is actually worth (as against our own estimation of the book value), whether we sell it, part-exchange it or scrap it.

The difference between our net book value and the value received for the asset is either over or under-depreciation, depending on whether we receive more or less than net book value. This over or under-depreciation is transferred to the profit and loss account at the end of the year: over-depreciation will *reduce* the depreciation charge for the current year, under-depreciation *increases* the depreciation charge for the year.

Example

An electronic typewriter purchased five years ago at a cost of £750 depreciated at the rate of 10% per year, is now part-exchanged, £200 being allowed as trade-in.

	£
Cost	750
Depreciation (5 years × 75)	(375)
Net Book Value	375
Proceeds	(200)
Profit and Loss under-depreciation	175

Stock Valuation

Closing stock is an asset and is shown in the balance sheet under **current assets**.

Bad Debts

When a credit customer does not pay and this is considered irrecoverable, the debt is written off.

The entry is to reduce the debtor's personal account and increase the bad debts account as follows:

Debit the Bad Debts Account

Credit the Personal Account

Bad Debts a/c

	£			£
A. Debtor	75			

A. Debtor's a/c

		£			£
Balance	b/d	75		Bad Debts	75

At the end of the accounting period, the total expense (bad debt) is charged to the profit and loss account. If a year end adjustment is made to write off an additional bad debt, this amount must be deducted from the debtors' figure in the balance sheet.

Provision For Bad Debts

It makes sense to assume that certain debtors will not pay us. By looking at our previous track record we can estimate that a certain percentage (usually between 2% and 5%) of debtors will not settle their accounts. Bear in mind that the profit is not really earned until the customer has actually paid! This is a continuing provision, so amounts are set aside each year from the profits to 'top up' the account.

Accordingly, when the percentage for the current year is determined, deduct the previous bad debt provision from that figure.

Example

	Provision set at 5% of debtors: Debtors last year £8000 Debtors this year £10 000	£
So	Bad Debt provision required this year	500
	Bad Debt provision from last year	<400>
	Difference posted to profit and loss account	100

Sometimes the position works in reverse so that we have already more bad debt provision than is now needed. In this case the surplus is written back to profit, usually by *reducing* the actual bad debt charge.

For bad debt provision, the **difference** between the **old** and **new** provision is charged to the profit and loss account. On the balance sheet the *new* bad debt provision is shown as a deduction from our debtors to give a more realistic figure of what we really expect to collect.

Example

Current Assets

	£	£
Debtors	10 000	
Less Bad debt provision	< 500>	9500

So we are showing how much we really expect to receive.

In practice, many accountants draw up a trial balance, make adjustments as necessary, and prepare outline final accounts before constructing the actual accounts themselves, as follows:

Trial Balance			Adjustments		Trading and Profit/Loss		Balance Sheet	
	£	£	£	£	£	£	£	£
Capital		4070						4070
Sales		9000				9000		
Purchases	3000				3000			
Stock	1000				1000			
Returns in	50				50			
Returns out		100				100		
Discount allowed	75				75			
Discount received		120				120		
Rent and rates	210		50	50	260			50
Motor expenses	320				320			
Salaries	2100				2100			
Insurance	95		25	25	70		25	
Drawings	1500						1500	
Debtors	2000						2000	
Creditors		1000						1000
Carriage in	170				170			
Carriage out	50				50			
Motor vehicles	4500						4500	
Bank	300						300	
Provision for depreciation		1200	900	900	900			2100
Bad debts	120				120			
Provision for bad debts			200	200	200			200
Closing stock			1100	1100		1100	1100	
	15 490	15 490	2275	2275	8315	10 320	9425	7420
Net Profit					2005			2005
					10 320	10 320	9425	9425

Note Adjustments:
- Closing stock   £1100
- Rent accrued   £50
- Insurance prepaid   £25
- Provision for bad debts to be created at 10% of debtors
- Depreciation on motor vehicles at 20% of cost.

Questions

1 Describe a balance sheet.

2 What are fixed assets? Give three examples.

3 What are current assets? Give three examples.

4 What are current liabilities? Give three examples.

5 How are prepaid expenses shown in the balance sheet?

6 One of our debtors, A. Clarke, is declared bankrupt, owing us £1000. We are informed that he can only pay 50 pence in the pound. What entries should we make to reflect this?

7 A firm depreciates its motor vehicles at 20% using the reducing balance method. One of its cars cost £10 000 three years ago.
a) What is the annual charge for depreciation for each of the three years?
b) What is its present written-down value?
c) If, as the result of a board decision, the company decides to adopt a different make of car for the fleet and the car is sold now for £4000, has it been over-depreciated or under-depreciated?
d) How would this over-depreciation or under-depreciation be treated in the profit and loss account?

8 The bad debt provision of G. Black for last year was £3000. His debtors were £50 000 at the end of this year and he wishes to make a bad debt provision of 7%. How much would be charged to the profit and loss account this year? What will be the balance sheet entry?

9 Prepare a balance sheet from the following information about W.T. Bray's business at 30 September 19–2.

	£
Cash in hand	50
Bank overdraft	190
Capital	20 000
Vehicles	2340
Land and buildings	14 700
Creditors	830
Debtors	1200
Stock in hand	2730

10 From the answer to Question 11, Unit 10, prepare a balance sheet for T. Bear on 31 March 19–3.

11 For each of the following items state whether it is included as a fixed or current asset, long-term or current liability or part of the capital in the balance sheet:

Loan from B. Bowker
Net loss for the year
Prepayment of insurance
Rent receivable in arrears
Electricity accrued
Bank overdraft
Provision for bad debts
Petty cash
Plant and equipment
Drawings
Depreciation
VAT owing to Customs and Excise

12 Record the following transactions in the appropriate books of J. Davidson, antique dealer, and then prepare a trial balance and a trading and profit and loss account for the month of January 19–3 and a balance sheet as at 31 January 19–3.

19–3

Jan 2 Paid £50 000 into a business bank account
    3 Bought shop premises £20 000 paid by cheque
    5 Bought shop fittings paid by cheque £2500
    9 Bought goods for resale £14 000 paid by cheque
  10 Withdrew £100 cash from bank
  12 Bought stationery paid in cash £20
  16 Bought a van paid by cheque £2500
  19 Sold goods for £8500 received payment by cheque
  23 Paid petrol bill for van £15 by cheque.
  26 Sold goods on credit to N. Mistry £3500
  28 Paid for shop cleaning £20 cash
  31 Received cheque from N. Mistry for £2000 in part payment of his account

Stock in hand at cost price was valued at £4000 on 31 January.

13 Arthur Smith has the following balances remaining in his books after preparing his profit and loss account for the year ended 31 December 19–7.
Draw up his balance sheet in good style to show his working capital and capital employed.

	£		£
Stock	4710	Debtors	6350
Arrears	230	Accruals	390
Advances	150	Prepayments	80
Creditors	7470	Motor vehicles (cost)	7260
Capital	36 930	Premises	25 490
Plant and equip(cost)	4200	Provision for bad debts	170
Depreciation P/E	1800	Net loss	2120
Depreciation M/V	2350	Drawings	4680
Bank overdraft	480	Cash	120
Bank deposit	5200	Loan outstanding	10 700

14 Prepare the balance sheet for Wendy Johnson-Bratt, Unit 10, Question 12.

15 Show the balance sheet entries at the end of the year resulting from the following situations. Ignore the effect on profits.
  a) Motor vehicles at cost at start of year £25 400
    Accumulated depreciation for vehicles at start of year £4200
    Cost of vehicle purchased during the year £6300
    Profit and loss charge for depreciation of motor vehicles £5500
  b) Total debtors at end of year £62 700
    Bad debt not yet written off £1300
    Provision for doubtful debts at start of year £2700
    Provision at end of year to be 5% of debtors
  c) Stocks at start of year £3700
    Purchases during the year £128 954
    Stocks at end of year £4265
  d) Gross profit for the year £27 600
    Net profit for the year £10 400

Capital at start of year £35 300
Additional capital brought in during the year £5000
Drawings made during the year £8700
Indicate in which section of the balance sheet each of the above entries would be included.

16 The following balances were extracted from the ledger of Arthur Holland on 30 June 19–6. Prepare his trading and profit and loss account and balance sheet for the year ending 30 June 19–6.

	Dr £	Cr £
Capital		90 020
Sales		130 720
Drawings	8228	
Stock	8020	
Purchases	85 584	
Wages	24 582	
Carriage outwards	1290	
Plant and machinery	40 350	
Bank	4216	
Fixtures and fittings	24 000	
Debtors	25 750	
Creditors		11 900
General expenses	5400	
Advertising	2400	
Rent and rates	2820	

Stock at 30 June 19–6 was valued at £7410. The general expenses balance includes £136 paid in advance.

17 From the following information prepare M. Goodley's balance sheet at 31 March 19–7.
Balances as at 31 March 19–7:

	£
Capital	61 188
Premises (cost)	32 000
Fixtures and fittings (cost)	10 000
Plant and machinery (cost)	14 800
Debtors	18 340
Bank	2540
Cash	60
Creditors	11 950
Drawings	3600

Additional information:

	£
Stock at 31 March 19–7	5250
Net profit for the year	10 440
Prepayments on insurance	120
Wages outstanding	235

Provision for bad debts 5%
Depreciation: Fixtures and fittings 5%
                    Plant and machinery 10%

18 Brian Wyse — Newsagent

Using the trial balance and notes at the end of the second year of trading for Brian Wyse (as shown in Unit 10) draw up his balance sheet on that date.

When you have completed the balance sheet, look at the Capital section. Has Brian been sensible in the level of drawings he has been taking out of the business in this year?

Now, consider his working capital. Are there likely to be any problems here, or is Brian using his resources wisely?

Answers

7 a) 1 £2000
   2 £1600
   3 £1280
   b) Net Book Value £5120
   c) Under-Depreciation
   d) £1120 charged as an expense to profit and loss.

8 Profit and loss: £500 Increase in Provision
   Balance sheet: Debtors £46 500

9 Net worth/capital £20 000

10 Net worth/capital employed £20 499

12 Trial balance totals   £62 000
   Gross profit   £2000
   Net profit   £1945
   Net worth/capital employed £51945

18 Brian Wyse — Newsagent

Brian Wyse's Balance Sheet on 30 April 19—0

			£
Capital	Opening Balance		5000
	Add Net profit		4145
			9145

			£	
	Less Drawings	Cash	6365	
		Stock	500	(6865)

	Closing balance	2280
Long-term liabilities: Loan		2000
		4280

Capital employed
Represented by:

	Cost	Depreciation	NBV
Fixed Assets			£
Motor Van	2000	400	1600

Current Assets

	£
Stock	2500
Debtors	150
Prepayments	230
Bank	2000
	4880

***Less* Current Liabilities**

	£	£	£
Creditors	2100		
Accruals	100	(2,200)	2680
Net worth			4280

Brian Wyse has taken out far too much capital during the year as his closing balance is less than half the opening balance. In a relatively new enterprise, capital needs to be increased in order to help the business grow and he has not been wise!

The working capital ratio is roughly 2:1 — the ideal situation. However, almost half his current assets are in the form of cash, which could perhaps be used to generate more business.

Unit 12

Final Accounts and Income And Expenditure Accounts

At the end of this unit you will be able to:

1 Appreciate how the preparation of final accounts conforms to the double-entry principles

2 Prepare final accounts from the trial balance

3 Understand the accounting for non profit-making organisations.

Final Accounts: Completing the Double-entry

In Unit 10, page 192 it was explained that although we are using the modern 'vertical presentation' of final accounts, all the entries still conform with basic double-entry principles.

At the end of an accounting period the accounts relating to revenue expenditure or receipts are closed off and the balances on these accounts transferred to the trading account or the profit and loss account. The accounts will then be re-opened to start the next accounting period.

Example

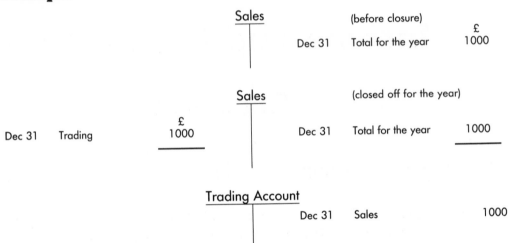

	Sales	(before closure)
		£
	Dec 31 Total for the year	1000

	Sales	(closed off for the year)
	£	
Dec 31 Trading 1000	Dec 31 Total for the year	1000

Trading Account

Dec 31   Sales   1000

Let us compare a trading and profit and loss account displayed in vertical presentation with the same figures shown in the traditional double-entry style:

J. Smith's Trading and Profit and Loss Account
for the year ending 31 December 19–2

		£	£	£
Sales				1000
Less Returns				(100)
				(900)
Turnover				
Less Cost of sales			£	
Opening stock		£	900	
Add Purchases		800		
Less Returns		(200)	600	
			1500	
Less Stock at end			(1000)	(500)
Gross profit				400
Rent receivable				50
				450

Less Overheads		
Administration	100	
Selling and distribution	60	
Financial	140	(300)
Net profit		150

Trading Account

	£		£
Opening stock	900	Sales	1000
Purchases	800	*Less* Returns	(100)
	1700	Net sales	900
Less Returns	(200)		
	1500		
Less Closing stock	(1000)		
Cost of sales	500		
Gross profit (balance	400		
transferred to			
profit and loss)	900		900

You will note that instead of debiting the trading account with £100 sales returns, we have deducted this figure from the credit side. This is done simply to give a clear picture of the actual sales for the year. Purchase returns and closing stock are also shown as deductions for the same reason.

Profit and Loss Account

	£		£
Administration	100	Gross profit	400
Selling and			
Distribution	60	Rent receivable	50
Financial	140		
Net profit (balance	150		
transferred to			
capital account)			
	450		450

The profit of the business belongs to the proprietor and the net profit figure is, therefore, transferred to the proprietor's account – the capital account. At the end of the accounting period, the drawings account will also be closed off and the balance transferred to the capital account.

Capital

		£			£
Dec 31	Drawings	200	Dec 31	Balance b/f	3000
	Balance c/d	2950		Profit and loss	150
		3150			3150
			Jan 1	Balance b/d	2950

The transfer of the net profit to the capital account will still need to be done when vertical presentation is used and, as shown in Unit 11, these changes to the proprietor's capital are also detailed in the balance sheet.

It is important to remember that the balance sheet is not an account but a *statement* showing the assets and liabilities of the business at a certain point in time. The entries in the balance sheet are the balances of accounts relating to capital expenditure and receipts. These accounts are *not* closed off.

Golden Rules for Preparing Final Accounts (including Adjustments)

The ledger is the summary of the firm's financial history over a period (usually a year) and from this we prepare a trial balance.
From the trial balance, and using additional information i.e. accruals etc. which are year-end adjustments shown as notes to the trial balance, we prepare the final accounts.

Stages in Preparation

Look down the trial balance and differentiate between capital and revenue items. Decide whether each item is put in the balance sheet, trading or profit and loss account and write B/S, T or P/L against each one.

It is important to remember that, in final accounts:

> **Trial Balance Items appear once only**
> *but*
> **Notes appear twice**

The reason for this is that these entries have not yet been included in the books and so both aspects must be shown. As we are concerned with double-entry they need to be used *twice*. The notes always indicate adjustments *to be done* and are an indication that *two* entries are needed.

Tick off each item in the trial balance as it is used in the final accounts.
Let us take another look at the way certain items are treated in the final accounts:

Returns in (Sales returns) must be deducted from the sales figure in the trading account.

Returns out (Purchases returns) must be deducted from the purchases figure.

Carriage in (Delivery expenses incurred in purchasing goods for re-sale) increases the cost of purchases and must be added in the trading account.

Carriage out (Delivery expenses incurred by a business in order to achieve sales) is an expense of the business and must be charged to the profit and loss account. It must never be added to the sales figure as it clearly does not increase income.

Discount Received is a revenue receipt and is added to the gross profit.

Discount Allowed is an expense.

It should be noted that, whereas all the final accounts we have looked at consist of a trading and profit and loss account and balance sheet, the final accounts of a professional firm (doctors, dentists, solicitors, etc.) would not include a trading account. In this instance, the profit and loss account (or revenue account) would comprise 'fees' less 'expenses'.

To sum up, here is an example of the preparation of final accounts for you to follow:

L. Hawke's Trial Balance
on 31 December 19–3

	£	£
Premises	15 000	
Debtors	6271	
Creditors		4137
Purchases	62 127	
Sales		82 902
Discount received		638
Discount allowed	457	
Vehicles	8100	
Stock	4619	
Capital		22 672
Lighting and heating	395	
Rates	517	
Telephone	252	
Drawings	1000	
Interest		84
Cash in hand	94	
Bank		391
Wages	6147	
Salaries	4016	
Shop equipment	587	
Garage rent	501	
Vehicle expenses	819	
Returns outwards		175
Returns inwards	97	
	110 999	110 999

The above trial balance was extracted from the books of L. Hawke on 31 December 19–3. We can draw up a trading account and profit and loss account for the year to that date, together with the appropriate balance sheet, taking into account the following matters:

- Stock in hand at 31 December 19–3 was valued at £4902.
- Prepayments of £90 had been made on rates.
- Accruals of £80 had been built up on garage rent.
- Depreciation on shop equipment to be provided for at 10% and vehicles at 25% per annum.
- Provision for bad debts to be 5% of the debtors.

L. Hawke's Trading and Profit and Loss Account
for the year ended 31 December 19–3

	£	£	£
Sales		82 902	
Less Returns inwards		(97)	82 805
Less Cost of sales			
Stock at 1 January 19–3		4619	
Add Purchases	62 127		
Less Returns outwards	(75)	61 952	
		66 571	
Less Stock at 31 December 19–3		(4902)	61 669
Gross Profit			21 136
Add			
Discount received		638	
Interest		84	722
			21 858
Less Expenses			
Wages		6147	
Salaries		4016	
Vehicle expenses		819	
Garage rent	501		
(Accrual)	80	581	
Discount allowed		457	
Rates	517		
(Prepayment)	(90)	427	
Lighting and heating		395	
Telephone		252	
Provision for bad debts		314	
Depreciation: vehicles	2025		
	59	2084	(15 492)
Net Profit			6366

L. Hawke's Balance Sheet
on 31 December 19–3

Fixed assets:	Cost £	Depreciation £	Net Book Value £
Premises	15 000	–	15 000
Vehicles	8100	2025	6075
Shop equipment	587	59	528
	23 687	2084	21 603

Add Current assets				
Stock		4902		
Debtors	6271			
Less Provision for				
bad debts	(314)	5957		
Prepayments		90		
Cash		94	11 043	
Less Current liabilities				
Creditors		4137		
Accruals		80		
Bank overdraft		391	(4608)	6435
				28 038

Financed by:	
Capital	
Opening balance	22 672
Net profit for the year	6366
	29 038
Less Drawings	(1000)
	28 038

Non Profit-Making Organisations

We will now look at the accounts kept by clubs and charities. Clubs are normally founded for the interest, social or sporting activities of its members, whereas charities are normally founded for the assistance of others.

Their rules generally provide that a statement of the financial transactions of the organisation should be presented to members each year. Because clubs and charities are non profit-making, they do not prepare a profit and loss account. Their accounts will consist of figures explained under the headings below.

Receipts and Payments Account

Because clubs do not normally have a great number of transactions (though this clearly depends upon the size of the organisation) they do not keep a ledger but prepare the final accounts directly from a cash book or receipts and payments account. As with the cash book of a profit-making organisation, the receipts and payments account (or book) will record *cash transactions* only (including cheques, standing orders, etc.) and will not include any credit transactions that take place within the accounting period. If a receipts and payments account is used *in addition to* a cash book, it will only show the totals of each type of income or expense.

Example

Globetrotters' Cycle Club
Receipts and Payments Account
for Year Ended 30 November 1987

19–6		£	19–7		£
Dec 1	Balance b/f	206	Nov 30	Rent	900
19–7					
Nov 30	Subscriptions	1340		Postage	64
	Refreshment sales	650		Travel	26
	Film receipts	500		Miscellaneous	62
	Miscellaneous	104		Refreshment costs	300
				Film hire	220
				Light and heat	200
					1772
			Nov 30	Balance c/f	1028
		2800			2800
Dec 1	Balance b/f	1028			

Income and Expenditure Account

This account is the equivalent of a trading organisation's profit and loss account. Many organisations show it as a ledger account with the income on the right hand side of the page and the expenses on the left-hand side. As clubs and charities are non profit-making, any 'difference' in this account is referred to as a 'surplus' if the income exceeds the expenditure, or a 'deficit' if the expenditure exceeds the income.

Any trading activities carried on specifically to make a profit (such as a bar) should be shown as a separate trading account. The profit from such a trading account is then transferred to the income and expenditure account, as for example, 'Bar Profits'.

As in the case of a trading organisation's profit and loss account, the income and expenditure account should reflect only the income and expenses relating to the period being accounted for, and some year end adjustments will normally be necessary. If, for example, the subscriptions of a club include £60 relating to the following year then this amount is deducted from the subscriptions total recorded in the receipts and payments account.

It is also customary in an income and expenditure account to show the net effect of items involving both income and expenditure. For example, sale of refreshments *less* the cost of these refreshments would be included under income, and telephone charges *less* any receipts for telephone calls would be included under expenditure.

Example

Income and Expenditure Account
for Year Ended 30 November 19–7

Income		£	£
	Subscriptions		1340
	Sale of refreshments	650	
	Less Expenses	(300)	350
	Film admission charges	500	
	Less Hire charges	(220)	280
	Miscellaneous		104
			2074
Less			
Expenditure			
	Rent and rates	900	
	Light and heat	200	
	Postage	64	
	Travelling	26	
	Miscellaneous	62	
	Depreciation	266	(1518)
	Surplus for the year		556

Balance Sheet

This is similar to that of a trading organisation with the following exceptions:
- Capital may be referred to as **The Accumulated Fund**

- Profits or losses are called **Surpluses** or **Deficits.**

As for a trading organisation, year end adjustments will need to be shown in the balance sheet.

Example

Balance Sheet on 30 November 19–7

	Cost £	Depreciation £	NBV £
Fixed assets:			
Equipment	1330	266	1064
Current assets:			
Cash			1028
			2092
Accumulated fund			1536
Add Surplus			556
			2092

Notes • The cash balance is the closing balance from the receipts and payments account.

• The accumulated fund will always equal assets less any liabilities. In this case it is made up of the cost of the equipment plus the opening balance from the receipts and payments account.

Questions

1 If the purchase of a fixed asset was shown as a purchase, would this affect the gross profit? If so, would the gross profit be understated or overstated?

2 Will capital be increased or decreased if the business makes a loss?

3 If a business hires machinery, will the value of that machinery be shown in the balance sheet?

4 If a business has some liabilities, will the proprietor's capital be more or less than the total assets?

5 Non profit-making organisations do not have a profit and loss account – what do they have instead?

6 Explain the meaning of a 'Surplus' of funds in a non-profit making organisation.

7 A summary of the Downtown Football Club receipts and payments account is shown below, together with various year end notes. Prepare an income and expenditure account and balance sheet.

Receipts and Payments

19–7	£		£
Members' subscriptions	2120	Purchase of equipment	1700
Collections at matches	897	Rent for football pitch	520
Sale of refreshments	540	Secretary's expenses	475
		Printing and stationery	193
		Repairs to equipment	86
		Footballs and strip	234
		Purchase of refreshments	211
		General expenses	79
		Balance 31 December c/d	59
	3557		3557

Note • The subscriptions include £105 for 19–8 (the following year).
• Depreciation is to be charged on equipment at 10% per annum; footballs and strip to be written off over two years.
• General expenses include £25 paid in advance for insurance.

8 The Quick-Fire Rifle Club's year ends on the 31 December each year. From the following receipts and payments account you are required to prepare an income and expenditure account and balance sheet for the year ended 31 December 19–7.

	Receipts			Payments	
19–7		£	19–7		£
Jan 1	Balance b/f	570	Dec 31	Ammunition purchases	600
Dec 31	Membership subs.	2750		Rates	660
	Ammunition sales	680		Rifles	1235
	Club visits	750		Electricity	350

Licences		100
Travel to clubs		700
Trophies		125
Maintenance & repairs		365
		4135
Dec 31 Balance c/f		615
	4750	4750

19–8
Jan 1 Balance b/f 615

Additional Information: £
Club assets at 31 December 19–6   Premises   15 000
                                   Rifles   4900
                                   Fixtures & fittings 1200
Depreciation as at 31 December 19–6 Rifles   980
                                   Fixtures & fittings   120

Membership fees include £150 paid in advance.
Rates include £120 brought forward from the previous year. This year they were paid in two equal instalments on the 1 April and 1 October.
The electricity account for December has not been received and is estimated at £40.
Depreciation is charged at 20% per annum on rifles and 10% per annum on fixtures and fittings.

9   From the following trial balance and adjustment notes, prepare the trading and profit and loss account and balance sheet for Patrick James for the year ending 31 December 19–.

Trial Balance as at 31–December 19–1

	DR £	CR £
Cash in hand	135	
Cash at bank	12 325	
Purchases	41 240	
Sales		68 060
Returns in and out	560	240
Stock at 1 January 19–1	3900	
Wages	5150	
Light and heat	2100	
Rent receivable		650
Telephone	600	
Insurance	1250	
Motor vehicles	6250	
Land and buildings	20 000	

Plant and machinery	7000	
Bank loan		15 000
Interest on bank loan	750	
Capital		17 310
	101 260	101 260

Stock was valued at £6250 as at 31 December 19–1.
Insurance amounting to £250 has been paid in advance.
Interest due on the bank loan amounts to £150.

10 From the details given for Danny Jutz, draw up his drawings and capital accounts as they would appear in the ledger and show how this information would be presented on the balance sheet.

> Net profit for the year £15 190
> Cash withdrawn for his own use £8520
> Goods taken from stock £410
> Opening balance of capital £54 000
> Competition Cash Prize paid into the business £10 000

Furthermore, it is agreed that 50% of his motor expenses are for his own private use. The total for these expenses is £1200.

11 St Hilda's Social Club provides the following information:

		£
Balances at 1 Jan 19–2	Accumulated fund	5000
	Bar stocks	2300
	Bar creditors	1800
	Equipment (NBV)	4300
	Bank	200

Cash Book Summary

19–2		£			£
Jan 1	Balance b/f	200	Dec 31	Bar wages	3240
Dec 31	Subscriptions	4230		Bar creditors	17 200
	Donations	1170		Whist drive expenses	330
	Bar takings	22 605		Disco fees	270
	Whist drives	310		Heating & lighting	460
	Disco	720		Equipment	2300
				Insurance & telephones	290
				Equipment repairs	160
				Rent	4020
				Balance c/d	965
		29 235			29 235

		£
Balances at 31 December:	Bar stocks	3500
	Bar creditors	2400
	Rent overpaid	140

Equipment is to be depreciated at 10% of net book value.
You are required to prepare the:

a) Bar creditors control account to calculate purchases for the year
b) Bar trading account to show the net bar profit
c) Income and expenditure account showing net figures wherever appropriate
d) Balance sheet on 31 December.

12 Ivor Wrench runs his own plumbing business. All goods purchased are for use on jobs undertaken so are included in his total charges. Using the following information, draw up his profit and loss account and balance sheet.

Trial Balance on 30 April 10–1

	£	£
Capital		25 000
Creditors		500
Bank	600	
Purchase of materials	2420	
Receipts for work undertaken		21 300
Stock of materials	250	
Wages for staff	7680	
Drawings	8350	
Heating & lighting	2110	
Motor vehicle	4800	
Tools and equipment	1200	
Repairs to equipment	85	
Motor expenses	1640	
Postage and telephones	415	
Advertising and stationery	870	
Mortgage interest	505	
Mortgage outstanding		8500
Premises	23 100	
Accountant's fees	1275	
	55 300	55 300

Note • Stock of materials on hand 30 April 19–1 £370
• Amounts still owed by customers £1785
• Wages not yet paid £310
• Depreciation on motor vehicles at 20%, tools and equipment at 40%

13 From the following receipts and payments account of the Westlea Sports and Social Club prepare the bar trading account and the income and expenditure account for the year ended 31 December 19–6.

Receipts		Payments	
19–6	£		£
Jan 1 Balance b/f	5098	Dec 31 Bar steward's salary	7000
Dec 31 Subscriptions	14 235	Rent and rates	6207

Annual dinner:	
Ticket sales	2565
Bar takings	17230
Hire of hall	2708

Heating and light	1685
Secretary's expenses	750
Bar purchases	8862
New furniture and fittings	4220
Repairs and maintenance	2675
Insurance	830
Annual Dinner expenses	2175
Balance c/f	7432

41836	41836

19–7
Jan 1 Balance b/f   7432

Note • Bar stocks at 1 January 19–6   £1882
      Bar stocks at 31 December 19–6   £1988

     • Rates prepaid   £52

     • Subscriptions include £555 paid in advance

14 The following balance sheet was prepared by James Watkins at 31 December 19–8.

	Cost £	Dep'n £	N B V £
Fixed assets			
Fixtures and fittings	2460	246	2214
Motor vehicle	6000	1200	4800
	8460	1446	7014
Current assets			
Stock		8460	
Debtors		11 196	
Bank		520	
Cash		120	
		20 296	
Less Current Liabilities			
Creditors	10 360		
Accruals	120	(10 480)	9816
			16 830
Financed by:			
Capital			16 000
Add Net profit			3220
			19 220
Less Drawings			(2390)
			16 830

After the above balance sheet was prepared, the following errors and omissions were discovered:

- An invoice for £224 relating to goods sold in December had been omitted
- The bank statement for December was received showing bank charges of £36
- Insurance of £320 paid on 1 April 19—8 for the forthcoming 12 months had been debited in total to the profit and loss account
- Stock had been under-valued by £253.

Draw up:
a) A statement showing the corrected net profit.
b) A revised balance sheet.

15   Brian Wyse — Newsagent

As Brian is now an established successful businessman, he has been elected Honorary Treasurer for his local church. At the end of the year he produces this cash book summary:

St Joseph's Cash Book

	£		£
Balance 1 January b/d	125		
Weekly collection	2500	Repairs to equipment	195
Covenants	12 250	Building maintenance	2520
Jumble sales takings	572	Minister's stipend	5500
Whist Drive entrance fee	123	Caretaker's wages	2790
Summer Fete income	791	Heating, lighting and cleaning	4210
Balance 31 December c/d	156	Organ repairs	860
		Refreshments:	
		Whist Drives	87
		Fete	35
		Printing church magazine	320
	16 517		16 517

Brian has also made the following notes:
- The equipment had no re-sale value so does not need to be depreciated
- A bill of £120 for building repairs is still unpaid
- Covenants paid by banker's order have not yet appeared on the bank statement £75
- An annual maintenance contract on the boiler for £120 has been paid for the next twelve months.

Draw up an income and expenditure account showing *net* income for the Whist Drives and Fete.

What is the significance of the closing balance in the cash book?

Answers

7 Surplus income/expenditure £1626
Net worth/Accumulated fund £1626

8 Deficit for year £122
Net worth/Accumulated fund £20 448

9 Net profit £19 750
Net worth/Capital employed £52 060

---

15 Brian Wyse – Newsagent

St Joseph's Income and Expenditure Account for the year ended 31 December 19–

		£
Income		
Covenants as cash book		12 250
not yet shown on statement		75
		12 325
Collections		2500
Jumble sales		572
Proceeds of Whist Drives	£	
Entrance fees	123	
Less Cost of refreshments	(87)	36
Proceeds of Summer Fete	791	
Less Cost of refreshments	(35)	756
		16 189
Less **Expenditure**		
Minister's stipend		5500
Caretaker's wages	£	2790
Heat, light and cleaning	4210	
Less prepayment on boiler contract	(120)	4090
Building maintenance	2520	
Accrual	120	2640
Organ repairs		860
Church magazine		320
Equipment repairs		195	16 395
Excess of expenditure over income		206

The **credit** balance in the cash book indicates an **overdraft**.

Unit 13

Manufacturing Accounts

At the end of this unit you will be able to:

1 Appreciate the need for manufacturing accounts

2 Prepare a manufacturing account

3 Understand the different types of expense.

The Manufacturing Account

So far in our studies we have dealt with businesses which buy stock for re-sale. This is reflected in the trading account, which shows the net turnover for a period and the cost of sales for the same time. However, as you can appreciate, there are many businesses of all sizes which are engaged in making goods. These manufactured goods are then sold, either directly to the public or to another company, a wholesaler or retailer, or for further processing, or a mixture of all of these.

In order to find out how much it has cost to produce our finished goods it is necessary to draw up a Manufacturing Account.

In order to calculate the total cost of producing goods over a period of time, usually a year, we need to include all the costs associated with the factory. Not only will these be such obvious items as raw materials and the labour directly involved in the finished articles, but also all the overheads, such as power, depreciation of the plant and machinery and other, indirect, labour costs: supervisors and cleaners, production and quality control, packaging and canteen staff. It should be noted that manufacturing accounts are *not* obligatory. Limited companies, for example, normally prepare trading and profit and loss accounts for publication and keep their manufacturing accounts purely for internal information and control purposes.

For the purposes of *costing* to help management keep control of expenses (and, therefore, profits) the expenditure must be classified into Prime Costs, Factory Overheads, and Factory Cost of Finished Goods.

Prime Costs

These are expenses which can be *directly* identified with a particular unit of production. For instance, if a furniture maker produces a table we can calculate exactly how much wood has been used, any special fittings, and how much time has been spent in the process by the craftsman. So, generally speaking, we can show **direct materials** and

direct labour as the main ingredients in prime costs. There may also be other **direct expenses** – these could include royalties applied to each unit produced, or hire of equipment needed for a special job.

As with the cost of sales in the trading account, in order to arrive at the true cost of direct materials used we have to include any opening or closing stocks of raw materials. There may also be other costs such as carriage, or freight and insurance associated with this item.

So, just like the calculation of cost of sales, the total cost of raw materials consumed in a period is arrived at by:

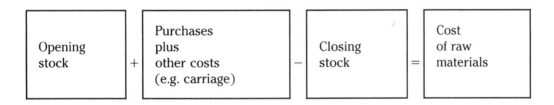

Factory Overheads

These will be all the other costs of running the manufacturing part of a business. Included in these will be **indirect wages and salaries** for people employed in the factory, but not directly engaged in the production process (as mentioned earlier). There may also be **indirect materials**, which are not worth costing out to each unit produced. Indirect materials are such things as cutting oils, cleaning rags, glue, screws and other small items. Note, however, that this does not mean that such materials may not be subject to normal stock control procedures.

Some costs, for instance rent and rates, heating and lighting and telephones may cover the whole business, including administration, sales and transport. In this case we have to *apportion* the costs on some realistic basis. For instance, rent and rates are usually apportioned on the basis of the floor area of each department. By apportioned we mean shared out in a fair way.

Factory Cost of Finished Goods

Any stocks of completed units, which are, therefore, available for sale, are shown in the trading account. These take the place of the normal stocks of purchases in a retail business.

Many factories are organised in a logical way, which is a practical reflection of the order in which the accounts are prepared. Raw materials and any purchases of finished goods (such as components or special fittings) come in at one end of the factory, go through the manufacturing process on a production line and are then stored in a warehouse at the other end ready for despatch to the customer.

When stocks are valued at the end of the year, there will probably be some units in the factory which are only partly completed. These are called **Work In Progress (WIP)**. To calculate the total cost of production of all goods completed in the period we have to make an adjustment in the manufacturing account for the opening and closing stocks (just like the cost of sales calculation, again).

Non-Manufacturing Costs

All the non-manufacturing costs of a business are shown in either the trading or the profit and loss account, just as before. The only difference is the way in which the items are grouped together.

Generally, there are three main headings for these:

Administration Costs
These include: staff salaries; office expenses; depreciation of office machinery and furniture.

Selling and Distribution Costs
These include: salesmen's salaries and commission; carriage out; warehousing of finished goods; transport; advertising.

Financial Costs
These include: discounts allowed; bank charges; loan interest.

Consider the following diagram:

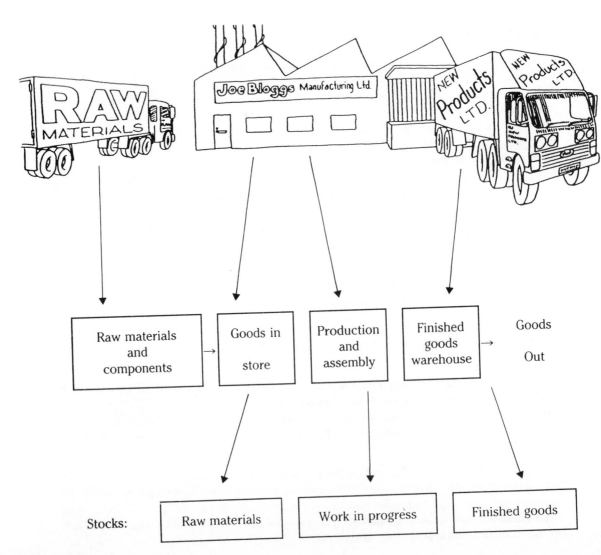

Now we can look at an example of a manufacturing account.
Remember that we would find all the following figures in a trial balance or the notes.

Example

Bogit Manufacturing Account for the year ended 31 December 19–7

		£	£
Raw Materials	Opening Stock		6000
	Add Purchases	22 500	
	Carriage in	1200	23 700
			29 700
	Less Closing stock		(7100)
Direct materials consumed			22 600
Direct wages			12 300
Direct expenses: Royalties			1200
Prime cost			36 100
Factory Overheads			
Indirect wages		11 200	
Rent and rates		5400	
Power, heat and light		6300	
Indirect materials		1800	
Loose tools		1700	
General expenses		2400	
Depreciation of plant		5900	34 700
			70 800
Add Work in progress at start			3100
			73 900
Less Work in progress at end			(4200)
Cost of production			69 700

This then leads straight into the trading account and then the profit and loss, in the normal way; the cost of production figure, however, replaces the 'purchases' figure. Remember, though, there may also be purchases of finished goods to be included in the trading account.

As this information is usually extracted from a trial balance, the figures may be subject to all the year end adjustments you have already seen in previous units, and treated accordingly.

Transfer at Market Value

Sometimes a business wants to know how much of the gross profit is earned by the production side and how much by actually selling the goods. In this case, the estimated gross profit is *added* to the cost of production figure to arrive at a higher value to be transferred to the trading account. It is usually shown as **Goods Transferred at Market Value.**

When the profit and loss account is prepared it will now show **two** gross profit figures, one for manufacturing and one for trading. This will have no effect on the final net profit, but does help management to make decisions about the value to the business of the various activities. This can be further modified if the final accounts (usually the manufacturing and trading) are prepared either on a departmental basis, or for each type of product. This, again, is part of the function of cost accounting.

When final accounts are prepared, it is always necessary to carefully observe the 'prudence' concept of accountancy, which stipulates that profits must not be anticipated by recording them prematurely. Thus, when the transfer price of the finished goods to the trading account exceeds their cost of production, it is necessary to take into account the unrealised profit element in the opening and closing stock figures.

Example

Bogit Manufacturing, Trading and Profit and Loss Account for the year ended 31 December 19–7

Details as for previous example.

	£	£
Cost of production		69 700
Gross profit c/d		10 000
		79 700
Transfer at market value c/d		79 700
		125 000
Sales		
Less Cost of sales		
Opening stock of finished goods	10 600	
Goods transferred at market value b/d	79 700	
	90 300	
Less Closing stock of finished goods	(11 200)	(79 100)
Gross profit on trading		45 900
Gross profit on manufacturing b/d		10 000
		55 900
Total		
Less Expenses		
Administration	9300	
Selling and distribution	6500	
Financial	1100	(16 900)
Net profit		39 000

The balance sheet is then completed in the usual way, except that there will now be **three** separate stock figures: raw materials, work in progress and finished goods.

Let us assume that in year ending 31 December 19–7, their first year of trading, a manufacturing firm decides to transfer their completed goods from their factory to their sales outlets, at an increase of 10% over the cost of production. (They have ascertained that this would be the normal cost of purchasing these goods, at trade price, from outside suppliers.)

At the end of their first year of manufacturing and trading the closing stock of goods in their sales outlets is valued at £9900. As these goods have been transferred at a mark up of 10%, there is an unrealised profit element of £900 in this figure. The true and fair value which must appear in the balance sheet is £9000.

A **Provision for Unrealised Profit on Stock** account is opened in the general ledger. The required accounting entries are:

		£
Debit	Profit and loss account	900
Credit	Provision for unrealised profit on stock account	900

This reduces the net profit figure by £900.
The balance sheet entry would be:

Balance Sheet As At 31 December 19–7 (Extract Only)

	£	£
Current assets		
Closing stocks		
Finished goods	9900	
Less Provision for unrealised profit	(900)	9000

In the general ledger:

Provision For Unrealised Profit On Stock Account

19–7		£			£
Dec 31	Balance c/d	900	Dec 31 Profit and loss	900
19–8			Jan 1 Balance b/d	900

At the start of the second year of manufacturing and trading (year ending 31 December 19–8), the firm's general ledger will contain the above Provision For Unrealised Profit On Stock account, which is still open.

At the end of this second year, the closing stock of goods in the firm's sales outlets is valued at £11 000. As these goods have been transferred at a mark up of 10%, their true and fair value for the balance sheet entry is £10 000 (i.e. £10 000 + 10% mark up = £11 000). Provision required £1000.

However, as we already have a provision for unrealised profit of £900 brought forward from last year, we will only require a further £100 provision to reach a balance of £1000.

The required accounting entries to increase the provision are:

		£
Debit	Profit and loss account	100
Credit	Provision for unrealised profit on stock account	100

Notice that this is exactly the same as increasing a provision for bad debts or depreciation. The balance sheet entry would be:

Balance Sheet as at 31 December 19–8 (Extract Only)

	£	£
Current Assets		
Stocks		
Finished goods	11000	
Less Provision for unrealised profit	(1000)	10 000

In the general ledger:

Provision for Unrealised Profit on Stock

		£				£
19–8						
Dec 31	Balance c/d	1000	Jan 1	Balance b/d	900
			Dec 31	Profit and loss	100
		———				———
		1000				1000
19–9			Jan 1	Balance b/d	1000

This Provision for Unrealised Profit on Stock account will continue to be adjusted at the end of each accounting year to conform with the new closing stock valuation of the finished goods.

Finally, before we work through a full set of final accounts, let us consider carefully the accounting entries necessary when we discover, at the end of an accounting period, that we must reduce an existing provision for unrealised profit.

If, at the end of the third year (year ending 31 December 19–9) the closing stock of finished goods is valued at £8800 (including the mark up of 10%) the provision for unrealised profit required will now be only £800.

As this provision account is already open in the general ledger with a credit balance of £1000, the required accounting entries are:

		£
Debit	Provision for unrealised profit on stock account	200
Credit	Profit and loss account	200

The profit and loss account entry will appear as an addition for **Reduced Provision for Unrealised Profit** £200, thus *increasing* the net profit figure by £200.
The balance sheet entry will be:

Balance Sheet as at 31 December 19–9 (Extract Only)

	£	£
Current Assets		
Stocks		
Finished goods	8800	
Less Provision for unrealised profit	(800)	8000

In the general ledger:

Provision for Unrealised Profit on Stock Account

		£				£
19–9						
Dec 31	Profit and loss	200	Jan 1	Balance b/d	1000
Dec 31	Balance c/d	800				
		———				———
		1000				1000
19–0			Jan 1	Balance b/d	800

We can now look at an example of a complete set of final accounts:

G. Brown's Trial Balance on 31 March 19–7

	£	£
Stocks Raw materials	3100	
Finished goods	5500	
Work in progress	1190	
Wages (direct 50%)	27 600	
Royalties	750	
Carriage in	320	
Purchases of raw materials	31 850	
Production machinery (at cost)	32 000	
Accounting machinery (at cost)	5600	
General factory expenses	1400	
Electricity	2400	
Factory power	3250	
Administrative salaries	12 600	
Salesmen's salaries	9480	
Commission on sales	2700	
Rent	3600	
Insurance	1200	
General administration expenses	850	
Bank charges	1100	
Discounts allowed	900	
Carriage outwards	840	
Sales		125 000
Debtors/creditors	15 970	9700
Bank	2400	
Cash	600	
Drawings	3000	
Capital		30 000
Provision for depreciation:		
Production		4000
Accounting machinery		1000
Provision for unrealised profit on stock		500
	170 200	170 200

Note • Closing stock of raw materials   £4200
      Finished goods   £6600
      Work in progress   £2160

Notes • Electricity, rent and insurance are to be apportioned: factory ¾, administration ¼.

• Depreciation on machinery at 10% per annum on cost.

• Finished goods transferred at 10% mark-up.

• General administration expenses accrued £170.

From the trial balance on the previous page and notes (the year end adjustments) we can prepare the manufacturing, trading and profit and loss accounts and the balance sheet.

G. Brown's Manufacturing, Trading and Profit and Loss Account for the year ended 31 March 19–7

		£	£
Raw materials	Opening stock		3100
	Purchases	31 850	
	Add Carriage in	320	32 170
			35 270
	Less Closing stock		(4200)
			31 070
Raw materials consumed			31 070
Direct wages (50%)			13 800
Direct expenses (Royalties)			750
Prime cost			45 620
Factory overheads:			
Indirect wages (50%)		13 800	
Power		3250	
Rent (¾)		2700	
Insurance (¾)		900	
Electricity (¾)		1800	
General factory expenses		1400	
Depreciation on machinery (10% of 32000)		3200	27 050
Factory cost			72670
Add Work in progress at start			1190
			73 860
Less Work in progress at end			(2160)
Cost of production			71 700
Gross Manufacturing Profit (10%) c/d			7170
Market value of goods produced c/d			78 870
			125 000
Sales			
Less Cost of sales:			
Opening stock finished goods		5500	
Add Market value of goods produced b/d		78 870	
		84 370	
Less Closing stock of finished goods		(6600)	(77 770)
Gross profit on trading			47 230
Gross profit on manufacturing b/d			7170
Total gross profit c/f			54 400

Administration Expenses:	£	£	£
Salaries		12 600	
Rent (¼)		900	
Insurance (¼)		300	
Electricity (¼)		600	
General	850		
Plus Accrual	170	1020	
Depreciation on machinery (10% of 5600)		560	
		15 980	

Selling and Distribution:			
Salaries	9480		
Commission	2700		
Carriage out	840	13 020	

Financial:			
Bank charges	1100		
Discount allowed	900	2000	

Increased provision for unrealised profit		100	(31 100)
Net profit			23 300

G. Brown's Balance Sheet on 31 March 19–7

	Cost	Accumulated Depreciation	Net Book Value
	£	£	£
Fixed assets:			
Production machinery	32 000	7200	24 800
Accounting machinery	5600	1560	4040
	37 600	8760	28 840

Current assets:	£	£	£
Stocks Raw materials		4200	
Work in progress		2160	
Finished goods	6600		
Less Provision for unrealised profit	(600)	6000	12 360
Debtors			15 970
Bank			2400
Cash			600
			31 330

Less Current liabilities			
Creditors	9700		
Accruals	170	(9870)	21 460
Net worth			50 300

Financed by:

Capital:		
Opening balance		30 000
Add Net profit		23 300
		53 300
		(3000)
Less Drawings		
Capital employed		50 300

Questions

1 What is the main purpose of a manufacturing account?

2 Name the three elements of prime cost.

3 Give three examples of factory overheads.

4 Where will you find opening and closing stocks of WIP?

5 What is achieved by transferring goods produced at market value?

6 What are the three sub-headings used in the profit and loss account?

7 From the following information, you are required to prepare a manufacturing account showing the prime cost and total cost of production.

		£
Stocks at 1 April 19–6	Raw materials	3100
	Work in progress	5200
	Finished goods	7400
Stocks at 31 March 19–7	Raw materials	4700
	Work in progress	5900
	Finished goods	6800
Raw materials purchased during the year		27 200
Cost of direct labour		33 950
Indirect labour		17 240
Factory rent, rates and insurances		9360
Heating, lighting and power		7450
Depreciation on plant and machinery		6500
Gross profit on manufacturing at 20%		

Note Some of these figures may not be needed in the manufacturing account.

8 John Murphy owns a manufacturing business. At the end of 19—8 he extracts the following information from his books:

	£		£
Stocks of raw materials		Purchases	
January 1	4400	Raw materials	88 600
December 31	3800	Finished goods	2300
Returns of raw materials	950	Sales of finished goods	169 100
Returns of goods sold	650	Discount allowed	1350
Discount received	1200	Direct wages	22 400
Work in progress		Factory power and light	1700
January 1	4500	Repairs to plant	1050
December 31	5400	Indirect wages	10 900
Depreciation of		Office expenses	4100
Machinery	5200	Bad debts written off	600
Office furniture	1400	Office salaries	9400
General office expenses	5700	Stocks of finished goods	
Insurances	2400	January 1	6700
Rent and rates	4500	December 31	6200
Bank charges and interest	950		

From this information and the necessary year end adjustments as shown below, construct the manufacturing, trading and profit and loss accounts for the business.

Note
- ⅓ of rent and rates, and ¾ of insurances should be apportioned to the factory.
- Indirect wages of £540 have not yet been paid.
- A bad debts provision of £150 is to be created.
- John Murphy has taken £200 worth of finished goods for his own use, but no entry has been made for this.

9 A. Bartlett owns a manufacturing company. From the following information prepare the manufacturing, trading and profit and loss accounts for the year ending 31 December 19—8 and the balance sheet as at 31 December 19—8.

Stock at 1 January 19—8

	£	£
Raw materials	20 000	
Work in progress	15 000	
Finished goods	25 000	
Rent and rates	23 000	
Purchase raw materials	320 000	
Fuel and light	20 000	
Factory wages	60 000	
Carriage out	2000	
Admin. salaries	13 000	
Sales		500 000
Returns in	6000	
Office expenses	10 000	
Capital account		456 000
Sundry creditors		42 000
Freehold premises	380 000	
Plant and machinery	80 000	
Debtors	18 000	
Cash at bank	6000	
	998 000	998 000

Note Make provision for the following:
- Stock in hand at 31 December 19–8

Raw materials	£24 000
Work in progress	£12 000
Finished goods	£28 000

- Depreciation on plant and machinery 10% straight line method
- 80% of fuel and light and rent and rates to be charged to manufacturing
- Wages outstanding £2000
- Rent paid in advance £3000
- Market value of finished goods £451 000. (You are not required to take into account the unrealised profit.)

10 Bill Dew shows you his final accounts as he is worried at his level of profit. Using these figures and the additional information, re-draft Bill's accounts to show the correct situation.

Profit and Loss Account on 30 April 19–3

	£
Stock of raw materials 1 May 19–2	1000
Stock of raw materials 30 April 19–3	1300
Purchases (including carriage in)	29 700
Salaries and wages	45 200
Overheads (inc. depreciation at 20%)	32 600
Stock of WIP 1 May 19–2	2400
Stock of WIP 30 April 19–3	3700
Stock of finished goods 1 May 19–2	4800
Stock of finished goods 30 April 19–3	3300
Total cost of production	124 000
Add Mark-up at 10%	12 400
Cost of sales	136 400
Sales	194 700
Gross profit	58 300
Less Expenses	(51 800)
Net profit	6500

Note
- Ignore adjustments for unrealised profit
- The purchases figure includes £10 000 for new plant
- Unpaid wages on 30 April totalled £1800
- Expenses include a salary which Bill has been taking for himself at the rate of £1000 per month
- 30% of salaries and wages are direct and 40% indirect labour.

Show all your workings.

11 For each of the following situations indicate the amount by which the prime cost, cost of production, gross or net profit will be increased or reduced when the matter is corrected.

a) Opening stock of raw materials was undervalued by £100
b) Closing stock of raw materials was overvalued by £200
c) Factory indirect wages showed an accrual of £150 which had been deducted from the trial balance figure of £5200

d) A new machine costing £1000 was included in the cost of raw materials. Depreciation is 25% of cost
e) Carriage out amounting to £450 was posted to carriage in
f) Plant repairs amounting to £4000 had been charged to the plant and machinery account. Depreciation is at 20%
g) £2500 worth of debts owed for credit sales have gone bad and are now written off
h) The office manager's salary of £12 500 had been coded to direct wages
i) A provision for unrealised profit of £2600 has been added to the gross profit
j) Closing stock of WIP has been undervalued by £480

12 Murray Mint has the following balances remaining in his books after preparing the year-end revenue accounts on 31 Dec 19–7. Draw up his balance sheet and indicate the level of capital at the start of the year.

	£		£
Debtors	10 900	Stocks	
Creditors	4870	Finished goods	2400
Accruals	580	Raw materials	3170
Prepayments	360	Work in progress	1690
Cash at bank	1410	Motor vehicles	14 100
Cash in hand	50	Plant & equipment	8620
Provisions		Premises	36 750
Bad debts	600	Depreciation:	
Unrealised profit	400	Motor vehicles	5200
Drawings	9200	Plant & equipment	4180
Capital introduced	5000	Bank loan	8640
Mortgage outstanding	16 400	Net profit	14 680
		VAT due to C & E	1460

13 V. Taylor is a manufacturer. From the following information prepare his manufacturing account and trading account for the year ended 31 December 19–8

		£
Stocks at 1 January 19–8	Raw materials	890
	Work in progress	1420
	Finished goods	5460
Stocks at 1 December 19–8	Raw materials	860
	Work in progress	1175
	Finished goods	5250
Purchases of raw materials		9280
Factory wages		25 360
Machinery maintenance		910
Depreciation on plant and machinery		2000
Factory power		855
Factory rent, rates and insurance		990
Factory lighting and heating		125
Factory salaries		3200
Sales		60 725

14 The following information was extracted from the books of Wainwright Manufacturing in respect of 19—3.

		£
Stocks at 1 January 19—3	Raw materials (3000 lbs)	1500
	Finished goods (450 units)	2025
Purchases of raw materials		18 750
Sales (6900 units)		55 200
Manufacturing wages		14 400
Raw materials cost 50p per lb		
Each unit manufactured requires 5lb raw materials		
During 19—3 7200 units were manufactured		
Finished goods are valued at prime cost		

Calculate the quantities and values of raw material stock and finished goods stock at 31 December 19—3.

15 Brian Wyse's cousin, Terry Mitson, has been in manufacturing for several years. His latest set of figures include these balances:

	£		£
Purchases of materials	21 000	Sales	98 000
Carriage on purchases	7000	Stocks at January 1	
Manufacturing wages paid	32 000	Raw materials	1700
Manufacturing wages owing	1500	Work in progress	4300
Direct manufacturing costs	3400	Finished goods	9200
Factory expenses	11 400	Stocks at December 31	
Factory indirect wages paid	9500	Raw materials	2200
Indirect wages owing	700	Work in progress	4100
Factory salaries	12 000	Finished goods	10 200
Depreciation on plant	6000		

Draw up his manufacturing and trading accounts for the current year.

Answers

7 Prime cost £59 550
Cost of production £99 400
Market value of goods produced £119 280

8 Prime cost £110 650   Cost of production £132 440
Gross profit £33 410   Net profit   £7360

9 Prime cost £378 000   Cost of production £421 000
Gross profit £76 000   Net profit   £43 000

15   Terry Mitson's Manufacturing and Trading Account for the year ended 31 December 19—

		£	£
Raw Materials	Opening stock		1700
	Purchases	21 000	
	Carriage	700	21 700
			23 400
	Less Closing stock		(2200)
Raw materials consumed			21 200
Direct wages		32 000	
Accrual		1500	33 500
Direct expenses			3400
Prime cost			58 100
Overheads			
Indirect wages		9500	
Accrual		700	
		10 200	
Salaries		12 000	
Factory expenses		11 400	
Depreciation on plant		6000	39 600
			97 700
Add Work in progress at start			4300
			102 000
Less Work in progress at end			(4100)
Cost of production c/d			97 900
Sales			98 000
Less Cost of sales			
Opening stock of finished goods		9200	
Cost of production b/d		97 900	
		107 100	
Less Closing stock of finished goods		(10 200)	(96 900)
Gross profit			1100

Unit 14

Stock Control

and

Stock Valuation

At the end of this unit you will be able to:

1 Appreciate why stock is controlled, and describe systems which are used

2 Understand how stock can be valued in different ways, and some methods which are employed

3 Understand how stock valuation affects the final accounts.

Stock Control

The process of receiving goods, storing them and later issuing them for use should be one of the most straightforward systems in a business. In practice, however, the control of stock has a number of pitfalls which may upset the effective running of a business. For instance, unauthorised personnel should not be allowed access to the store, as materials taken in an emergency can lead to the store's system being upset and goods getting misplaced or damaged. Staff from other departments often do not bother to update stock records so the information is unreliable, which means that any stock calculations will be inaccurate. The store should be a secure place and admittance restricted to authorised personnel.

For effective stock control, accurate and up-to-date records are required. Every issue and receipt should be accompanied by proper documentation, such as Goods Received notes or Stock Issue forms. The records should be updated immediately on receipt or issue of stock data to avoid a backlog of details to be entered. Stock should be clearly labelled, with similar items stored in the same area to make issues quick and accurate.

Rotation of stock is also essential so that older units are issued before more recent deliveries. This eliminates any problems of deterioration or obsolescence. To help this practice it is useful to date-stamp items whenever possible. This, of course, is essential when dealing with perishables, such as food.

To summarise, effective control of stock will be maintained if:
- A secure storage area is provided
- Access is allowed to authorised personnel only
- There is a properly authorised and updated documentation system
- Stock is rotated on a regular basis
- Care is taken with all paperwork.

Stock Recording

The main requirements of any stock recording system are:
- Accurate data
- Prompt and regular updating
- Accessibility for the users
- Posting of information restricted to trained and authorised staff
- Security from fraud
- Regular stocktaking to check actual quantities against the recorded levels.

Systems used for stock control vary, but usually fall into one of the following categories:
- Bin cards
- Computer systems
- Stock record cards.

Any good system depends on regular and accurate recording of actual stock movements, which requires trained staff, particularly in the case of computers.

Bin Cards

Example

Item No/Material		Location		
Date	Issues	Receipts	Balance	Initials
19–8 Mar 1 2 3 4	 1 3	 6 5 	 6 5 10 7	*LP* *LP* *LP* *LP*

This type of record gives details of quantities in each bin or rack; it is often kept in the stores area with the stock. The card indicates receipts, issues and running balance for each item. If this type of card is used properly, simple but effective stock control is created.

Bin cards can, however, have one major drawback: they tend to be less accessible to other departments such as purchasing or accounts who may need the information on a regular basis.

Computer Systems

These tend to be the most accurate way of recording stock movement. Details of balances can be made available almost immediately on a screen (VDU) or hard-copy printer. On-line systems allow instant updating which ensures that stock demands are not duplicated and important items do not run out of stock.

Many larger retail outlets combine stock control with the normal cash till procedures to provide constantly updated records by coding all items sold. There are many commercial hardware and software packages available, but it is important to make sure that only trained staff use the equipment.

As computer systems are amended more easily, they are more susceptible to transcription errors. Therefore it is equally important that a regular stock reconciliation system is followed and back-up files provided, in case of computer breakdown.

Stock Record Cards

This system is normally maintained in a central location, but is sometimes found in the stores area. The records are very similar to bin cards but contain more information about suppliers, customers, stock check reconciliations, unit costs and stock levels.

Example

Item No: 1236			Maximum level: 25			
Description: Brass 2" Union			Minimum level: 2			
Location: Row C; Bin 5 Reorder level: 5						
Customers: Clarkes, Dipstick and Tweed. Jes Hall.						
Suppliers: White and Twist Ltd.						
Date	Issues		Receipts			Balance	Initials
	Order No	Qty	Delivery Note	Qty		
19–8 Mar 1 2 4 9	3257 3369	9 6	AB 121 AB 230	12 18	12 3 21 15	*J.P.* *J.P.* *J.P.* *J.P.*

As these stock records are usually kept within the main office area, they are more readily accessible than bin cards. However, they can suffer from lack of physical checks, particularly by store personnel, who may not notify the office that items have run out of stock.

If this is the only system used, the first sign of an error or problems could be a shortage of vital parts which could lead to lost production or sales.

Stock Levels and Ordering

For any business it is important that optimum stock levels are assessed to maintain a balance between being too low and too high. If stock is *too low* there is a risk to sales or production which inevitably results in hold-ups in the factory or loss of profit on sales. If stock is *too high* there is a risk of idle capital (unnecessary finance being tied up), extra costs of storage and insurance, risk of deterioration and obsolescence in the stock as well as encouraging pilfering by staff.

It is good business practice to determine the following:

Maximum stock level

This is the highest level of permitted stockholding and should be exceeded only in exceptional circumstances e.g. favourable buying situations.

Minimum stock level

Stock should not fall below this level as this is a buffer stock in case of emergencies.

Re-order level

At this level of stock a requisition should be passed by stock control to purchasing: this level depends on the amount of stock used and the length of time it takes for orders to arrive.

Re-order quantities

These should be assessed to take maximum advantage of trade or quantity discounts, but with due regard to the other levels above.

Stock Taking or Inventory

The actual counting of stock can be quite an arduous task because it means checking each item of stock, pricing it (pricing policies are discussed later), multiplying the price by the number of items in stock, and then adding all the totals.

In a retail business, prices are often reduced for a pre-stocktake sale in order to minimise the amount to be counted. This can also clear out slow moving items and leave a nucleus of good profit-making lines.

Continuous Stocktaking

One method in a large warehouse or store is to check some items each week, or even each day, throughout the year. This method has the following advantages:
- Regular stocktakers can be employed to improve stocktaking quality

- More time is available to take stock

- Greater accuracy is achieved in stocktaking

- Storekeepers are encouraged to be more accurate

- Stock inaccuracies are revealed sooner

- Changes in procedure are highlighted sooner

- Production hold-ups are kept to a minimum.

Errors can occur for the following reasons:
- Poor storekeeping, leading to failure in recording transactions or mistakes in figures, for example

- Pilferage and falsification of figures

- Unrecorded losses due to theft, damage or deterioration ('shrinkage')

- Clerical errors in paperwork

- Incorrect procedures.

Even if this method of continuous stocktaking is not adopted, it is still necessary to make sure that each item of stock is checked at least once during the financial period.

Annual Stocktaking

Annual stocktaking, which usually takes place at the end of the financial year when business is relatively quiet, involves checking actual quantities of all stock, including raw materials, work in progress and finished goods. This method has some disadvantages compared with continuous stocktaking.

To be done effectively and organised properly, annual stocktaking should adopt the following principles:
- It should be organised well in advance to minimise any disruption in production.

- The store area should be closed during the stocktake so that nothing is removed or delivered.

- The store should be sectioned off and specific staff given responsibility for each section.

- Working copies of stock sheets should be prepared and coded.

- Stocktakers should work in pairs : one to count and the other to complete the sheets.

- Stock that has been counted should be marked to make sure that nothing is omitted or counted twice.

- Opened boxes should not be presumed to be full, but individually checked.

- Items in store already charged out to a cost centre should not be counted but clearly labelled.

- Identification of items sold to a client but not yet despatched should be clearly marked.

- When completed, the working sheets must be summarised on final stock sheets so that materials of the same type are combined.

- Stock sheets should be checked against stores record sheets to show up any discrepancies.

- Finally, stock sheets should be priced, extended and totalled to give the closing stock value.

As this method is normally carried out at week-ends to avoid disturbance of normal business, it can be expensive in overtime payments to staff.

Pricing of Stock

When charging for materials issued, the question is: which price? This is assuming that prices have altered during the year. However, if there have been no price changes, there is no problem.

The three most common methods of pricing are listed below.

FIFO (First in First out)

This method assumes that the cost of the first batch received is used until all units from that batch have been issued, then the price of the next batch received is used, and so on.

The advantage is that this tends to be realistic by assuming that issues are made in order of receipt. The disadvantage is that the issue price may not reflect the current replacement price.

LIFO (Last in First out)

This method uses the price of the last batch received until all units from that batch have been issued, then the price of the previous batch is used.

This should not be confused with actual *issuing* of stock. The oldest items should always be *issued* first, to prevent deterioration, except for particular items of stock, such as whisky or champagne, which improve with age.

Advantages are that this system keeps value of issues close to present day prices, stock valuation is usually conservative and, as with FIFO, no notional profits or losses arise from the pricing policy.

Disadvantages are that, as with FIFO, it can be awkward to operate and may be misleading in respect of physical issues. LIFO valuation may not be acceptable for Corporation Tax assessments and if issues are made from older receipts, they will be valued at out-of-date prices.

Weighted Average

This method averages prices after 'weighting' the quantities at each price.
For example: 10 units @ £10
20 units @ £20
30

Weighted average $\dfrac{(10 \times 10) + (20 \times 20)}{30 \text{ units}}$ = £16.67 per unit

Advantages:
- Logical: it assumes items have identical values
- Calculations are less difficult than LIFO or FIFO
- Allows for fluctuations in purchase pricing
- No notional profits or losses arise.

Disadvantages:
- Issues may not be at current economic value
- Issue price is usually notional
- Issue price may run to a number of decimal places to ensure accuracy.

Examples

Here are examples of each of the three pricing methods.

F. Smith commenced business as a coal importer on 1 July 19–0.
Purchases were made as follows:

	Tonnes	Price per tonne £
1 July	20	38
5 August	30	40
12 September	25	35
20 October	40	42
11 November	15	43
10 December	10	44
Total received	140	

In December 100 tonnes were sold.

Although it is clear that 40 tonnes are still held in stock, the value placed on that stock will depend on the pricing policy used, and this has a direct effect on the profit which will be calculated in the trading account.

FIFO Using this method, the 40 tonnes would be valued at:

		£
15 tonnes @ £42 =	630
15 tonnes @ £43 =	645
10 tonnes @ £44 =	440
40	Total	1715

LIFO   This gives the valuation of:

$$\begin{array}{lll} & & £ \\ 20 \text{ tonnes @ £38} = & 760 \\ 20 \text{ tonnes @ £40} = & \underline{800} \\ \underline{40} \qquad \text{Total} & & \underline{1560} \end{array}$$

Weighted Average   This gives an average price per tonne of:

$$\begin{array}{ll} & £ \\ 20 \times 38 = & 760 \\ 30 \times 40 = & 1200 \\ 25 \times 35 = & 875 \\ 40 \times 42 = & 1680 \\ 15 \times 43 = & 645 \\ \underline{10} \times 44 = & \underline{440} \\ 140 & \underline{5600} \end{array}$$

$$\frac{5600}{140} = \underline{£40}$$

So the 40 tonnes would be valued at £1600 (40 × 40)
For this to work properly, an accurate check has to be kept on how many items have been issued at each price.

Date	Receipts			Issues			Balance	
	Qty	Price	Value	Qty	Price	Value	Qty	Value

The Stock Account

Once the closing stock has been valued (technically after the trial balance has been prepared), it is posted to the trading account and shown as a *debit* balance (an asset) in the ledger.

Stock Account

19–8		£	
Dec 31	Closing stock	1715	

Normally, no other entry is made on this account until the end of the next financial period, when the closing stock is posted back to the new trading account as **opening stock** and the latest closing stock figure shown on the debit side.

Example

Stock Account

19–8		£		19–9		£
Dec 31	Closing stock	1715		Jan 1	Opening stock	1715
19–9						
Dec 31	Closing stock	2345				

Closing stock is always shown as a year end adjustment, usually as a note. The figure included in the trial balance is the *opening* stock.

Points to Remember

Whichever system is used, a business should always stick to one system in an account period to maintain constant pricing/valuation levels, although different methods may be used for various types of stock.

It is also mandatory for tax purposes for large companies to be consistent in their methods of valuation and the policy must be stated in the accounts. If it is decided to change the method, this must be reported and the profit for the previous year re-calculated to show the effect of such a change.

You can see from the examples that using different methods such as LIFO and FIFO not only alters the closing stock figure but also results in different profits. However, since the closing stocks of one year become the opening stocks of the next, this difference is compensated in future years provided there is a consistent approach.

Questions

1 What are the main stock recording methods and their advantages and disadvantages?

2 What is meant by stock levels? What are the main levels determined for any item?

3 Describe briefly the two main forms of stocktaking, mentioning the features of each type.

4 What are the advantages and disadvantages of the main types of stock valuation methods?

5 Where is the closing stock figure shown in the trial balance and where does this figure appear in the final accounts?

6 John McLeod is an oil distributor. In the table below, his purchases of stock for six months from 1 August 19–1 are shown:

			Litres	Price per litre (Pence)
1	August	19–1	2300	56
2	September	19–1	9600	52
3	October	19–1	11 500	57
6	November	19–1	7200	55
9	December	19–1	9700	58
12	January	19–2	12 750	60

His sales were:

3	August	1750	litres sold for	£1078
9	November	25 200	litres sold for	£15 800
16	January	20 500	litres sold for	£13 530

Record this information on a stock record card. The information can be shown with columns for receipts, issues and the balance, giving details of quantities and values in each case, or the closing stock figure value can be calculated separately.

Using FIFO, calculate:
a) closing stock value
b) total profit made.

7 Roy Flowers sells Growquick Fertiliser to local farmers and has been concerned about the method he uses to price his stock.

Using FIFO and LIFO, calculate:
a) his closing stock values
b) his profits with each method.
Decide which method you would advise Flowers to use, giving your reasons.

Receipts		Tonnes	Price per tonne (£)
5	March	2100	16
6	April	2600	17
1	May	7200	14
2	June	5700	15
3	July	6200	16
4	August	5900	18

Issues		Tonnes	Sales price (£)
20	April	4300	80 410
14	June	9200	151 800
16	August	12 300	243 540

8 Jean Harrow trades as a sugar merchant. Her purchases for part of 19–3 are listed below:

		Tonnes	Price per tonne (£)
2	January	3600	38
3	February	7700	40
4	March	5600	37
6	April	9200	41

Her sales were:

On 3 January 2800 tonnes for £117 040
On 10 April 22 500 tonnes for £1 014 750

Using LIFO, calculate:
a) closing stock value
b) total profit made.

9 Nell E. Dean uses the weighted average method for costing her stock issues. Record the following details in a suitable format to show her closing stock valuation.

Note The weighted average must be re-calculated after each receipt. This value is then used with all issues until the next receipt.

Item 3½″ floppy disks in boxes of 10

19–9
March 1 Opening balance 25 boxes
       Weighted average price £8.00 per box
       3 50 boxes received at £8.30 per box
       7 18 boxes issued
      11 45 boxes issued
      16 48 boxes issued at £8.70 per box
      18 13 boxes issued
      23 22 boxes issued
      27 50 boxes received at £8.90 per box
      29 11 boxes issued
      31 Stock-take reveals 3 boxes missing

10 Aart de Villiers is not sure which is the most appropriate method of stock valuation to use in his business. From the information which Aart provides, draw up comparative trading accounts for the two years 19–1 and 19–2 to show the effects of using FIFO, LIFO and weighted average valuations.

Stocks (in units) at 31 Dec   19.0 1000
                               19.1 1500
                               19.2 2000

Unit cost of stock at year end (£)

	FIFO	LIFO	W A
19.0	1.20	0.80	0.90
19.1	1.30	0.90	1.20
19.2	1.60	1.20	1.50

Total cost of purchases   19.1 £27 800
                           19.2 £39 400

Total sales income   19.1   £55 300
                                19.2   £74 200

Your answer should be in the form of two separate trading accounts for the two years, with three columns in each to show your calculations using the three different methods of stock valuation.

11   Don Lamprecht maintains a full stock control system in his stores. For one particular item he has set a maximum stock-holding level of 300 units, a minimum of 60 and re-order at 100, since average usage over a 5-day week is 20 per day and it normally takes two working days for the order to arrive.

Draw up a stock record card for this item to show the movements indicated below. Note on the card the date orders are placed, and use the foregoing details to calculate the appropriate re-order quantity under normal circumstances. Assume orders arrive on time.

19.3
Opening Balance on 1 May   150 units

Issues	May 2	30 units	May 16	15 units
	3	25 units	18	20 units
	5	45 units	19	35 units
	8	40 units	23	30 units
	10	30 units	25	35 units
	12	25 units	26	30 units
	15	35 units	30	20 units

Note   The re-order quantity should take the stock level back to maximum. It is calculated as the difference between maximum and minimum levels.

12   The following sales and purchases were recorded by Malcolm Ball for the first quarter of 19–2:

	Sales	Purchases
19–2		
10 January		2500 articles @ 75p
29 January	3000 articles @ £1.00	
16 February		2500 articles @ 78p
19 February	2500 articles @ £1.05	
2 March		2000 articles @ 80p
25 March	1800 articles @ £1.10	

At 1 January 19–2 the opening stock was 1500 articles which had cost 72p each. On 31 March 19–2 the stock included 50 damaged articles, 40 purchased in January, 10 purchased in March. These will be sold at half their cost price.

Using FIFO, calculate:
a) closing stock value
b) the gross profit for the quarter.

13   Barbara Anderson's financial year ends on 31 March. She is, however, unable to carry out her stock taking until 3 April. During the period 1–3 April the following transactions take place:

		£
Takings	April 1	261
	2	396
	3	450
Purchases	April 2	800
Goods returned by customer on April 1		57
Goods returned to supplier on April 1		40

The stock at close of business on 3 April was valued at £3565.
The gross profit is 20% of sales. Calculate the value of stock on 31 March.

Answers

6 a) £3360
   b) £3697

7 a) FIFO £70 200
       LIFO £55 400
   b) FIFO £76 450
       LIFO £61 650

8 Jean Harrow

Date	Receipts			Issues	Balance
19–3	Qty	Price	Value		
		£	£	£	£
Jan 2	3600	38	136 800		3600
3				2800	800
Feb 3	7700	40	308 000		8500
Mar 4	5600	37	207 200		14 100
Apr 6	9200	41	377 200		23 300
10				22 500	800

Total   £1 029 200

a) Closing stock value:
    800 @ £38 = <u>£30400</u>

b) Sales (£117 040 + £1 014 750)   £1 131 790
    Cost of sales:
       Purchases   £1 029 200
       Less Closing Stock   (£30 400)(£998 800)
    Gross profit   <u>£132990</u>

Unit 15

Revision And Examination Preparation

This unit will enable you to:

1 Look at revision procedures and see why they are necessary

2 Consider examination techniques

3 Liaise any book-keeping problems.

Revision

Why do we need to revise? Once we have learned something new, unless we use that knowledge constantly, or go back to basics from time to time, that knowledge gradually leaves us. You have probably heard people say that they have forgotten all they ever knew! This is not necessarily true for a practical skill, like riding a bicycle, but is nearly always the case with academic knowledge. If we graph the amount of knowledge retained over a period of time, it will look something like this:

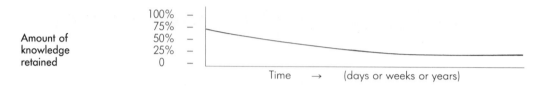

To be fully prepared for an examination, we obviously need to have the maximum amount of knowledge just before being tested. The best way of doing this is to revise at the same time as learning new material. In Unit 1, you may remember, we saw that **repetition** is an aid to learning effectively. By repetition, we gradually retain more and more information over the length of a course such as this, and the knowledge gained will hopefully look something like this:

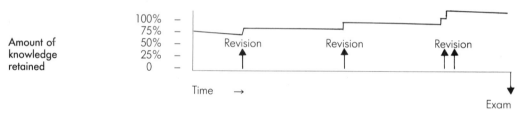

As you can see, the nearer we get to the end of the course, the greater the total amount of information you should have.

Now, just to remind you of some of the basics of book-keeping, here are **Ten Golden Rules** to remember:

1 Every debit has a credit.
2 Recording transactions twice gives control.
3 When money is received, debit the cash book, credit the ledger account.
4 When money is paid, credit the cash book, debit the ledger account.
5 When goods are bought on credit, debit purchases and credit the supplier (a creditor).
6 When goods are sold on credit, credit the Sales and debit the customer (a debtor).
7 To reduce an account, put an entry on the opposite side.
8 Capital is what the business owes to the owner.
9 A balance is the difference between the two sides of an account.
10 Items in the trial balance are used once, and notes are used twice when preparing final accounts.

You do *not* have to be able to repeat these word for word, but you should be able to *apply* them.

Planning Your Revision

It is essential to plan your revision well. It may help if you bear the following points in mind:

- As far as possible you should have revised *each topic* as soon as possible after each lesson. When you go back to it later you will find that much more has 'stuck' than if you had just left it without thoroughly learning it at the time.

- Leave yourself plenty of time for your final revision before the examination.

- Try to decide how much attention you are going to give to each topic on which you are likely to be examined.

- Don't cram your revision. Many people achieve little or nothing by late night revision sessions. When you are tired, you learn little and you are certainly not going to do well if you go into an examination tired through overwork.

- Do not just read through your notes. This is very time-consuming and in itself is not particularly efficient. Only one full read-through is really necessary. At the same time as reading through you should make brief notes. Write down main points about each topic in brief. After you have done this, look back over a topic and, without reference to your notes, attempt to summarise it, then check to see how accurate you have been. Work through all your material in this way and you will find that, not only can you remember it, but, what is more important, you can understand it. Having a full and flexible understanding of your material is essential for a good examination performance.

The Examination

Just Before the Examination

You need to have as much information as possible about the examination to be taken. Not only should you know what topics the examination is going to cover, but also where it is to be held, and what time it starts and finishes. You should know what type of questions you will have to answer and you should have a rough idea how long you will have to answer the questions. Make sure you have all the necessary equipment (pens, ruler, pencils, calculator). There is nothing worse than having to stop during an exam to fill a pen, or to discover that you have left your calculator behind.

Make sure you arrive at the examination in good time. On no account be late. On the other hand, don't arrive there too early so that you spend a long time hanging around getting more and more worried. It is very easy to say, but you should try to stay as calm as possible. There is no point in taking your notes along with you, attempting to do a last minute cram before you start. If you don't know the material by then, then you never will, and attempting a last-minute revision will add to your anxiety and will probably confuse you.

When you go into the examination room, find your place as quickly as possible and check that you have on your desk everything that you will need: examination paper, stationery etc. If you haven't everything you need, tell the invigilator before the examination starts.

Examination Procedure

Read The Paper

When you are allowed to start, read the question paper **fully**, making sure you have understood all the instructions.

Decide What To Answer

You should now begin to select the questions you will answer. There is a good case to be made for answering your best question first. It gives you self-confidence, gets you off to a good start and, as you will probably spend less time struggling on this one, gives you more time to answer the more difficult questions.

Think

For each question you answer you should not just 'jump in'. You should take time to think about the answer and work out a rough plan if necessary.

Answer The Question

You should read the question carefully and all the time you are writing your answer refer back to see that you are actually **answering the question**. No marks will be given for the wrong answers, even if what you are saying is right.

Check The Time

Make sure you don't run over your allotted time for each question. If you are sure that you are producing a very good answer, then you can probably allow an extra few minutes on it safely. But remember that 'extra minutes' mount up, and then you can find yourself with no time to answer the last question. Do *not* let this happen. Clearly, there are no marks for unanswered questions. Even a poor attempt at a question may pick up a few marks.

Check Your Work

Although it may be difficult, you should try to check over your paper at the end to correct any mistakes you may have made (for example, arithmetic, spelling, layout etc.) and to see that your paper is presented as well as possible.

Presentation

It is very difficult when writing at speed to keep your handwriting neat and legible. But it is well worth the effort. Book-keeping and accounting are a means of communicating, so if your writing is difficult to read you are not getting your message across clearly.

Preparation

These notes are suggestions that have been found useful for examinations. They are *not* an infallible guide to examination success. This is largely in your hands, because no amount of skill in examinations can make up for poor preparation.

Topics Covered

As a further reminder, turn back to the Contents page and look once again at the list of topics that you have covered in this book. Are there any areas that you feel you do not properly understand? Now is the time to review any weak areas which might need further revision.

A Final Word to Future Book-keepers

By the time you reach this stage of the course, you should have a good working knowledge of the basic terminology of book-keeping and accounts, the ability to prepare ledger accounts and simple final accounts, and the necessary skills to become a book-keeper. However, this does not mean that you are a fully qualified accountant! You may remember that we said, right at the start of this course, that it can take several years of hard work and intensive study to gain admission to one of the recognised accounting bodies. If this course has whetted your appetite, and you would like to continue studying, your local library can give you information about further courses you can follow.

However, as with any skill, practice makes perfect: if you want to improve you will need to *use* your newly acquired skill. The best way to do this is to get involved with everyday book-keeping, either by working with accounts or by acting as the treasurer for a local club or church.

Whether or not you pass the examination and obtain the Scheidegger Diploma, you have studied an interesting subject which can help you in many ways in the future. Hopefully, you have gained from the course what you originally expected.

Even though many businesses are increasingly turning to computerised accounting packages, it is still very useful to know what the computer is *doing* with the figures it is processing.

Good luck with your examination and future career.

Revision Exercises

1   The trial balance extracted from the books of I.P. Macleod on 30 November 19–1 is shown below.
Prepare a trading and profit and loss account for the year, together with the balance sheet.
In addition you are informed that:
a)   Stock on hand at 30 November 19–1 was valued at £6750
b)   Prepayments on rates were £100
c)   Accruals on electricity were £50 and on telephone expenses £30
d)   Depreciation is to be provided for on vehicles at 25% and on machinery and office equipment at 10% per annum
e)   The debtors' balance includes a bad debt of £540.

I.P. Macleod's Trial Balance
on 30 November 19–1

	£	£
Sales		17 519
Purchases	7000	
Bank	560	
Cash	39	
Drawings	600	
Premises	10 000	
Machinery	2600	
Office equipment	700	
Vehicles	3300	
Discount received		819
Discount allowed	716	
Stock	6100	
Creditors		3719
Debtors	4560	
Capital		26 291
Insurance	196	
Rates	301	
Telephone	193	
Wages	7000	
Salaries	3000	
Electricity	516	
Returns in	713	
Returns out		506
Vehicle expenses	760	
	48 854	48 854

2 At 30 September 19–3 the following trial balance was extracted from the books of Joseph Lee:

	Debit £	Credit £
Machinery	3400	
Vehicles	2600	
Capital		10 500
Drawings	3250	
Purchases	15 602	
Sales		22 904
Opening stock (1.10.–2)	4600	
Rent and rates	1063	
Salaries	2906	
Debtors	1674	
Creditors		967
Bank		595
Cash	76	
Provision for bad debts		250
Bad debts	45	
	35 216	35 216

Prepare his trading and profit and loss account for the year and the balance sheet at the end of the year, taking into account the following:

a) Closing stock was valued at £3075
b) Provision for bad debts is to be increased to £350
c) Accrual on salaries of £60.

3 Felicity Down's cash book on 31 March showed a balance at the bank of £456.48. On attempting a reconciliation with her bank statement the following matters were discovered:

a) A Payment from D. Green to Felicity of £40 by credit transfer had not been recorded in the cash book
b) Cheques drawn but not presented to the bank were: A. Buck £21.60; B. Mills £36.00
c) A paying-in slip dated 29 March totalling £372.30 was not credited by the bank until 2 April
d) A standing order for £21.60 payable on 20 March for rental of photocopier had been paid by the bank but not entered in the cash book
e) Bank charges £15 had not been entered in the cash book

Open the cash book and make the additional entries as appropriate. Prepare a statement reconciling the revised cash book balance with the balance shown by the bank statement.

4 Prepare a sales ledger control account from the following information:

				£
19–2	March	1	Balances b/f	8620
		31	Goods sold during the month	13 570
			Goods returned	265
			Cash and cheques received	11 925
			Discount allowed	230

Bad debts written off	170
Balance set off against a	
creditor account	320

5 A new motor vehicle was purchased on 1 June 19–0 for £8000. If the financial year end is 31 May, and vehicles are depreciated at 25% on the reducing balance method, calculate the depreciation charges for the three years it is retained by the business.

If, at the end of the three years, the vehicle is traded in for a replacement and a trade-in allowance of £3750 is given, how much will be shown on the next year's profit and loss account as *under* or *over*-provision for depreciation?

6 The following **Multiple Choice** questions cover a wide range of topics. Consider each one and decide on the most appropriate answer, which can be indicated by the letter shown.

i) Which one of the following accounts would be found in the sales ledger?

A sales
B returns
C H. Jones, a debtor
D F. Smith, a creditor.

ii) A credit note received from a supplier would be recorded in

A the cash book
B the journal
C the returns inwards book
D the returns outwards book.

iii) The bank column of the cash book shows a credit balance. This would appear in the balance sheet as a

A current asset
B long term liability
C current liability
D fixed asset.

iv) A trader purchased goods from a supplier at a cost of £1000. The terms stated on the invoice are trade discount 10% and cash discount 5% for payment within 7 days.
If the trader pays within the 7 day period he will send the supplier a cheque for

A £850
B £855
C £900
D £950.

v) To prepare the sales ledger accounts, the ledger clerk could use copies of the

A customers' orders
B works requisitions
C sales invoices
D despatch notes.

vi) A petty cash account has an imprest of £25. Currently the account has a debit balance of £3. How much cash is needed to restore the imprest?

A £3
B £22
C £25
D £28.

vii) A suspense account can be used as a temporary measure to balance the

A trading and profit and loss account
B manufacturing account
C trial balance
D appropriation account.

viii) The correct heading for an annual balance sheet is

A balance sheet on 31 December
B balance sheet for year ending 31 December
C balance sheet for period ending 31 December
D balance sheet for year as at 31 December.

ix) The amount of a firm's gross profit is calculated in

A the profit and loss account
B the trading account
C the balance sheet
D the manufacturing account.

x) The cost of goods sold is arrived at by finding the

A amount of the purchases *less* returns, *less* opening stock
B amount of sales *less* returns, *less* closing stock
C closing stock *plus* goods purchased *less* opening stock
D opening stock *plus* goods purchased *less* closing stock.

xi) The balance on the accumulated fund of a club can be established at any date by

A preparing a balance sheet
B looking at the bank statement
C preparing an income and expenditure account
D calculating the balance on the subscription account.

xii) Totals for a period in the purchases day book are posted to

A purchases ledger and VAT account
B nominal ledger and VAT account
C purchases account and VAT account
D creditors account and VAT account.

xiii) A bank reconciliation statement is usually prepared by

A the bank clerk
B the petty cashier
C the cashier
D the chief accountant.

xiv) Depreciation of fixed assets is entered in

    A trading account and profit and loss account
    B profit and loss account only
    C balance sheet only
    D profit and loss account and balance sheet.

xv) Day books are used

    A because of legal requirements
    B to avoid too many entries in the ledger
    C because the double-entry is incomplete without them
    D to give basic work to unqualified staff.

xvi) Which of the following errors is normally revealed by a trial balance?

    A a transaction completely left out of the books
    B a sale on credit to Smith Bros entered in Smith & Co.'s account
    C an asset sold in part-exchange entered only on one side of the accounts
    D a payment for expenses entered on an asset account.

xvii) Information for control accounts comes from

    A the ledger
    B books of original entry
    C final accounts
    D bank statements.

xviii) Which of the following has a credit balance in the ledger?

    A capital
    B drawings
    C carriage in
    D carriage out.

xix) Working capital is

    A fixed assets *less* current assets
    B fixed assets *plus* current assets
    C current assets *less* current liabilities
    D current assets *plus* current liabilities.

xx) A business may make a loss, yet still have more money in the bank at the end of the year. This could be because

    A drawings have been more than the previous year
    B fixed assets have been sold during the year
    C more stock has been purchased during the year
    D debtors owe more than at the start of the year.

7 Konstantin Lapskin starts up a business with £5000 in the bank. Open up a three-column cash book, sales, purchases and nominal ledger to record his first month's transactions. Draw up Konstantin's trial balance at the end of the month. Day books are not necessary.

19–5
April 1 Withdrew £100 from the bank as a cash float
      2 Paid 3 month's rent in advance £1200 by cheque
      3 Bought goods on credit from the following:
          S.O'Hara £800 – 25% trade discount

R.Butler £250 – 20% trade discount
B.McQuinn £240 – 33⅓% trade discount
All subject to VAT at 15%

5   Paid wages in cash £75; banked week's cash takings £460 which included VAT

8   Sold goods on credit to:
    M.Bros   £120
    R.Stones   £250
    E.John   £70
    Trade discount is not given to customers. All sales are subject to VAT.

11   Banked week's cash takings which totalled £644 (VAT inclusive) after paying out wages of £82 and taking cash for himself £120

14   Returned faulty goods to Butler at the list price of £40

19   Received cheques in full settlement from Bros £134.50 and John £78.50

24   Bought motor van for £4100 on credit from Blakes paying £500 deposit by cheque. The VAT on this cannot be reclaimed by Konstantin

25   Bank cash takings for the week £655.50 including VAT, after paying wages £85.70 and sundry expenses £103.50

30   Sent out cheques to settle the accounts with O'Hara and Butler in order to obtain the 2% cash discount offered

8   Draw up the personal account for Jenny Wren in column style and indicate in which part of the ledger it would be found. Presuming that a full set of day books is maintained, use suitable folios to indicate when the original entries would be found.

19–9			£
Feb	1	Balance	1620 Dr
	2	Invoice 01234	360
	5	Credit Note 1057	24
	7	Invoice 01239	246
	11	Credit Note 1063	31
	13	Cheque 501678	910
		Discount	7
	17	Invoice 01254	412
	19	Invoice 01263	629
	24	Adjustment re invoice 01234 undercast £10	
	27	Interest charged on overdue amount £5	

At the end of the month Jenny informs you that she has sold her business to Jack Crow and asks for her outstanding balance to be transferred to his account. This is confirmed by Jack.

9 Explain the difference between capital and revenue items. What tests could be applied to determine the nature of a particular item?

Indicate for each of the following whether it should be considered as capital or revenue:
a) Purchase of plant and equipment for a factory
b) Repairs to motor vehicles for a greengrocer
c) Purchase of motor vehicles by a car dealer
d) Rebuilding a factory destroyed by fire, covered by insurance
e) Payment of solicitor's fees for purchase of property.

For each of the errors indicated, state whether net profit would have been over-stated or under-stated, or not affected at all:

a) Purchase of delivery vehicle included in purchases figure
b) Drawings posted to the wages account
c) Bricks purchased for new buildings charged to raw materials
d) Royalties included in selling and distribution expenses
e) Proceeds from the sale of equipment at net book value posted to sales.

10 On 1 April a company had in store 200 units of an item valued at £50 per unit. Issues and purchases were subsequently made as shown:

Issues	Purchases
15 April 400 units	9 April 600 at £58 each
18 May 600 units	2 May 400 at £64 each
24 June 200 units	18 June 600 at £72 each

Prepare the stores records to show this information when the weighted average cost is used for pricing stores issues.
If the selling price of these goods was £100 each, how much gross profit was earned in the period?

11 At the year end Edna Way has the following information available:

	£
Total of balances in the sales ledger	45 100
Total of balances in the purchases ledger	63 260
Balance on the sales ledger control account	45 710
Balance on the purchases ledger control account	63 130

After compiling her trial balance there is a difference of £2128 on the credit side.

Edna subsequently finds the items detailed below. Adjust or correct as necessary to reconcile the sales and purchases ledger figures and draw up the suspense account to show the effect of these errors.

a) An account of £200 in the sales ledger is to be set off against an account of £400 in the purchases ledger.

b) An invoice for a customer £100 has not been posted to the personal account.

c) Discount allowed £150 and discount received £270 have not been included in the totals for the year.

d) A payment of £567 for motor expenses was posted to the ledger account as £675.

e) A page in the purchases book was undercast by £400.

f) £250 rent received was posted to the debit of the rent account.

g) Bad debts of £360 have not been included in the control figures.

h) Bank charges of £80 were recorded only in the cash book.

i) Purchases returns of £60 have not been recorded anywhere in the books.

j) The balance on the provision for bad debts of £1000 has been posted as a debit on the trial balance.

Note Some of these adjustments affect more than one figure.

Answers

		£
1	Net loss	2576
	Net worth/Capital employed	23 115
2	Net profit	1603
	Net worth/capital employed	8853
3	Cash book balance	459.88
	Bank statement balance	145.18
4	Sales ledger balances	9280
5	Year 3 net book value	3375
	Over-depreciation	375

6 Multiple-choice answers

i)	C	vi)	B	xi)	A	xvi)	C
ii)	D	vii)	C	xii)	C	xvii)	B
iii)	C	viii)	A	xiii)	C	xviii)	A
iv)	B	ix)	B	xiv)	D	xix)	C
v)	C	x)	D	xv)	B	xx)	B

Glossary of Useful Terms and Abbreviations

a/c	Account.
Account Rendered	Amount owing, brought forward, usually notified by a statement (qv).
Accrued Expenses	That portion of expenditure of a recurring or day-to-day nature which has become due since the last payment was made, e.g. gas, electricity, telephone.
Assets	Property in general, but see Fixed, Liquid and Current.
Balance	The difference between the two sides of an account, usually calculated at the end of an accounting period (e.g. monthly, annually).
Balance Sheet (B/S)	A summary of assets and liabilities on a certain date showing the state of a business.
Balancing Off	The process of calculating the balances in a set of books.
Bank Reconciliation Statement	An agreement between the bank column of the cash book and the bank statement allowing for cheques not presented and deposits not credited.
Bankers Order	An arrangement with a bank whereby periodical payments will be made by the bank without a fresh request being made each time.
b/d	Brought down, e.g. a balance on a page, at the start of a new accounting period.
Bearer	The person in possession of a cheque made out 'Pay ... or Bearer'.
b/f	Brought forward, e.g. a balance from a previous page or a previous year.
Bought Ledger	see Purchases Ledger.
Capital	Any asset invested in the business by the owner(s).
Carriage In	The expense of bringing purchases into a business, charged to the trading account.
Carriage Out	The expense of delivering sales, charged to the profit and loss account.
Cash Book	Part of the ledger containing the cash and bank accounts.
Cash Discount	see Discount.
Casting	Addition of a column of figures.
Casual Labour	Part-time or occasional work carried out by a person not permanently employed by the particular organisation.
¢	A contra entry – one appearing on both sides of an account – most commonly found in the cash book.
c/d	Carried down, e.g. a balance on a page at the end of an accounting period.
c/f	Carried forward, e.g. a balance to a following page or year.
Cheque	A written order to a banker to pay a named sum on the writer's account to a named person or to bearer.
Clearing House	Bankers institution where cheques drawn on various banks are exchanged and only balances paid.
Control Account	An account drawn up periodically using total figures taken from the books of original entry to act as a check or to provide missing figures.
Cost of Production	The total amount it has cost to produce manufactured goods completed in a period, as calculated in the manufacturing account (qv).
Credit	In book-keeping the right hand column or side of an account.
Creditor	A person to whom a debt is owing.
Creditors Ledger	see Purchases Ledger.
Cross-Casting	Addition of a line of horizontal figures.
Current Assets	Assets of such a nature as to be easily converted into cash, e.g. stock, debtors.
Debit	The left hand column or side of an account.
Debtor	A person from whom a sum is owing.
Debtors Ledger	see Sales Ledger.
Depreciation	The reduction of an asset in value as a result of wear and tear or obsolescence, charged to profit and loss.

Discount	A deduction from the price payable for goods or services, hence: *Cash Discount* – an allowance for prompt payment. *Trade Discount* – an adjustment to the list price, usually to a trader or business. *Quantity Discount* – an allowance from the list price for a large volume of purchases.
Double-Entry	A system of book-keeping where every debit has a credit which gives control over the arithmetical accuracy.
e.g.	For example (Latin – *exempli gratia*)
Endorsement	Signature of the person to whom a cheque is made payable, usually on the reverse.
Excess	The amount by which expenses exceed income in an income and expenditure account.
Finished Goods	Those units of production which have been completed in a period and are available for sale.
Fiscal Year	The revenue year which ends on 5 April for income tax and corporation tax purposes.
Fixed Assets	Items intended for continuing use in a business over a number of years, e.g. premises and motor vehicles.
Fixed Costs	Those expenses of a manufacturing business which have to be incurred regardless of how many units are produced e.g. rent and rates, salaries.
Float	A fixed sum usually provided to pay expenses e.g. petty cash float, till float.
Fo	Folio page in ledger, identified by letters and/or numbers.
General Ledger	That part of the ledger containing all those accounts not in the cash book, sales ledger and purchases ledger. Also known as Nominal Ledger.
Gross Profit	Normally the excess of the amount of sales over the cost of such sales, involving carriage in and any other necessary costs.
i.e.	That is (Latin: *id est*).
Imprest	Usually applied to a float of cash or stock which is to be kept at a fixed level by periodical reimbursement of the exact amount used or spent.
Income and Expenditure Account	An account for a non profit-making organisation for a period which contains the whole of the transactions during that period, as opposed to a receipts and payments account which deals only with cash transactions: the difference being a surplus or an excess.
Indirect Expenses	Those expenses of a manufacturing business which do not vary in proportion with the numbers of units produced and cannot be identified with a specific unit manufactured.
Inventory	A detailed list of stock; the act of physically counting stock.
Invoice	A document showing details of goods and/or services supplied and charges, including discount (qv) and VAT.
Ledger	The book containing all the accounts of an organisation, usually sub-divided into the cash book, sales ledger, purchases ledger and general ledger.
Liabilities	Debts or monetary obligations. Amounts owing.
Liquid Assets	Assets of a cash or quasi-cash nature, e.g. investments, bank deposit accounts.
Loan	Money lent, usually at an agreed rate of interest.
Manufacturing Account	The final account which includes all costs associated with production to give the total cost of producing finished goods in a period.
Net Loss	The amount by which expenses exceed income in a profit and loss account.
Net Profit	The amount by which income exceeds expenses in a profit and loss account.
Nominal Ledger	see General Ledger.
Notional Expense	An assessed amount.
o/d	Overdrawn.
Overdraft	The sum owing to a banker on current accounts.
PAYE	Pay-as-you-earn (income tax).
Paying-in Slip	Form provided by banks etc. for customers to enter details of sums paid into their accounts.
Personal Account	A ledger account for an individual or an organisation, usually contained in the sales or purchases ledger.
Prepayments	Payments (periodical or otherwise) which have not expired at the date of a balance sheet, e.g. rates, insurance, licences.
Prime Costs	Those manufacturing expenses which can be directly related to an individual unit of production e.g. raw materials, direct wages (skilled labour) and direct expenses (royalties).
Profit and Loss Account (P/L)	An account for a trading organisation detailing income and expenses, where the net profit or loss is calculated.

Glossary of Useful Terms and Abbreviations

Profit Margin — The difference between the cost and selling price of goods, compared to the selling price.

Profit Mark-Up — The difference between the cost and selling price of goods, compared to the cost price.

Purchases Ledger — That part of the ledger containing all the personal accounts for credit suppliers (creditors).

qv — Which see (Latin: *quod vide*). Cross reference.

RD — Refer to drawer (used by banks when cheques are returned unpaid).

Remittance Advice — A summary of items included in a payment to a creditor.

Sales Ledger — That part of the ledger containing all the personal accounts for credit customers (debtors).

Shrinkage — Loss of stock due to theft, damage or deterioration.

Sold Ledger — see Sales Ledger.

Statement — An account of transactions between two parties, usually sent by a creditor to a debtor or a bank to a customer. It is in fact a copy of a personal account (qv) normally sent at the end of a month.

Statutory Deductions — Applied to wages and salaries; deductions which are made with legal authority, e.g. PAYE and National Insurance contributions.

Surplus — The amount by which income exceeds expenditure in an income and expenditure account.

Total Account — see Control Account.

Trading Account — An account which shows the gross profit (qv) made on transactions during a period: a summary of sales and purchases adjusted for opening and closing stocks and certain expenses.

Trial Balance — A list of all the balances remaining in a set of books after balancing off (qv); if the totals of the debit and credit columns agree, it is prima facie evidence of their arithmetical accuracy. However, it is not proof of the accuracy of the accounts themselves.

Variable Costs — Those expenses of a manufacturing business which increase in proportion with the amount of goods produced e.g. raw materials.

w/o — Written off. That is, an expense charged against income in the profit and loss account.